Greenhill Books

Stilwell the Patriot

Stilwell with Chiang Kai-Shek and Madame. A rare happy photograph, which contrasts dramatically with their later estrangement

David Rooney

Stilwell the Patriot

Vinegar Joe, the Brits and Chiang Kai-Shek

Foreword by Robert Lyman

Greenhill Books ★ London
Stackpole Books ★ Pennsylvania

Greenhill Books

Stilwell the Patriot: Vinegar Joe, the Brits and Chiang Kai-Shek

First published 2005 by Greenhill Books/Lionel Leventhal Ltd
Park House, 1 Russell Gardens, London NW11 9NN, England
and
Stackpole Books, 5067 Ritter Road, Mechanicsburg PA 17055, USA

British Library Cataloguing-in Publication Data

Rooney, David
Stilwell the patriot: Vinegar Joe, the Brits and Chiang Kai-Shek
1. Stilwell, Joseph Warren, 1883
2. United States. Army – Officers – Biography
3. Generals – United States – Biography
4. Generals – China – Biography
5. World War, 1939–1945 – China
6. World War, 1939–1945 – Campaigns – Burma
I. Title
940.5'425'092

ISBN 1-85367-632-2

Library of Congress Cataloging-in Publication Data available

For more information on our books, please visit www.greenhillbooks.com, email
sales@greenhillbooks.com, or telephone us within the UK on 020 8458 3614.
You can also write to us at the above London address.

Maps drawn by Derek Stone
Printed and bound in the UK by CPD (Wales), Ebbw Vale

Contents

Illustrations

Maps

Foreword

The story David Rooney describes in this fine study is concerned with the extraordinary endeavours of one of the leading Allied characters of World War II, Lieutenant General 'Vinegar' Joe Stilwell. Stilwell ranks alongside Great Britain's General 'Bill' Slim and a very small group of senior Allied commanders who spent all their service between 1941 and 1945 engaged in the long war against Japan in South East Asia, and whose names will be indelibly connected for their contributions to the destruction, after years of unremitting hardship, of Japanese militarism in Asia.

During World War II, across every theatre, forces from a variety of nations, with differing and sometimes competing cultures, national perspectives and strategies were forced to co-operate together to an extent never before experienced. These relationships were not always easy, and the development of effective collaboration – not always achieved – became a critical objective of higher command in the war. The tensions between Wavell and de Gaulle in the Levant in 1941, and between Eisenhower and Montgomery in northwest Europe in 1944 and 1945, are but two of many examples. It was in South East Asia that probably the most complicated set of international relationships developed anywhere in the war, involving the British, Americans and Chinese at every level, from the tactical – with Chinese and British and Chinese and American fighting alongside each other through monsoon jungle, muddy trail and heat-scorched rice paddy – to the highest realm of intergovernmental decision making. The United States representative in this diverse and dynamic theatre was the infantry soldier, whose courage and professionalism was already a byword in the pre-war United States Army, and his service in India, Burma and China between 1941 and 1944 has for ever associated his name with the long war against Japan fought from China.

History and historians have tended to treat Stilwell, as is often the case with enigmatic characters of his ilk, with passion, prejudice and precious little balance. Stilwell, like that other aberrant personality Orde Wingate, seems fated to attract the extremes of comment, and a full consideration of his contribution to the ultimately successful prosecution of the war against the Japanese can too easily be lost. Like Wingate, Stilwell has suffered this loss to his reputation, but by no means all of it has been deserved. Rooney redresses this imbalance and rehabilitates Stilwell through an analysis of the core drives and values that motivated him to commit so much of his life and health to such difficult and seemingly unrewarding endeavours in China. He captures Stilwell's full-orbed personality and recognises in the man much more than the simple hard-living infantryman of legend, but the true patriot of American interests at a time when even patriotic Americans seemed not to understand that their interests were being ill-served by pandering to the warlords of the Kuomintang. The passion of his defence of United States interests against the blatant depredations of the nationalist Chinese, who sought only their own selfish advantage, and those of imperialising Britain, which appeared to seek only the recovery of lost grandeur, can easily be lost amidst the noise generated by his letters and diary, which has often hidden the clear motivations for Stilwell's attitudes and behaviour. It was this patriotic mission that gave Stilwell the oft-observed 'fire in his belly', not his penchant for self-publicity or hard living, and it is the key factor against which his achievements must be judged. This is the singular success of David Rooney's new study. It should do much to allow a reappraisal of Stilwell's achievements in the light of the failure of United States policy towards China in the years that followed the end of the war, as well as enable a new understanding of the complex relationships Stilwell established not just with his fellow Americans but with 'Limey' and Chinese alike.

ROBERT LYMAN

Preface

Having served in India in 1945 at the end of the Burma War, and having studied and written about the Burma campaign for more than ten years, I am familiar with the career of Vinegar Joe Stilwell. A dramatic and abrasive character, he inspired deep loyalty and an equally strong antagonism. His character and actions impinge on most aspects of the war in Burma, and particularly on the great issue of American involvement with Chiang Kai-Shek in China. In attempting to assess Stilwell's character and his achievements, the only interpretation that makes sense is that he was driven all the time by a strong patriotism. He tried to ensure that the vast American investment of men, money and supplies in helping China should be properly and effectively used in fighting the Japanese. He met Chiang Kai-Shek early in 1942 – before the Burma retreat – and realised that Chiang was double-dealing on a colossal scale. He was using Lend–Lease supplies not to fight the Japanese but to strengthen his position among the Chinese warlords and to stockpile ready for the showdown he expected with the Communists after the Allies had defeated Japan. Stilwell devoted the rest of his life, until his untimely death in 1946, to an attempt to alert the American people to Chiang's chicanery and to the reality of the situation in China. Unfortunately for America and the world, his views, which could have had great significance for the history of China, were stifled and then extinguished by his early death.

In addition to the China issue, I have attempted to give a balanced appraisal of Stilwell's military achievements, taking into account both American and British views, and to assess his contribution in the wider context of the Burma War. I trust that this book will be clear, lucid and readable. To assist the reader who may be unfamiliar with the geography of either Burma or China, there is a series of sketch maps which contain almost all the place names that appear in the text. Since 1945 place names in China have changed, as have those in Burma (Myanmar). To avoid confusion I have used the contemporary names from the time of the Second World War.

Finally I should like to express my sincere thanks for help in preparing this book to my daughter, Kathy Rooney; to the staff of the Cambridge University Library; to Diane and Jim Gracey, formerly of Blackstaff Press, for their greatly appreciated typing and computer skills; and to Michael Leventhal, David Watkins and their colleagues at Greenhill Books for their encouragement.

DAVID ROONEY

Stilwell the Patriot

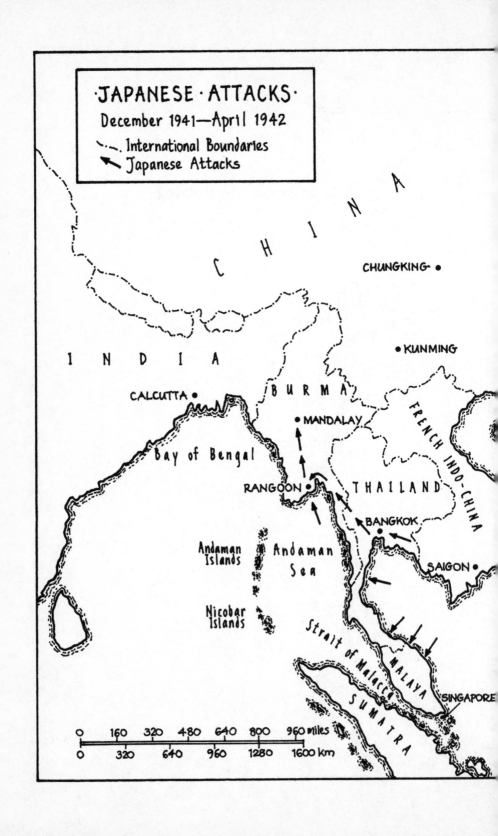

·JAPANESE · ATTACKS·
December 1941—April 1942
·-·-· International Boundaries
← Japanese Attacks

CHINA

CHUNGKING ·

KUNMING ·

INDIA

CALCUTTA ·

BURMA

· MANDALAY

Bay of Bengal

RANGOON ·

FRENCH INDO-CHINA

THAILAND

BANGKOK ·

SAIGON ·

Andaman Islands

Andaman Sea

Nicobar Islands

Strait of Malacca

MALAYA

SUMATRA

SINGAPORE

| 0 | 160 | 320 | 480 | 640 | 800 | 960 miles |
| 0 | 320 | 640 | 960 | 1280 | 1600 km |

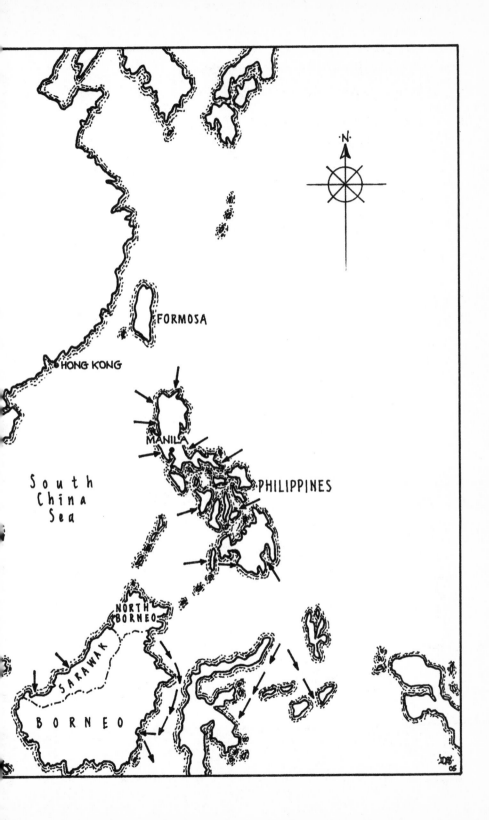

CHAPTER 1

Early Days

Joseph W. Stilwell – known for several decades of his military service as Vinegar Joe – was a lieutenant general commanding III Corps in California when the Japanese attacked Pearl Harbor. A gifted linguist, fluent in French and Spanish, he had served in China on different postings and in different capacities on and off since 1911. No senior American officer had Stilwell's wealth of experience in China, yet in the weeks after Pearl Harbor it appeared that he was destined for the European or North African theatre of operations. He was called to Washington and had urgent discussions with Eisenhower about possible landings at Dakar or Casablanca.

We know his thoughts and his acerbic comments about every aspect of the war because, during a career characterised by prolonged and acute frustration, he kept a diary, which he used to let off steam and ease his frustrations. The diary was never intended for publication but, fortunately for posterity, after his death in 1946, which occurred tragically soon after his retirement, it was published as *The Stilwell Papers*,★ which have been used extensively since. They have contributed substantially to the image of a tough, competent, irascible, colourful and opinionated commander who reserved his fiercest criticism for Chiang Kai-Shek and, equally, for the snooty upper-class English officers – the 'Limeys' – with whom he came into contact. This image is unfortunate, for although his colourful comments are indisputable, he was an outstandingly able commander with an unrivalled knowledge of the whole China situation, and if he had

★ Theodore White (ed.), *The Stilwell Papers*, Macdonald, London, 1949. Unless otherwise stated, Stilwell's quotations in this book are from *The Stilwell Papers*.

not been sacrificed by Roosevelt in 1944 for political expediency he could have saved the American administration from major and costly blunders in the years after 1945.

Stilwell was born in 1883 into a wealthy and old-established American family. Bright and precocious, he was expelled from school for a prank, and this led to him joining the army. From his entry to West Point in 1900 he was always a loner, rejecting the heavy-drinking group and becoming a fitness fanatic. He was commissioned into the infantry in 1904. Substantial changes in army administration were then taking place as a result of the blunders that happened during the Cuban campaign of 1898.

Fighting still continued in the Philippines, and Stilwell volunteered to serve there as the only place he was likely to see action. He rapidly established a reputation as a highly professional officer who was fiercely concerned for the welfare of his men. He took part in several campaigns in jungle territory against rebel groups and was commended for leadership and initiative.

He studied Spanish seriously, and in 1906 he returned to West Point as a language instructor and then spent summer leaves visiting the downtrodden areas of South America and Mexico. He always took an intense interest in the conditions of the people and made notes about every aspect of their lives. He fiercely criticised the corrupt and uncaring regimes, usually backed by American big business, that kept the people in abject poverty – a view shared by Che Guevara some fifty years later.

At this stage of his career he was eager for overseas postings and, after marrying in 1910, he and his wife Winifred (Win) sailed for the Philippines in 1911. After a short stay there, while his wife returned home he briefly visited Japan and then travelled on to China, the country that was destined to be the backdrop to the most dramatic part of his career. He arrived in Shanghai, the largest of the so-called Treaty ports, lying on the Yangtze river, which to his surprise had the appearance of a western city. From the start he studied and took notes on every aspect of this new and fascinating experience and began the difficult task of learning the language.

During the nineteenth century when, after the Opium Wars, the European powers grabbed the Treaty ports, China's isolation was slowly broken down and her weakness exposed to the predatory powers of the West. In the 1880s, with European arrogance, France took part of Indo-China, Britain took part of Burma, and Japan, already emerging as a threat, took Korea, Formosa and a foothold on the mainland of Manchuria. Greedy western nations grabbed commercial concessions and naval bases, and the United States joined in with economic penetration and vigorous missionary activity. 1899 witnessed a wild flare-up by the Chinese against western domination, and the rebels, in the Boxer Rebellion, launched powerful attacks on the foreign legations in Peking. European armies rescued the legations, spread fire and destruction, and exacted further humiliating concessions. The uprisings, some led by Sun Yat-Sen, caused widespread chaos across the country. This was the historical background to the situation which Stilwell found when he arrived in 1911.

Always eager to eschew the cocktail-party circuit, Stilwell obtained permission to travel from Shanghai to the far south to visit Canton and Wuchow, where there had been serious uprisings, and also Hong Kong. Here he admired the British soldiers but made the first of many critical comments about the foppish upper-class English officers. He returned to Shanghai with a valuable collection of meticulous observations and colourful comments. In December 1911 he returned to the Philippines, and then to the USA.

His intellectual, academic and linguistic ability had been recognised and in 1912 he was reappointed to the staff of West Point. He always disliked the humdrum routine of army life, and almost immediately he obtained a transfer to Madrid to brush up his Spanish. He was still in Spain when he heard the news of the murder in Sarajevo of the Austrian Archduke Franz Ferdinand in June 1914. When war was declared, seeing the chance to observe war at first hand, he applied – unsuccessfully – for a posting as an observer with the French army.

The American public, accustomed to seeing war as a frontier skirmish or modest foreign adventure in Cuba or the Philippines, with no likelihood of a threat to the homeland, had never accorded the military a high priority, and in 1914 the army was ill-prepared to take part in a modern war. Something of a dress-rehearsal had taken place in 1916 when General Pershing led a punitive expedition against

Mexico with infantry, cavalry, artillery and even some air squadrons, but their enemy, the Mexican insurgent Pancho Villa, was hardly of the calibre of the German army. By 1916 the US forces had increased to more than 200,000, but, in addition to the task of training huge numbers of officers and men, the whole apparatus of command and staff had to be created almost from scratch. There had been little organisation for action at division level, let alone at corps or army level, and no machinery existed for the co-ordination of infantry, artillery and cavalry. It was a remarkable achievement that within a few months of the USA entering the war in April 1917, seven divisions were able to cross the Atlantic and hurry forward to bolster the Allies on the western front. Pershing, an aggressive cavalryman, saw the American task as conducting a war of movement, and he correctly and resolutely refused the urgent pleas from the Allied commanders to use American units to plug the gaps in their ranks caused by the hundreds of thousands of casualties.

Stilwell arrived in France with the main force late in 1917. Early in 1918, after a brief liaison with a British division – which stimulated some pithy comments – he joined a French unit near Verdun. He was about to witness and take part in the dramatic finale of the war. Despite the sickening casualties of the previous years, in March 1918 Ludendorff launched an offensive with forty divisions released from the eastern front by Russia's withdrawal from the war after the Bolshevik revolution. Ludendorff hoped to use the eastern divisions to achieve victory before the American forces could be fully and effectively mobilised on the western front, and he nearly succeeded. Under the pressure of the crisis created by the Ludendorff offensive the Allies at last agreed to a unified command under Foch, and Pershing, always sensitive to issues of independence, reluctantly agreed.

Frustration played a large part in Stilwell's later life, and it started on the western front when, because of his fluent French and staff experience, he was forced to undertake the necessary staff work and his applications to join a combat unit were refused. An ambitious professional soldier, it galled him to see officers who were considerably junior to him rising to higher ranks because of the losses in the fighting units.

In spite of his frustrations, Stilwell played a significant role in the major American operation of the war. Promoted to lieutenant colonel, he supervised the training and organised the main intelligence briefings in preparation for the attack of the American First Army that took place at St Mihiel on 7 September 1918. Described by John Keegan as 'an undoubted victory',★ the American divisions not only defeated the opposing German units but captured 13,000 prisoners. This operation, in which Stilwell, Marshall, MacArthur and Patton all took part, showed that the American forces were trained and ready to play an effective part in the war. With the ultimate failure of the Ludendorff offensive, this American battle had a significant impact on the German attitude to surrender.

In January 1918, President Woodrow Wilson had put to Congress his idea of an honourable settlement at the end of the war based on his Fourteen Points, and this was the basis on which Germany and other countries approached the Allies with peace feelers. In October Ludendorff, who had come so close to achieving victory, publicly advocated the rejection of the Fourteen Points, and was dismissed. By the beginning of November 1918, from the Baltic states in the north that sought nationhood, through eastern Europe threatened by Bolshevik revolution, through the ramshackle Hapsburg dominions stretching across the Balkans, most countries and aspiring countries sued for peace. In Germany, against the threat of red revolution supported by soldiers and sailors, the Kaiser abdicated, and the future of the country lay in untried hands. Facing this chaotic background, Wilson came to the Versailles Conference with his Fourteen Points, in response to which the cynical but realistic French premier Clemenceau commented, 'The Good Lord needed only ten.' Against the hard determination of Clemenceau and Lloyd George to 'squeeze Germany till the pips squeak', Wilson's idealism was doomed. Throughout much of the world, expectations of justice and self-determination were raised only to be bitterly disappointed, and fudged decisions laid up dire peril for the future. The hopes of Ireland under Michael Collins were dashed. Lawrence of Arabia, who had

★ John Keegan, *The First World War*, Hutchinson, London, 1998, p. 441.

masterminded the Arab revolt against the Turks based on a British promise of independence, saw those promises broken, and the foundation was laid for a century or more of conflict in the Middle East. Wilson, who commented ruefully that new nations were popping up every day that he had never heard of, had no solution to the cauldron of expectations and disappointments.

Stilwell, serving as part of the occupation force in the pleasant wine-growing area of the Mosel valley and, like most serving soldiers at the end of a war, impatient to get home, made his usual stark comments. He regarded Wilson as 'an addle-pated boob' and showed little interest in the deliberations at Versailles. However, one part of those deliberations was to influence his career directly.

When the war started in 1914, in the Far East both China and Japan joined the Allied cause hoping that the Allies would win and that the eventual peace settlement would bring them valuable benefits. In China the chaos and upheavals, which Stilwell had witnessed during his informative visit in 1911, had spread across the country as the so-called warlords profited from the lack of central control. The feeble government in Peking continued to clash with the Kuomintang, the government led by Sun Yat-Sen, which was based in the south and centred on Canton. Japan, which had already given evidence of its expansionist aims, clearly hoped that the war would provide the opportunity to increase its severe demands on China and, as well, to take over the Russian and German concessions. Under considerable Japanese pressure at the peace conference, Wilson unwisely agreed to the Japanese demand for Shantung. This small but crucial peninsula, pointing across the Yellow Sea towards Korea, lay just south of Peking. It had immense tactical and strategic military significance. The Shantung award caused riots and violent protest across China, which went some way to making the rival factions overcome their differences. In America, outbursts of strong anti-Japanese feeling were led by the already powerful Chinese lobby in Washington and by the widespread Chinese missionary support groups.

In both the American and British armies many officers who had survived the carnage and gained higher rank were, when the war ended, reduced to their substantive rank and faced years of stagnation and frustration. Stilwell, back home in 1919 and reduced to the rank of captain, was relatively fortunate. Because of the excellent reports from both corps and divisional headquarters about his work in the final operations on the western front, together with his earlier successful posting to China, he was appointed as a military attaché in China. First, however, he had to spend a year at Berkeley to learn Chinese. Always fascinated by systems and methods – and usually able to suggest ways of improving them – he commented that although the course was adequate it should have taken place in China. In August 1920, after successfully completing the course and before they left for Peking, he and his wife Win bought a piece of land at Carmel near Monterey in California, intending to build a home for their family and retirement.

The situation in China had seriously deteriorated since Stilwell's visit in 1911. Rival military gangs led by bandits roamed the towns and countryside, and bullets and shells often landed in the affluent areas of Peking where the expatriates lived. Fighting raged over much of northern China, and Sun Yat-Sen, with the Kuomintang, tried without success to establish nationwide control. He felt he had been shamefully let down by the Allies in the post-war settlement, and he turned, briefly, to an alliance with the new Russian Communist party.

Stilwell found routine headquarters life in Peking both boring and stultifying, and he was delighted when he had the opportunity to join a road-building operation in Shensi Province, about 400 miles southwest of Peking. A famine relief committee, backed by the Red Cross, supported the scheme, which was designed to assist the distribution of food during famines. He spent several months working on the project as an engineer adviser, living a hard life, little different from the Chinese coolies who formed his workforce. He revelled in the total immersion in Chinese life and language. At the time China was suffering from a severe famine, and Stilwell described the thousands of gaunt skeletons roaming the countryside and the putrefying corpses left by the roadside. He commented vividly on the suffering of the local people from starvation and also on the effect of opium, to which vast numbers were addicted. He castigated local officers and rulers for not dealing with the opium problem. His views were generally ignored, but he did meet one governor who was making a sincere attempt to improve the conditions of his people – although even his work was overwhelmed and destroyed by the usual warring factions.

While Stilwell was stationed in Peking in 1922, the Five Power Conference met in Washington and made significant decisions. Agreement was reached to ban the use of poison gas in war and attacks by submarines on merchant ships. Japan agreed to give up all rights and territories in China that had been acquired through the defeat of Germany and also agreed to the limitation of her naval rearmament. These decisions had a direct effect on Stilwell, who was sent to observe how well the provisions of the Washington Agreement were being carried out. He revelled in the opportunity and travelled, recording his acute observations, to Manchuria, Korea and Japan. Wherever he went in the Japanese-occupied areas he found the Japanese to be obstructive and unpleasant. He compared them to the Germans, though without the ability, summing them up as 'arrogant little bastards'. After this fascinating and enlightening period of travel, which also took in the Yangtze valley, he, his wife and their young family returned home in 1923.

CHAPTER 2

The China Station

On his return home in 1923, Stilwell spent several years improving his military credentials and qualifications, first at Fort Benning in Georgia and then at the more demanding General Staff School at Fort Leavenworth. Here he tackled a highly pressurised staff course in a more relaxed fashion than most. Eisenhower passed out first. After sharing in the 1918 victories, America seemed to breathe a sigh of relief, with the result that army numbers were reduced, finance for defence was whittled down and prospects of promotion almost disappeared. Stilwell faced this situation with foreboding, but his outstanding previous work in China and reputation gained in 1918 as a dedicated professional officer brought him an opportunity which he seized enthusiastically. He was offered the command of a battalion in the American force at Tientsin, the port city close to Peking, and, after a summer leave at Carmel in 1924, he and his family embarked again for China.

Every time Stilwell returned to China he found dramatic and unexpected changes. While he had been back in the USA the turmoil caused by irresponsible warlords and bandits had worsened, and the influence of Russia on Sun Yat-Sen and the Kuomintang had grown more powerful. With few options open to him, Sun Yat-Sen had gone along with the Russian advisers and had initiated a political policy, but in 1925 he suddenly died of cancer. The removal of his restraining hand created the chance for the advancement of Chiang Kai-Shek. Chiang had joined Sun Yat-Sen's party in 1918. He became Commandant of the Whampoa Military Academy in 1923, and after Sun's death in 1925 took over the Kuomintang.

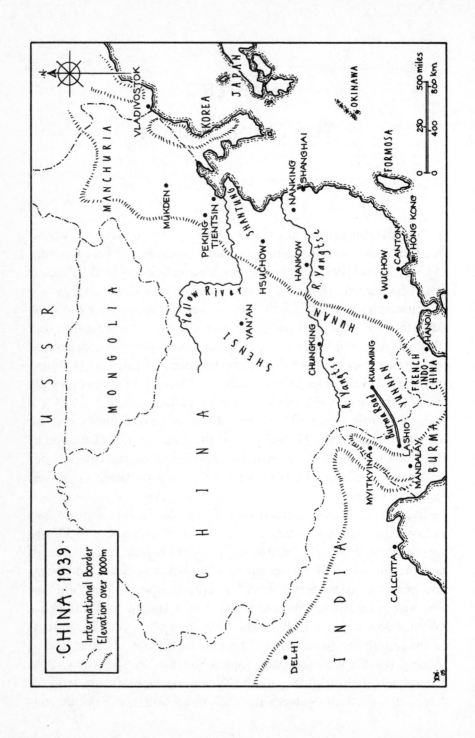

CHINA · 1939 ·
International Border
Elevation over 1000m

Several bloody incidents in 1925 and an effective left-wing propaganda campaign had whipped up countrywide fury against American and British influence and against the superior, condescending attitude of Christian missionaries.

When the Stilwell family arrived in Tientsin in 1926, the Kuomintang forces were driving north towards Nanking and Shanghai. The period of uneasy alliance between the Communists – among whom Mao Tse-Tung was prominent – and the Kuomintang leaders was soon to end. Mao, whose insistence that guerrilla fighters should respect the people had contributed to the success of the revolutionary forces, now left the Kuomintang – just before Chiang turned on his erstwhile allies and wiped out most of the leadership in Shanghai. The expatriate communities became gravely and increasingly concerned as the warring Chinese troops approached Shanghai. In Nanking angry crowds attacked foreign people and property, and while the leaders dithered a massive exodus of expatriates took place – especially missionaries, of whom there were 12,000 in the country. Missionaries faced a dilemma, for they tended to support the Kuomintang because Sun Yat-Sen had been a Christian, and they faced embarrassment when Chiang's nationalist forces demanded that people and companies in the Treaty Ports should be taxed and that the unjust Treaty regulations should be changed.

Expatriate groups in Tientsin watched these developments with growing apprehension, and serious plans were made by the American army and marines to rescue expatriates from Peking should it be necessary. Somewhat to the chagrin of the army, the marines arrived with guns, tanks and planes. In a highly volatile situation the American forces needed reliable, accurate information, and they chose Major Stilwell as the obvious person to travel through the war-torn area to observe and gather information. Glad to escape the stuffy and static military life of the legation, which he had always disliked, Stilwell was nevertheless anxious about leaving his pregnant wife and four children.

He and a Chinese colleague set out by rail for Hsuchow, about 300 miles south of Tientsin and more than halfway to Nanking and Shanghai. On this long journey Stilwell faced very real danger. Rival armed gangs disputed control at the stations and on the trains, and crowds panicked at the approach of any armed group. As far as possible Stilwell kept himself hidden because of the violent, xenophobic feelings among the tightly packed crowds on the train. Many wanted him taken off and shot. After facing appalling danger in Hsuchow, he and his colleague managed to board a train going south towards Shanghai. They went through an area where the Kuomintang forces dominated and, although they were less anti-American, the crowds at the stations and on the train were, if anything, more hostile. Again, many demanded that the foreigner should be taken off the train and shot. His Chinese colleague probably saved Stilwell's life by demanding to be taken to Chiang Kai-Shek himself, saying that there would be serious trouble for anyone who tried to stop them. They kept up this bluff until they reached Shanghai, where, starving, dehydrated and totally exhausted, they left the train and ran for their lives. They managed to reach the International Settlement, and from there they were able to get to the USS *Pittsburg*, which was lying off shore and where at last they found safety.

Stilwell sent in a detailed report backed up by acute observations about the Kuomintang forces and comparing them favourably to the rabble under the warlords in the north. He was highly commended by the senior American commanders for his bravery and determination and for his excellent report.

In 1928, in a bizarre situation that arose when the General Officer Commanding became mentally unstable, Stilwell was promoted to lieutenant colonel and became his chief of staff. He rapidly became the leader and mentor of the American community, giving lectures and writing articles that displayed his outstanding grasp of Chinese affairs. He commented shrewdly on the sinister incident when Japanese forces deliberately tried to provoke a fight with Chiang, who, realising his weakness, wisely withdrew. The Chinese people deeply resented the insult and boycotted Japanese goods. Stilwell warned that the Japanese could easily overrun the ports, the railways and the developed areas along the east coast. Chiang was not able to challenge the Japanese, but he was strong enough to push aside the northern warlords and he arrived at Tientsin with the Kuomintang forces. Although he was now nominally leader of China, the reality was different. He called the warlords to a disbandment conference, but, as long as they commanded hundreds of thousands of troops, they simply ignored his pleas. Mayhem and chaos continued across China. Stilwell, now established as a recognised and respected expert on China, returned home with his large family in 1929.

Many of the American army commanders of the Second World War had, like Stilwell, served under General Pershing on the western front in 1918. Pershing, an inspiring leader, had created a nucleus of forward-thinking leaders, who would wield great influence in the world to come. Among these George Marshall was the most influential, and he was destined to play a vital role in Stilwell's career.

Marshall severely criticised the rigid textbook attitude of much military training in the army and, after serving in China, where he had witnessed Stilwell's outstanding work, he returned to the USA to take command of the infantry school at Fort Benning. From this key position Marshall determined to carry out a revolution in the training of infantry officers. He picked out Stilwell to be his second-in-command because he knew of Stilwell's cogent and forceful attitude to stuffiness and mediocrity.

Stilwell relished the opportunity this gave him to break away from the shackles of training manuals, and he focused the training of young infantry officers on the need to make decisions in the uncertain chaos of battle, when the view of the platoon or company commander, who can see the ground, is very different from that of more senior commanders further back. He used the thickly wooded country around Fort Benning to reinforce this point. Marshall considered Stilwell to be an absolutely outstanding instructor who stimulated his students to face the real problems that junior infantry commanders would face in war. The passion to see and understand the problem of the infantry commander on the ground never deserted Stilwell, and even when in 1944 he was Deputy Commander of South East Asia Command, surrounded by the pompous ceremonial he hated, he frequently returned to his Chinese battalions trudging through the Huckawng valley of northern Burma. Widely respected at Fort Benning as an inspiring instructor, he was also renowned as a severe critic of those who did not reach his exacting standards, and this led to his nickname of Vinegar Joe – which he treasured.

While Stilwell was establishing himself at Fort Benning, events took place in the Far East that led ultimately to the Pacific war in which he was to play a significant role. In 1931, Japan, having created a phoney incident, seized Mukden and began a systematic advance through Manchuria. This proved a damaging blow to the Kellogg–Briand Pact of 1928, which the major powers, including Japan, had signed, and which renounced the use of war except in self-defence. In the USA the government announced the Stimson Doctrine, under which agreements achieved by force would not be recognised, and the League of Nations despatched a commission under the British peer Lord Lytton. While the Lytton Commission was on its way to the Far East, Japan defiantly set up the puppet state of Manchukuo under a Chinese boy emperor. The Chinese spontaneously rose up against the Japanese aggression and threatened the 30,000 Japanese troops stationed in Shanghai. Claiming to act in self-defence and for the protection of its citizens, Japan used ground, naval and air forces to attack the Chinese part of the city. After several months of increasing international pressure, Japan accepted a cease-fire and withdrew. Stimson considered the Japanese action to be the greatest shock to international morality since 1914. In Japan the war party won an overwhelming election victory. The Japanese government claimed that, because of the chaos in China, the Kellogg–Briand Pact was not binding. Claiming again that it was acting in self-defence, it rejected the Lytton report and withdrew from the League of Nations. The Manchuria crisis presaged the downfall of the League of Nations and should have warned the world of Japan's aggressive intent. In the face of the Japanese military advance Chiang Kai-Shek, who was in too weak a position to oppose it, shrewdly withdrew and concentrated instead on opposing the guerrilla attacks of the Chinese Communists under Mao Tse-Tung.★

In 1934 Stilwell concluded his stint at Fort Benning but found himself faced with few attractive options. After applying unsuccess-

★ Martin Gilbert, *History of the Twentieth Century*, HarperCollins, London, 2001, Vol. 1, p. 825.

fully for an overseas appointment, he accepted a posting to San Diego to a training assignment with a reserve corps. He was seriously depressed – as was Marshall at this time – and felt that as a lieutenant colonel aged fifty-one he had little future in the army. Although his work with Marshall was to stand him in good stead and he had left Fort Benning with a reputation as a very able instructor, he was also known as a character who was prickly, over-sensitive and pernickety. He was renowned for his caustic comments about pettifogging rules and for his outspoken contempt for what he called 'the machine'. However, the San Diego posting at least enabled him and the family to oversee the building of their home at Carmel. He even considered retiring from the army but, with the massive unemployment of the early 1930s, he realised that staying in the army was probably his best option.

The army rescued Stilwell from his gloomy situation by offering him the post of military attaché in China. He was overjoyed at the prospect of returning to China, though the whole situation had gravely deteriorated since his last visit. The Japanese, those 'arrogant little bastards', had continued their penetration of northern China. In the south Chiang had organised a major attack on the Communist forces and driven them, under Mao's leadership, far to the west and then to the north, on what became known as the Long March, after which the Communists established a precarious base in the remote northern territory of Yan'an.

In 1936 Stilwell and his family arrived back in China, and almost at once he set out on another of his forays to gain information and to assess the real situation. As usual he eschewed first-class rail travel, preferring to move about by bus and boat to meet more of the people. He travelled north to check on Chiang's preparations for defence against the Japanese incursions and, finding they were pathetic, was publicly critical of the Kuomintang leader. In the following year he travelled even more widely, visiting Chinese army training centres and studying the situation in Nanking.

Visiting the Japanese puppet state of Manchukuo, he found that the Japanese were trying to gain support for their policy by stressing the danger of Russian Communism spreading through eastern Asia.

The world was slowly learning about the Communist system under Mao, who by this time was established in the bleak northern area around Yan'an after the prolonged suffering of the Long March. Mao's firm discipline and his insistence that Communist forces respect the local people, which was part of his overall policy on guerrilla war, impressed outside observers and gave him a huge advantage over Chiang's corrupt and brutal soldiery. Stilwell observed the effect of Mao's philosophy and his training on the Chinese soldier. In December 1936, in a bizarre incident, a local warlord kidnapped Chiang to force him to co-operate with the Communist forces in a united front against the Japanese. This caused international concern because most observers feared chaos across China if Chiang was removed. He gained his freedom by offering some dubious promises, and there was a brief semblance of unity against the Japanese aggressors. Stilwell, now increasingly recognised as America's China expert, observed these incidents at quite close quarters but realistically dismissed the protestations about unity and democracy.

In July 1937 Stilwell witnessed the 'contrived incident', when Japanese troops clashed with the Chinese outside Peking and which Japan used as an excuse to start its war in China with the aim of taking over the northern part of the country. He immediately set up a network of contacts to keep him informed of Japanese progress, and he was determined to publicise details of the Japanese aggression. The Japanese forces advanced almost unopposed, daily committing dreadful rapine and other atrocities. Stilwell fumed at Chiang's total failure to take effective action and at the pusillanimous American attitude. Chiang decided to withdraw his forces to tempt the Japanese to move south and attack Shanghai. He hoped that this would give the incursion maximum publicity in the outside world and force the western powers to act. This was a signal failure – and then Chiang, against military advice, decided to defend Nanking.

As Japanese forces took over Peking and most Chinese territory stretching down to Shanghai and Nanking, Stilwell's criticism, both of Chiang and of the American government, became more strident. By the end of 1937 Chiang's HQ had been withdrawn to Hankow, about 200 miles southwest of Nanking. Stilwell had to follow. Thus

he was close at hand when, in December 1937, the Japanese perpetrated the rape of Nanking, in the course of which their troops raped
and massacred nearly 200,000 people. All women and girls were
brought in for mass rape by platoons of soldiers and then shot. The
world shuddered but took little action. The Japanese then bombed an
American ship, but quickly apologised. 'Bastards,' said Stilwell.

The rape of Nanking, whose horror still stands out despite all the
horrors that have happened since, brought to an end a period in
which the democratic powers, in the grip of appeasement, suffered
disastrous setbacks and the fascist powers appeared to be able to act
with impunity. In March 1936 Hitler, choosing a weekend when he
thought, correctly, that the British cabinet would not be meeting,
marched into the Rhineland in defiance of the Versailles settlement.
Mussolini had already marched into Abyssinia, where he bravely
overcame spear-throwing tribesmen with artillery and mustard gas.
Britain could have stopped the Italians by denying them use of the
Suez canal, but it feared to do so. In the same year Franco led his
Fascist forces, backed by the army and the Roman Catholic Church,
against the elected government of Spain. Then, to the delight of
the other fascist leaders, who backed him with troops, weapons and
aircraft, in April 1937 he carried out the destruction of Guernica in
an experiment to determine whether a town could be completely
wiped out by aerial bombing. These horrors perpetrated by the
fascists in Europe perhaps helped to deflect attention from the worst
aspects of Japanese aggression in China.

Stilwell grew increasingly frustrated and bitter at the craven attitude of the Washington administration and at the restrictions which
both the Chinese and the Japanese placed on his travels as a military
attaché. Infuriated by what he saw as the stuffy, blinkered attitude of
most of the embassy staff, he made contact with any free spirit –
including charity workers and journalists – who could bring him
reliable information. During 1938 he overcame some of the obstacles
and was able to resume his travels to the different war fronts. As he
saw more of the Chinese armies his admiration grew for the tough,
long-suffering, uncomplaining Chinese soldier, but he despaired of
the poor quality of leadership and the feeble, defeatist attitude of the

officers and commanders of the Kuomintang. As he tried to extend his travels, he was again curbed by 'the interfering bastards in Washington'. His frustration was so intense that once again he considered throwing up the job and resigning his commission.

During this depressing time, Stilwell did manage to obtain details of Russian supplies coming by air to the Communist forces in the north under Mao and, to his surprise, the Chinese won a significant battle against the Japanese. To the chagrin of their German military advisers, the Chinese commanders failed to follow up their victory and threw away the advantage they had gained. As the Japanese resumed their advance after their brief defeat, Chiang sought to delay them by blowing up the dams on the Yellow River. This certainly slowed the Japanese advance, but – and this was apparently a matter of indifference to Chiang – it made two million Chinese people homeless and caused countless civilian deaths. Stilwell observed Chiang's military failings and despaired further as he and his glamorous, western-educated wife emerged as the heroes of the missionary-based Chinese lobby in Washington.

By the end of 1938 Chiang had transferred his capital from Hankow to Chungking in the far southwest of China. Here he felt confident that, 'having exchanged space for time', he could hold out until the Japanese threat wilted. During this period the ruthless Japanese advance against the ineptly led Chinese forces enjoyed a double victory: they captured Hankow in the north, and in the south, in close proximity to Hong Kong, Canton, effectively cutting off Chiang from the eastern seaboard. This coincided with the nadir of the western democracies at Munich, on 29 September 1938, when Czechoslovakia was abandoned to Hitler.

Stilwell transferred his small team from Hankow to Hunan, the area around Chiang's new capital Chungking, where some desultory military action still continued. Stilwell spent a short time in Chungking, where he met Chiang and his wife. Stilwell was already looking to the future. He began to think that only America would be strong enough to face Japan, but he argued in some detail that the Chinese might be able to face the enemy if they had American equipment and supplies and if they were led by American officers.

In May 1939, in a mood of profound depression, Stilwell and his family left China on an American troopship for the long sea voyage home. In his mid-fifties and still a colonel, he reluctantly faced the prospect of retirement, but once again he was rescued from this fate. When the ship reached Honolulu in August 1939 he received a message that his old friend George Marshall had become the US Chief of Staff and had promoted him to brigadier.

After a brief leave, and after urgent discussions with Marshall on how to overcome America's fateful unpreparedness, Stilwell was posted to Texas to command a brigade and to bring some harsh reality into the training. Because of cut-backs during the 1920s and 1930s, when America faced no obvious military threat, in 1939 there were only three active divisions, and even these were not at full strength. Stilwell was increasingly concerned that the threat of fascism in Europe masked the growing danger from Japan in the Pacific. The Nazi blitzkrieg in 1940 at least assisted Roosevelt in obtaining the support of Congress for the necessary back-up and for a dramatic increase in military expenditure.

Stilwell rapidly gained a reputation as one of the best and most aggressive commanders in corps and army exercises, and he fiercely criticised the establishment for its slowness in learning from the German Panzer attack and the fall of France. The dramatic defeat of the democracies in Europe in the summer of 1940 soon had its effect on the situation in the Far East. The war party in Japan stepped up its provocation and pressure, and it forced France to agree to concessions in Indo-China. Within weeks of Dunkirk, Britain, under Japanese pressure, reluctantly agreed to close the Burma Road, which ran from Mandalay and Lashio up to Chungking and was by that time the main supply route for Chiang in Chungking. In September 1940 Japan joined the Rome–Berlin Axis.

In July 1940, Stilwell was promoted to major general and he took over command of 7 Division. He was already talking openly of the need for America to fight Japan and was suggesting a mixture of American and Chinese divisions. Before the end of 1940 America had begun its huge world-wide financial and military support for the democracies, and in Chungking Chiang Kai-Shek had started to play his unscrupulous and deceitful game. He constantly increased his demands for money and supplies, and he backed up these demands by hinting that things were desperate and he might be forced to do a deal with the Japanese.

In October 1940, Chiang, egged on by Claire Chennault, who was later to become Stilwell's *bête noire*, formally requested American planes and pilots so that he could to attack Japanese sea lanes and military movements. Chiang's protestations were rarely the whole truth, and even in the extremity of 1940, instead of facing the Japanese, he covertly attacked the increasingly powerful Communist forces under Mao. Chiang was to be severely criticised as a military leader, but he must be given credit for his decision to retire to Chungking, which gave him time and enabled him to keep China in the war against Japan. His demands for American planes, pilots and other support – initially rejected as fanciful – gradually built up a wave of support from the China lobby in the USA and their ginger groups. The scheme received a major boost from the Lend–Lease Act of 1941. Throughout this period Chiang's case was masterminded by his brother-in-law, the immensely wealthy and influential T. V. Soong, who made an astronomic fortune from Lend–Lease deals. The notion gradually grew that by arming and supplying thirty Chinese assault divisions America might keep China fighting effectively and deter Japan from attacking elsewhere. To oversee this colossal operation Washington set up an American military mission to China.

During 1941, Japan put pressure on the weak Vichy government and gained further concessions for the use of airfields in French Indo-China, including Saigon. This time Washington reacted to the move and froze Japanese assets. Belatedly it started to reinforce its bases in the Philippines, but both Congress and the country remained deeply divided about the prospect of war. As the war scenario widened and Roosevelt became more involved with Churchill, Chiang was infuriated by his exclusion from top-level discussion. This attitude continued and provided the bleak backdrop to inter-Allied co-operation until 1945. America, despite warnings, continued to believe that with positive support China would mount an effective attack on Japan. Towards the end of 1941 Chiang, in the hope of gaining more supplies, again warned that another defeat by the Japanese or the loss of Kunming could force China to withdraw from the war. The mistrust and misunderstanding between China, which felt it had spent years fighting the cause now supported by the democracies, and America, which believed it had been munificently generous in providing supplies for thirty divisions with scant result, continued through 1941. This enabled the war party in Japan to complete its planning and gave it time to make the decision on where and when to attack.

CHAPTER 3

Pearl Harbor and After

The *Stilwell Papers* give a vivid, colourful daily record of Stilwell's life during the Burma war, together with his equally colourful views and comments. A preface to the *Papers* explains that on Sunday, 7 December 1941, the day of the attack on Pearl Harbor, the Stilwells were entertaining some of the officers of III Corps HQ at Carmel when a friend telephoned and said, 'Listen to the radio.' That is how they heard the news of the Japanese attack.

Stilwell, as the commander of III Corps, was responsible for the defence of southern California. With the psychological impact of the Pearl Harbor catastrophe, it is understandable that people imagined other Japanese attacks to be imminent. In a tense and apprehensive atmosphere, rumours abounded. Southern California, with more than half of all the USA's aircraft factories, was responsible for three-quarters of the country's bomber production and a substantial part of its oil production, so it was an obvious target for the Japanese.

Within hours of the news breaking reports came in of attacking aircraft and ships. Feverish rumours spread wildly. It was reported that the main Japanese fleet was approaching San Francisco – a report which turned out to be totally false. As the overall commander, Stilwell had to take such reports seriously, but his role quickly emerged. It was reflected in his diary entry, 'Calm 'em down.' Commenting that common sense was being thrown to the winds and that any absurdity was believed, he added, 'The higher the H.Q. the more important is calm.'

From his comments there is no doubt that if the Japanese had indeed planned an attack on California to coincide with Pearl Harbor the area would have been almost defenceless. At the top level, Stilwell had to retrieve the reality from the fantasy. Even so, there was enough dire news in that fateful month of December 1941. On 10 December the British warships *Prince of Wales* and *Renown*, with no air cover, were sunk off the coast of Malaya by a Japanese air attack. 'My God. Worse and Worse.' The Japanese made rapid advances in the Philippines. Germany and Italy declared war on the USA, and Guam and Wake Island fell. The Japanese occupied Thailand. In July 1941 the Vichy government weakly agreed to the occupation of Indo-China. On Christmas Day 1941 Hong Kong, one of the bastions of British power in the Far East, fell to the Japanese.

In Chungking, Chiang Kai-Shek was delighted at the news of the attack on Pearl Harbor because it instantly brought the United States into the war against Japan. He quickly produced fanciful plans for all the countries involved in the war to centre their efforts on his HQ in a combined effort to defeat the Japanese during 1942. Stilwell's diatribes about the 'Limeys' – the British – are well known. Less well known is Chiang's hatred for the British, who he believed were taking away Lend–Lease supplies that were rightly his. Central to this issue was the Burma Road, which ran from Rangoon through Mandalay, Lashio, and through the mountains to Kunming and Chungking. Britain, in response to Japanese political pressure, had temporarily closed the road in 1940, but after Pearl Harbor it became the crucial supply route for much of the Lend–Lease material that was sent to Chiang.

While the frantic reaction to the Japanese attack continued, Marshall called Stilwell to Washington. On Christmas Eve he left his family in Carmel. He was immediately involved in earnest discussions about a possible American attack on the Axis forces in North Africa. He made caustic comments about Roosevelt, whom he called the 'Big Boy', and the diary entry for 27 December is clear:

> The Big Boy thinks it isn't yet the 'ripe time' for Casablanca. Good news to me, with 1,100 German planes in Sardinia and Sicily, and 185,000 troops in Morocco, and 80,000 French in North Africa,

twenty-eight divisions (German) in France and 400 planes in Spain etc. The plain truth is we can do one thing and not several and we'll have to pick it out.

During this time his diary is augmented by letters to his wife, which fortunately have survived and which give a stark description of Washington at this critical time.

My impression of Washington is a rush of clerks in and out of doors, swing doors always swinging, people with papers rushing after other people with papers, groups in corners whispering in huddles, everybody jumping up as soon as you start to talk, buzzers ringing, telephones ringing, rooms crowded with clerks all banging away at typewriters. 'Give me ten copies of this AT ONCE.' 'Get that secret file out of the safe.' 'Where is the Yellow Plan (Blue Plan, Green Plan, Orange Plan, etc.)?' Everybody furiously smoking cigarettes, everybody passing you on to someone else, etc., etc. Someone with a loud voice and a mean look and a big stick ought to appear and yell 'HALT. You crazy bastards. SILENCE. You imitation ants. Now half of you get the hell out of town before dark and the other half don't move for an hour.' Then they could burn up all the papers and start fresh.

He remained highly critical of Roosevelt, considering that he was a complete amateur on all military issues and dangerously impulsive. Once again his views on the British are clear-cut. He considered that they had far too much influence on Roosevelt. 'It took the disaster in Hawaii to stop the flow of all our stuff to the Limeys ... We'll do this, we'll do that. Blow hot, blow cold. And the Limeys have his ear, while we have the hind tit.' Amid a welter of discussion about what America should do and where its first efforts should be directed, Stilwell was seriously critical about the lack of a general strategic plan and of a top-level decision on what should have the highest priority.

Urgent discussions continued in Washington through January 1942, and it gradually emerged that Stilwell was being considered, not for a command in North Africa, but in China. He reacted adversely. He felt that Chiang and his entourage would remember him as a 'small fry colonel that they kicked around'. In mid-January Stimson, the Secretary of War, interviewed him and asked him what he thought of the possibility of commanding the Chinese venture. With a notable lack of enthusiasm he replied that he would go where he was sent. On 23 January he was offered the appointment of Chief of Staff to Chiang Kai-Shek and Commander of American forces in the China–Burma–India (CBI) theatre. His previous experience with Chiang stood him in good stead, and he immediately demanded to know his exact powers. T. V. Soong, who was to play a key role in the tortured relationship between America, Stilwell, Chiang and the Chinese, cabled Chiang and received firm, clear promises. Stilwell was to receive many such promises.

Before his appointment was officially confirmed, Stilwell continued to take part in high-level discussions on the general strategy of the war. In the brief jottings in his diary his strong feelings about the British constantly recur. He saw a copy of the notes of a meeting between Roosevelt and Churchill and commented: 'It demonstrates the tremendous hold the Limeys have on Our Boy … We must keep up the Lend–Lease torrent to our British cousins, even though our people go without.' At another conference in January 1942: 'All agreed on their disgust at the way the British were hogging all the material.' In contrast to his official worries, he told his wife in a letter that he had seen the movie *How Green Was My Valley* and that it was one of the best he had ever seen.

Early in February 1942 Roosevelt called Stilwell to the White House. Of this encounter Stilwell wrote:

> F.D.R. very pleasant and very unimpressive. As if I were a constituent in to see him. Rambled on about his idea of the war … 'a 28,000 mile front is my conception,' etc., etc. 'The real strategy is to fight them all,' etc., etc. Just a lot of wind. After I had enough I broke in and asked him if he had a message for Chiang Kai Shek. He very obviously had not, and talked for five minutes hunting around for something world shaking to say. Finally he had it – 'Tell him we are in this thing for keeps, and we intend to keep at it until China gets back all her lost territory.' He was cordial and pleasant and frothy.

After the White House interview, Stilwell went to his old friend Marshall to discuss the serious problems that would have to be faced in the CBI theatre. His experience in China, and above all his observations of Chiang, had already alerted him to the latter's methods and plans. Stilwell demanded that all the supplies and weapons for the proposed thirty Chinese divisions should be sent through him and be placed under his control. Expecting more advances by the Japanese, he obtained the agreement that if they captured Rangoon the Lend–Lease supplies would be diverted through Calcutta but remain under his control. At the same time he asked for large-scale provision of transport aircraft so that, if necessary, supplies could be flown up to Kunming or Chungking. At this stage his main aim was to oversee the training and equipping of the thirty Chinese divisions in preparation for a major ground offensive against the Japanese.

Stilwell left for the Far East on 14 February 1942 and travelled via South America and West Africa. In Lagos, Nigeria, he heard that Singapore, with its 60,000 British troops, had surrendered. 'Christ. What the hell is the matter?' At another stop he added: 'Usual Limey stories everywhere. Apathetic and snooty.' He continued his journey, passing through Cairo, Jerusalem, Baghdad and Karachi before stopping in Delhi.

By this time General Archibald Wavell, the British commander in the Far East, had met Chiang in Chungking and had grossly offended him. Reflecting the long-standing fear in Burma of Chinese occupation, Wavell tactlessly refused the offer of Chinese help when discussing the defence of Burma. This blunder exacerbated Chiang's seething resentment about control of the huge amounts of Lend–Lease material piled up in Rangoon and infuriated the Americans, who feared that Chiang might pull out of the war. Stilwell, now in Calcutta, met Wavell, 'a tired, depressed man, pretty well beaten down'. He added, 'When I think how those bowlegged cockroaches have ruined our calm lives it makes me want to wrap Jap guts around every lamp-post in Asia.'

Stilwell's prolonged journey continued. He flew from Calcutta to Lashio, on the southern part of the Burma Road, where Chiang gave him a cordial welcome. After a brief stop he went on to Kunming, where he met Chennault. His comment, 'He'll be OK,' he may later have regretted since Chennault gained great influence with Chiang and, equally significantly, with Madame Chiang Kai-Shek (subsequently 'Madame'). Chennault, with his powerful ambition, had persuaded them of the fanciful notion that a vast bomber force, provided by America, flown by American pilots and based in southern China, could knock Japan out of the war. From Kunming Stilwell flew on to Chungking, where he met Chiang and held the first serious discussion about his exact responsibilities. Chiang was incensed by the British retreat and their lethargy, and he suspected their motives. He appeared relieved when he was assured that Stilwell and not the British would command the American–Chinese forces in Burma. In this first crucial interview the translator proved inadequate and Madame took over. She made caustic remarks about the British and then discussed the role of Chennault and the American Volunteer Group (AVG), which she supported.

During the next few days Stilwell urgently sought information and intelligence on Japanese plans. He wondered why they had not attacked Rangoon and if they were too weak. He was soon to have the answer. He felt that if all the Chinese warlords, who generally commanded divisions as if they were a personal fiefdom, could be persuaded to pool their resources it could create a respectable force. Once again, Stilwell could not resist a dig at the British. He recounted how, after a state visit to India, Chiang and Madame were more impressed by Gandhi and Nehru than 'the whole damn British Raj'. The next day Stilwell had a further long discussion with Chiang and Madame, who appeared to have the sharper mind. Chiang dominated this frustrating session by explaining why China could not attack and continued with more bitter criticism of the British, during which he threatened to pull the Chinese divisions out of Burma. Stilwell felt that at least he had made some progress because he, a foreigner, had been given command of Chinese troops in Burma – something that had never happened before – but in a letter to his wife he wrote, 'My job is just endless grief.'

After Pearl Harbor and the capture of Hong Kong and Singapore, the Japanese attacked Burma in January 1942. This physically inhospitable country, with its long eastern border with China, stretched in the north into the foothills of the Himalayas. From here the great rivers, the Irrawaddy and Chindwin, flowed south through dense tropical forest, dominating the terrain and ensuring that all communications ran from south to north. The rivers, which joined near Mandalay, flowed into the sea west of the capital Rangoon. The main railway, built by British engineers in earlier years, ran almost due north from Rangoon, past Mandalay and up to Myitkyina (pronounced Michen-ar) near the northeast border with China.

During the 1930s the British administration had neglected defence issues, and there was no overall defence plan. The 1st Burma Division – thus called in the hope that an enemy might imagine there was a second – was trained for little more than internal security. The 17th Indian Division, now also stationed in Burma, had been trained for action in the sands of North Africa and was made up of only two brigades. It had been hurriedly diverted to Burma in the face of the sudden Japanese threat, as was 7 Armoured Brigade, which had already gained fame in the Desert Campaign in North Africa. In contrast, the Japanese attacked with two experienced and battle-hardened divisions – 33 and 55 – and very soon added three more. Certainly Britain was to suffer a humiliating defeat, but it should be remembered that the defence of Burma was placed in the hands of two inadequate, understrength divisions, one of which had been trained for a totally different theatre of war.

General Slim arrived in Burma in the same month as Stilwell, March 1942, and like him had no responsibility for the dire situation they faced. He took over what was called Burcorps, though this consisted of substantially less than two divisions and there was no corps headquarters or staff. Slim, like Stilwell, had briefly met Wavell when he passed through Delhi, and it had been stressed that above all he should not allow his forces in Burma to be cut off. Should it prove necessary, he should retreat northwards to defend the approaches to India and to maintain contact with the Chinese–American divisions in northeast Burma. By the time Slim reached the front, 17 Division had suffered a grave defeat at Sittang bridge and, on 6 March 1942, Rangoon had fallen to the Japanese. By the middle of March the

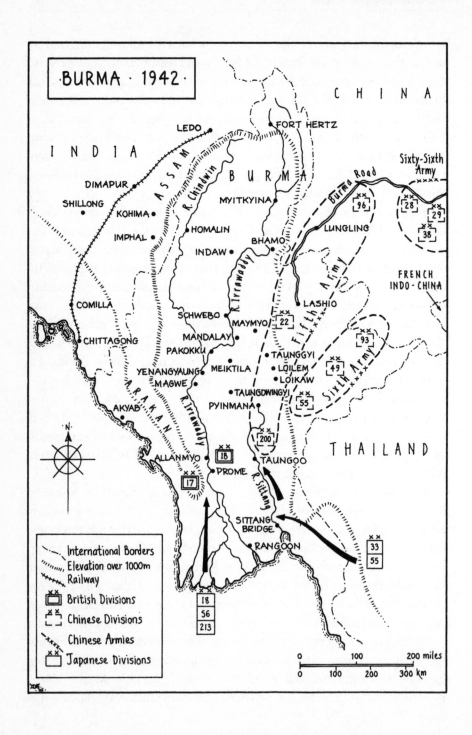

· BURMA · 1942 ·

CHINA

INDIA

LEDO   FORT HERTZ

ASSAM   BURMA

DIMAPUR   Sixty-Sixth
                    MYITKYINA   Army
SHILLONG
         KOHIMA   Burma Road
                                              96   28
         HOMALIN   LUNGLING   29
IMPHAL   BHAMO   38
              INDAW
                                                 FRENCH
                                               INDO-CHINA
COMILLA
              SCHWEBO   LASHIO
                      MAYMYO   Fifth Army
CHITTAGONG   MANDALAY   22
                                              93
         PAKOKKU
                    MEIKTILA   TAUNGGYI   49
YENANGYAUNG   LOILEM
     MAGWE   LOIKAW   Sixth Army
                    TAUNGDWINGYI
AKYAB   PYINMANA   55

         N   200
                                        THAILAND
                          TAUNGOO
     ALLANMYO   18
              PROME
            17   SITTANG
                              BRIDGE
                                              33
                    RANGOON   55

.... International Borders
         Elevation over 1000m   18
         Railway   56
         British Divisions   213
         Chinese Divisions
         Chinese Armies   0   100   200 miles
         Japanese Divisions   0 100 200 300 km

Japanese 55 and 33 Divisions had driven north and had been joined by three more – 18, 56 and 213 – which were brought in as soon as Rangoon was captured. As the five divisions moved north they faced the badly mauled 17 Indian Division, 1 Burma Division and the Chinese 200 Division from the Chinese Fifth Army.

By 12 March Stilwell was at Maymyo, a pleasant hill-station that was the British military HQ just northeast of Mandalay. Here he started his long and frequently acrimonious relationship with the British in Burma. On his arrival he met the Governor of Burma, Sir Reginald Dorman-Smith, of whom one critic remarked that his powers of self-deception were almost infinite. Stilwell was not impressed. The next day he met the British Commander-in-Chief, General Sir Harold Alexander, who was later to command the British forces in the Desert Campaign. Stilwell wrote of Alexander:

> Rather brusque and stand-offish. Let me stand around while waiting for Shang Chen to come. Uninterested when Shang did come. Astonished to find ME – mere me, a goddam American – in command of Chinese troops. 'Extrawdinary.' Looked me over as if I had just crawled out from under a rock.

Later that night a British major came to Stilwell's bedroom and told him to report to Flagstaff House at 10 a.m. He was furious and made a significant comment, 'It's just the superior race complex, for which they will pay dearly.' When Stilwell explained that he was the independent commander of the Chinese–American forces, Alexander said, 'That makes *my* position impossible from the start.' Stilwell wrote: 'So I gave him a dirty look and said I wasn't exactly on a bed of roses myself. He just stared blankly at me as much as to say, "I wonder what that bounder means."'

After tense meetings with Alexander, during which he learnt about the latest Japanese advances, Stilwell radioed for two Chinese divisions – 22 and 96 – from the Chinese Fifth Army to come south to help 200 Division, which was defending Taungoo. This message illustrates the problems over the powers of command that had been so readily promised him by Chiang. As Chief of Staff he had direct access to

Chiang, but during the fighting in Burma his orders went through General Lo, who was commander of the Chinese Expeditionary Force. When Stilwell gave orders in the field General Lo, as well as the army and divisional commanders, would pick and choose which to accept. In addition, Chiang had a personal representative at Lashio who decided what information should be passed on to Chiang, who, significantly, was referred to as 'Generalissimo'. Stilwell discovered later that Chiang, with his philosophy of refusing to attack, was in the habit of directly countermanding orders he had given so as to conserve his divisions.

Chiang's chicanery and double-dealing are further illustrated by a conversation Dorman-Smith had with the Chinese General Tu, who said, 'The American general only thinks he is commanding. In fact he is doing no such thing. You see, we Chinese think that the only way to keep the Americans in the war is to give them a few commands on paper. They will not do much harm as long as we do the work.'

After his visit to Maymyo, Stilwell was able to assess his real situation. He had been given command of two Chinese armies, the Fifth and the Sixth. The Sixth, with three divisions, occupied an area in the Shan states along the eastern border of Burma with Thailand and the Chinese province of Yunnan. The Fifth Army also had three divisions – 96, 22 and 200 – which were stretched more widely. 200 Division faced the Japanese at Taungoo, 22 Division was based on Lashio, and 96 Division was stationed further north in Chinese territory east of Myitkyina. A Chinese division consisted of about 8,000 men, but this included one-third who were porters and carriers. The troops were armed with rifles and light machine guns, with a few mortars but almost no artillery. There were no medical services and motor transport was non-existent.

Having been briefed as fully as possible at Maymyo, Stilwell flew back to Chungking on 18 March for discussions with Chiang, 'the stubborn bugger', who appeared to give approval to Stilwell's proposal to move two divisions of the Fifth Army – 22 and 96 – southwards to assist 200 Division, and also to move part of the Sixth Army towards Maymyo. He left this interview feeling 'It's pretty bad but maybe it will get better. All I can do is try.' He added, 'The Chinese accept my status, which is close to a miracle, since it is the first time in modern history that a foreigner has commanded Chinese troops.' After these discussions he wrote a memo. He had argued that if the three divisions of the Fifth Army were concentrated at Taungoo, the Japanese could be halted or even defeated. Chiang had strongly countered this, arguing that Mandalay was the key to the defence of Burma. Two divisions must be held back for its protection, and if necessary 200 Division must be sacrificed at Taungoo. Chiang stated clearly that five Chinese divisions were needed for a successful attack. In a significant comment Stilwell wrote:

> This was the doctrine that the Chinese Army was saturated with: with the G-mo [Generalissimo] giving such a lead, the fearful and the incompetent always had a good reason for retreat … The G-mo gave me further instructions in psychology and tactics, and told me that if I would observe him and listen for only six months, I could myself learn something of both arts.

He returned to Maymyo on 22 March to take command of the Chinese forces that faced the rapidly advancing Japanese.

CHAPTER 4

The Retreat from Burma

By 23 March 1942 Stilwell was back in Maymyo, desperately trying to organise the defence of Taungoo against a strong Japanese attack. He was attempting to arrange for 22 Division from the Fifth Army and 55 Division from the Sixth Army to advance and support 200 Division fighting effectively around Taungoo, but by the next day the Japanese had already advanced north of the town.

As the fighting continued around Taungoo, Slim was carrying out a similar rearguard action near Prome, almost directly to the west. Slim, like Stilwell a tough fighting commander, sent a strong force from 17 Indian Division and 7 Armoured Brigade – which he could ill afford to do without – to assist Stilwell at Taungoo. These suffered heavy losses without achieving much, but Slim never complained. He became the one British commander whom Stilwell liked and respected. When things were going badly for Slim in the fighting around Magwe, Stilwell sent the Chinese 38 Division under General Sun to assist. This division had hurriedly come down the Burma Road from Yunnan and, under the command of Sun, who had been trained at the Virginia Military Institute, proved itself to be one of the best Chinese divisions in the campaign.

During these frantic days of trying to stem the Japanese advance Stilwell, who remained convinced that the concentration of three divisions at Taungoo could have halted the Japanese, was constantly frustrated by the attitudes and the dithering of the Chinese army and its divisional commanders. General Tu, GOC of the Fifth Army, made one excuse after another. He was highly temperamental, and in a fit of depression he would shut himself away and refuse to speak to anyone.

General Liao, commander of 22 Division, which could have saved the day at Taungoo, made one trivial excuse after another to prevent his division from advancing. Stilwell later discovered that these commanders had secretly corresponded with Chiang, who advised them not to commit their divisions too heavily. Stilwell's seething frustration shows up in his comments:

> The basic cause is Chiang Kai Shek's refusal to let me concentrate at Pyinmana [a village just to the north of Taungoo]. Everything trails from that and the delay by Chiang Kai-Shek of the 22nd at Mandalay. Some bastard at Pyinmana stopped the move ... to think that a victory can be compromised by a goddam slip on the railroad ... Christ. The mental load on a commander who has strings tied to him.

At Taungoo 200 Division continued to fight bravely until 30 March, and for the last three days of fighting Stilwell suffered even further frustrations as the Chinese generals prevented any effective movement. Every day they came up with new excuses for not attacking. Stilwell considered resigning because he could not command troops that would not attack. He had a showdown with Chiang about General Tu, but this achieved nothing. On the 28th he went back to Maymyo to meet Alexander and to communicate with Chiang, who had now agreed to Alexander having overall command in Burma. In Maymyo Stilwell learnt that the few remaining Royal Air Force units, which were heavily outnumbered by the Japanese, had withdrawn from Burma altogether, and the rest of the retreat from Burma was conducted with no air support at all. In Maymyo he got hold of Tu and once more tried to force some action. Tu agreed to attack the next day but thought they had lost the opportunity! The next day came:

> As usual they are dogging it. General Liao, 22nd Division's commanding general, is a colourless bird. He wants to wait for the 96th division and I suppose the commanding general of the 96th for the 55th etc. Full of excuses – how strong the Jap positions are, and how reinforcements are coming to them etc. Two days ago it would have

been easy, but now … They'll drag it out and do nothing unless I can somehow kick them into it … Hot as hell. We are all dried out and exhausted. I am mentally about shot. Merrill* back at 9.00. Limeys will attack in force with tanks. Good old Slim. Maybe he's all right after all.

By the end of the battle for Taungoo, Stilwell was at the end of his tether:

By Jesus I'm about fed up … Alternatives now at hand. Let it ride and do nothing. Resign flatly. Ooze out and demand own forces … Liao and Tu have dogged it again. The pusillanimous bastards. No attack at all. Front quiet, no Jap reaction. Just craven. Miao moved command post back a mile. Tu ordered him not to attack.

The results of Tu's obstruction became clear on 30 March when 200 Division, having suffered 3,000 casualties, was completely surrounded by the Japanese, was forced to abandon its vehicles and heavy equipment and broke out through the jungle in small parties. This good division was sacrificed by Tu and Liao in spite of all Stilwell could do.

The British forces were having an equally hard time. The force sent to help the Chinese at Taungoo – three battalions, a squadron of tanks and a gunner battery – was surrounded at Schwedaung and, in the attempt to break out, suffered very heavy losses. The Japanese, not for the last time, took some of the British prisoners, tied them to trees and used them for bayonet practice. The Japanese attacks at Taungoo, Schwedaung and around Prome clearly illustrate their general tactics. Whenever their advancing troops met opposition, they immediately sent out aggressive fighting patrols on both flanks. These patrols moved swiftly and attempted to join up and set up a road block behind the defenders' position, subjecting them to fire from two directions. This often caused chaos and panic.

After the defeat at Taungoo, Stilwell saw that the crucial issue was that the Chinese commanders would not accept his orders. On 1 April,

* Major Frank Merrill, who later commanded Merrill's Marauders.

saying 'Am I the April Fool', he went to Chungking and threw down the gauntlet to Chiang. In the course of many stormy interviews Stilwell's humour did not entirely desert him. 'I have to tell Chiang Kai Shek with a straight face that his subordinates are not carrying out his orders, when in all probability they are doing exactly what he tells them ... however it is expecting a good deal to have them turn over a couple of armies in a vital area, to a goddam foreigner they don't know.' Madame, who was present at these discussions, was more sensitive to these issues and, more able to understand the western viewpoint, suggested that Chiang went down to Maymyo to deal with the matter. As a result, Chiang appointed a tough character, General Lo, to enforce Stilwell's authority. Stilwell appreciated Madame's support, but ultimately he realised that the whole presentation by Chiang to back up his authority was a great charade.

At the time of his visit to Chungking, Stilwell produced a memo which he entitled 'THE SYSTEM' and which gives a clear outline of his thoughts:

> Chiang Kai Shek says 'J. W. Stilwell can command the Fifth and Sixth Armies.' Then I get a lengthy harangue on the psychology of the Chinese soldier, and how the Fifth and Sixth must not be defeated or the morale of the Army and the nation will crumble, together with a cockeyed strategical conception based on the importance of Mandalay ... Then the flood of letters begins. To Tu. To Lin. To me. All of them direct. I never see half of them. They direct all sorts of action and preparation with radical changes based on minor changes in the situation. The Chinese commanders are up and down – highly optimistic one minute; in the depths of gloom the next. They feel, of course, the urgent necessity of pleasing the Generalissimo, and if my suggestions or orders run counter to what they think he wants, they offer endless objections. When I brush off these objections they proceed to positive measures – for instance, stopping the move of a regiment until it is too late to bring it to bear – or just fail to get the order out, or getting it out with a lot of 'ifs' and 'ands' in it, or when pushed, simply telling lower commanders to lay off and not carry it out. Or just put on a demonstration and report opposition too strong. I can't shoot them,

I can't relieve them; and just talking to them does no good. So the upshot of it is that I am the stooge who does the dirty work and gets the rap.

The memo on The System was accompanied by a shrewd description of Madame Chiang Kai-Shek, whom he called Madamissima:

> A clever, brainy woman. Sees the Western viewpoint. (By this I mean she can appreciate the mental reaction of a foreigner to the twisting, indirect and undercover methods of Chinese politics and war making.) Direct, forceful, energetic, loves power, eats up publicity and flattery … Great influence on Chiang Kai Shek mostly along the right lines too. A great help on several occasions.

On Chiang himself he was blunter: 'He is not mentally stable … My only concern is to tell him the truth and go about my business. If I can't get by that way the hell with it; it is patently impossible for me to compete with the swarms of parasites and sycophants that surround him.'

In the confused fighting around Taungoo and Prome there was more inter-Allied co-operation than one might have imagined from the caustic and critical comments, and this was the start of a firm relationship between Stilwell and Slim that lasted until the eve of final victory. Slim recorded that on one occasion during the retreat they were sitting down conferring when Stilwell said, 'At least you and I have an ancestor in common.' Slim asked, 'Who?' 'Ethelred the Unready.'* Slim, in his own book *Defeat into Victory*, paid a balanced and thoughtful tribute to Stilwell:

> These were my first active contacts with Stilwell, who had arrived in Burma a few days after me. He already had something of a reputation for shortness of temper and for distrust of most of the rest of the world. I must admit he surprised me when, at our first meeting, he said, 'Well General I must tell you that my motto in all dealings is buyer beware,'

* R. Lewin, *Slim*, Leo Cooper, London, 1972, p. 141.

but he never as far as I was concerned lived up to that old horse-trader's motto. He was over sixty, but he was tough, mentally and physically; he could be as obstinate as a whole team of mules; he could be, and frequently was, downright rude to people whom, often for no very good reason, he did not like. But when he said he would do a thing he did it … He had a habit, which I found very disarming, of arguing most tenaciously against some proposal, and then looking at you over the top of his glasses with the shadow of a grin and saying, 'Now tell me what you want me to do and I will do it.' He was two people, one when he had an audience, and a quite different person when talking to you alone. I think it amused him to keep up in public the 'Vinegar Joe Tough Guy' attitude especially in front of his staff. Americans, whether they liked him or not – and he had more enemies among Americans than among British – were all scared of him. He had courage to an extent few people have, and determination, which, as he usually concentrated it along narrow lines, had a dynamic force. He was not a great soldier in the highest sense, but he was a real leader in the field. No one else I know could have made his Chinese do what they did. He was, undoubtedly, the most colourful character in South East Asia – and I liked him.★

When Stilwell returned from Chunking and masterminded the conference at Maymyo (7–8 April) with Chiang, Madame, the Chinese generals and Alexander, his entourage included Clare Luce, the distinguished journalist from *Life* magazine. Her reports went far to create the public image of Vinegar Joe. Despite grave setbacks, the military issued reports that were as up-beat as possible. The press seized on these and, as in the Iraq war of 2003, produced inaccurate and unhelpful headlines. Barbara Tuchman, in her admirable book *Sand against the Wind*, neatly summarises how Stilwell was being presented to the newspaper-reading public:

'Vinegar Joe' was becoming a public personality. He made good copy and the press made the most of it, developing a picturesque stereotype,

★ Field Marshal Viscount Slim, *Defeat into Victory*, Cassell, London, 1956, p. 51.

the crusty cracker–barrel soldiers' soldier, tough, leathery, wiry, down-to-earth, wise-cracking, Chinese speaking, a disciplinarian loved by the troops, with lack of swank and a warm smile, an American 'Chinese Gordon', an 'Uncle Joe'.★

Stilwell's own comments were less flattering. He wrote: 'Deathly afraid of this damn publicity; what a flop I'll look if the Japs run me up in the hills.'

In the days after the conference Stilwell had serious discussions with General Kan, commander of the Sixth Army in the Eastern Shan states, and with General Tu, commander of the Fifth Army. They planned for the Fifth Army to concentrate at Pyinmana and the Sixth Army at Loikaw to defend the eastern flank and the approaches to the Burma Road. There was now almost unrestricted Japanese bombing of all the major Burmese towns. In the weeks before the start of the monsoon – usually in mid-May – the towns with their predominantly wooden buildings were tinder dry and the carnage caused by the fires was horrifying. Stilwell in his daily, staccato jottings often mixed high strategy with the humdrum, the horrifying and the bizarre. On 11 April he wrote, 'Kan put on a good dinner serving *crème de menthe* as wine. Good sleeping.' And two days later: 'All day playing rummy. Hot night. Ants all over me.'

The military setbacks continued. On 15 April Alexander called Stilwell to Maymyo for an urgent conference to discuss tactics. Two days before this, Chiang had promised that 96 Division from the northern sector of the Fifth Army area would hold the small but important town of Taungdwingwi. At the last moment he reneged on this undertaking and Alexander ordered Slim to try to hold it. This failed because the Japanese moved too quickly. In his diary Stilwell continued to be caustically critical of the British. On 14 April he merely noted that the British were pulling out of Taungdwingyi but omitted to say that the Chinese had promised to defend it. His comments on the conference with Alexander are equally pungent.

★ B. Tuchman, *Sand against the Wind*, Macmillan, New York, 1970, p. 281.

'Did Aleck have the wind up? Disaster and gloom. No fight left in the British … Alex calls me "Joe" now. Letter from G-mo full of crap and nonsense.'

By now hordes of terrified Burmese and Indian refugees were clogging up the roads and adding substantially to the military problems. The Japanese used the situation to their advantage and infiltrated their forward troops among the refugees. The Japanese advance was so rapid that on the day Alexander and Stilwell were conferring at Maymyo (15 April), Slim was facing a strong attack on the main Burmese oilfield at Yenangyaung. As the Japanese forces approached, Slim had the dismal task of blowing up over a million gallons of oil to deny the enemy its use.*

Slim's destruction of the Yenangyaung oilfields was the prelude to a fiercely fought battle involving close Allied co-operation. To help Slim in a crisis situation Stilwell sent the Chinese 38 Division under General Sun. Sun's help was crucial, and Slim paid him a high tribute by putting part of the available artillery and armour under the General's direct command. In spite of the help from the Chinese, the Burma Division faced dire peril and had to fight its way out of the Japanese encirclement and abandon much of its transport and heavy weaponry. For four days a bitter battle raged in temperatures well above 100°F amidst the smoke of the burning oil wells. The Chinese intervention resulted in the rescue of a main part of the Burma Division and freed over 200 British prisoners, but it was not enough to halt the Japanese advance.

The situation in the western sector was grave enough, but now Stilwell faced an even greater threat on his eastern flank. The Sixth Army had already infuriated him, and he had demanded that its commander, General Kan, should be reprimanded for incompetence in failing to control his divisional commanders, for failing to obtain intelligence about Japanese movements, and for failing to supply his forward troops. Stilwell had gone further and demanded the dismissal of General Chen, who commanded 55 Division. Chen had withdrawn from a vital feature in the face of a very weak Japanese attack,

* After the war the oil company tried, unsuccessfully, to sue Slim for damages.

and he had refused to attack a Japanese position despite having six battalions facing one enemy battalion. Stilwell ordered 93 Division to move south, but the commander refused. Meanwhile 55 Division, after conducting an unnecessary retreat, settled into bivouacs without even posting sentries.

Security in the Chinese divisions was notoriously lax and, during the fighting around Taungoo, the Japanese managed to obtain details of the Chinese strategic plan to concentrate their main defence around Mandalay. This was Chiang's plan, which Stilwell had substantially changed, and the Japanese response on discovering it was swift and effective. They had five effective divisions – now well-supplied through Rangoon – and, keeping three divisions to maintain the momentum of their central attack, they detached 56 Division, substantially reinforced with tanks, artillery and additional motor transport, to wheel around the eastern flank of the Chinese forces and make a swift thrust towards Lashio. If it succeeded, this brilliant strategy would not only cut the vital Burma Road but would also make possible a wide pincer movement to surround and destroy most of the Chinese and British forces in Burma. The clear command decision of the Japanese and its speedy execution are in stark contrast to the baffling and frustrating situation faced by Stilwell. In theory, he had six divisions under his command, but because of Chiang's machinations, the defeatist attitude of the Chinese divisional commanders and their refusal to obey Stilwell's orders he was powerless to stem the Japanese advance.

The Japanese made their first move against the Chinese 55 Division, ineptly commanded by General Chen. Chen's troops were still sitting idly in their undefended bivouacs when the Japanese struck. The main body of the Japanese 56 Division moved rapidly through the jungle east of the road, while another group, more than a battalion strong, made a pincer movement to the west. Then the whole of the division attacked the unsuspecting Chinese and all but wiped them out. Chinese troops fled into the jungle and Chen's division effectively ceased to exist. They had paid a very heavy price for their commander's incompetence. When the fighting was nearly over the Chinese 93 Division approached, but when they saw the situation

they quickly retreated without fighting. In three days of carefully controlled and aggressive fighting, the Japanese had destroyed a Chinese
division and advanced nearly 80 miles north of Loikaw. Lashio and
the Burma Road lay within their grasp.

Stilwell's appalling situation was further illustrated by the behaviour of the other Chinese commanders during that critical battle.
General Tu simply disappeared, and General Lo, who should have
been cracking the whip over the divisional commanders, had gone
off to Maymyo, ostensibly to confer with Alexander. Stilwell's diary
notes explain his feelings. 'Someone has to control the mess and I am
the goat. ... If C.K.S. [Chiang Kai-Shek] continues his tactical master-
pieces the mess will merely get worse. He has made it impossible for
me to do anything and I may as well acknowledge it now.' He
described Tu as 'a crybaby, not a commander', and added, 'That
bastard Tu came in. Same old crap. Can't take the responsibility ...
Christ, he's a headache.' When on 20 April Stilwell heard the first
rumours of the defeat of Chen and 55 Division, he wrote, 'Wild tales
of the Jap tank division at Loikaw. Aiming at Lashio? Jesus. This may
screw us completely.'

Stilwell's anguish at the Japanese advance towards Lashio reflected
his fundamental belief that the whole campaign should focus on
defending the Burma Road and the crucial supply route to Chiang's
forces – and, later, the attempts to reopen it. He and most American
officials were highly critical of the British attitude and assumed that
the British never seriously intended to defend Burma. They pointed
to the thousands of Indian Army troops, who could have been sent
in to defend Burma had the will and determination been there. They
also expressed strong feelings about their forces being used to prop
up the pre-war British Empire.

Even in the crisis situation that faced the Allied troops in Burma
in April 1942 there was far more co-operation between Slim and
Stilwell than would appear from his diary entries. Before the news of
the total defeat of 55 Division under Chen reached him he offered to
send 200 Division, which had already fought so well, to help Slim and
the beleaguered Burma Division. Slim went personally to welcome
the Chinese troops, only to discover almost immediately that they

were packing up to leave. Stilwell had sent Slim an urgent message, which did not reach him, explaining that a new crisis had arisen and that he had therefore had to recall 200 Division. There followed one of Stilwell's really outstanding achievements during the miserable days of the retreat. He rapidly concentrated most of 200 Division and a few other units and, although he was the overall commander of all Chinese forces – and was nearly sixty – he personally led a counter-attack against the Japanese who had captured Taunggyi and defeated them. Even then his vigour, leadership, rank and personality were not enough, and he had to offer the Chinese a bribe of 50,000 rupees to retake Taunggyi. The battle lasted through 23 and 24 April, Taunggyi was taken and he drove his forces on and recaptured Loilem. This was a fine achievement and illustrated what happened all too rarely in the Burma retreat, that the Japanese could be halted and driven back if they were opposed resolutely. Stilwell later received the Distinguished Service Cross for his leadership and bravery in this action, which throws an interesting light on his situation and his character. He was not always popular with fellow American generals, his achievement at Taunggyi is hardly mentioned in American war histories and he did not mention it in his diaries. In contrast, there is a full account in Slim's *Defeat into Victory*, and Slim paid tribute to Stilwell's bravery and leadership. In further contrast to Slim's generous tribute, Stilwell could not resist another dig about the Limeys running away.

During this time of crisis, Stilwell found time to write a letter to his wife. He had to be rather vague, and explained that he had been very busy, without much sleep, though food was plentiful. He added, 'Carmel! I don't dare think too much about that, or even about the family. But I am happy in knowing you are all there together. Enjoy it and someday I'll be back and look you up. With a long white beard and a bent back!!'

His diary entries in these hectic days record his desperate efforts to force the Chinese divisions to fight, or even to obey his direct orders. In the confusion of the retreat northwards towards Meiktila and Mandalay he had a brief, hurried meeting with Alexander. 'Alexander will do anything I tell him to. Had him radio Wavell for two reconnaissance planes.' Confused fighting continued around

Taunggyi and Meiktila. As Stilwell tried to move his units to halt the Japanese advance, he found that Chinese civilian contractors had commandeered most of the transport and were loading the trucks with rice, petroleum and other valuable items and were hurrying to get them back to China to sell at a huge profit. The group of Chinese contractors caused the one serious rift between Stilwell and Slim. The Chinese had requested a British unit to guard a train in case another Chinese gang attempted to take it away. Stilwell did not know of this request and, when a British unit took over the train, he assumed that the British were moving out. As his diary shows, he was too ready to believe that the Limeys were running away, and he sent a bitterly critical message to Slim. At the time the British were fighting a difficult rearguard action further south and Slim replied with, in his words, 'a very astringent refutation'. Shortly afterwards Stilwell withdrew his remarks, and Slim commented that this was the only time they fell out.

Under the pressure of the Japanese advance, discipline in the Chinese divisions rapidly crumbled. This added to the chaos of a situation in which Japanese planes, almost unchallenged, bombed at will, civil administration broke down completely, and roads to the north were blocked by thousands of terrified refugees.

On 25 April Alexander agreed to send part of 17 Indian Division to assist Stilwell at Meiktila, but at the same time news came that the Japanese had advanced 40 miles north of Loilem and were now less than 50 miles from Lashio, the key terminal of the Burma Road. There were few Chinese units to oppose them. On the same day, Stilwell noted that the commanding officers of units increasingly refused to follow orders from headquarters. He tried to galvanise 96 Division, but found that the commander, Yu, 'is a pitiful object. Entirely oblivious of his troops he was drinking tea and fanning himself. Cried all over the place. I got disgusted and left.' Increasingly, both the Americans and the British contemplated the dire necessity of withdrawing north of Mandalay. On 29 April Stilwell heard a report that the Chinese garrison was leaving Lashio. If Lashio fell, the key to the massive Allied withdrawal to the north would be Mandalay, the Irrawaddy and the Ava bridge. Stilwell heard that the

British were going to blow up the bridge on the night of 30 April in order to delay the Japanese advance.

On that dramatic night when the Ava bridge was blown, an intrepid British officer, Mike Calvert, who later, as a Chindit commander, came to have a close relationship with Stilwell, was involved in a brave but hare-brained attempt to confuse and mislead the Japanese. Calvert, accompanied by Wavell's ADC and Peter Fleming (later to gain fame as an author) carried out the exploit. They were provided with a briefcase, purporting to be Wavell's, full of orders to British units and giving details of large army and naval reinforcements that were about to arrive. Calvert drove the staff car southwards over the Ava bridge until they came under Japanese fire. He then quickly turned the car round, sped off and overturned the car on a corner. Purposely leaving the briefcase in the car, the three officers hurried off over the bridge just before it was blown up.*

Conferences between Stilwell and Alexander, or with his Chinese commanders, now concentrated on how to prevent the complete surrender of their forces and on whether the surviving units should aim to reach China or India. With Lashio in the hands of the Japanese, the route to China would be via Myitkyina, a town that was to feature largely in Stilwell's plans for the rest of the war. Nominally there were now three Chinese armies – the Fifth, the Sixth and the Sixty-Sixth – amounting to over 100,000 men in eastern Burma under Stilwell's command. By the end of April 1942 the Fifth and Sixth Armies had virtually disintegrated. The Sixty-Sixth, which so far had not been fully involved in the fighting – except for 38 Division under General Sun, which had been sent to support Slim – now moved to Lashio with orders to hold it at all costs. Troops of the Sixty-Sixth Army manoeuvred tentatively around Lashio, but they were strongly imbued with Chiang's defeatist attitude and had no desire to become too heavily involved. When the Japanese advanced towards the town with a few squadrons of tanks and two battalions of motorised infantry, more than 3,000 Chinese troops made a rapid withdrawal. Their task had been made more difficult by

* David Rooney, *Mad Mike*, Leo Cooper, London, 1997, p. 36.

the undisciplined rabble of the Fifth Army which, refusing to stay and fight, poured through the town in a desperate effort to get away from the Japanese. The rest of the Burma campaign illustrated, whether from the Japanese or the Allied perspective, the great advantage of defence over attack – notably at Imphal, Kohima, Mogaung and Myitkyina – making even more remarkable the craven defeatism shown by the Chinese divisions. It seems surprising too that, after all the Japanese atrocities of the 1930s, such as the attack on Shanghai and the rape of Nanking, the Chinese troops appeared to have little urge to wreak revenge on the Japanese aggressors.

In a final conference between Stilwell and Alexander they faced two alternatives: to retreat northwards up the Irrawaddy valley, which was also the approximate route of the railway from Mandalay to Indaw and Myitkyina; or to take a route further to the west, following the valley of the Chindwin, which led up to Assam, northeast India and the centres of Imphal and Kohima. Even at this stage Stilwell had some sanguine moments. After Chiang agreed to Chinese troops being trained in India, Stilwell wrote, 'God, if we can only get those 100,000 Chinese to India, we'll have something.' In addition to his direct responsibility for the Chinese divisions, he never wavered from his basic view that the main purpose of the CBI campaign should be to keep open, or to reopen, the Burma Road to supply Chiang Kai-Shek and the proposed 30 Chinese divisions around Chungking.

His thinly veiled contempt for Alexander continued. 'Alex has 36,000 men to take out. Where the hell have they been?' After their final meeting, Alexander left in a staff car to go over to the Chindwin valley, where the battered remains of 17 Indian Division and 1 Burma Division – now with few heavy weapons and little transport – continued to retreat. Stilwell had determined that he would stay loyally with his Chinese divisions, even refusing to fly out in an aircraft that had been sent especially to collect him. He sent out most of his staff and then started on the long march towards Myitkyina, realising that the Japanese might reach it before him.

His group of about 100 included more than 20 Americans, the redoubtable Dr Gordon Seagrave and some Burmese nurses from the doctor's mission hospital. Leaving Shwebo, his party soon found that the railway was completely blocked. There had been a serious train smash, when a Chinese general had taken over a train at gunpoint for his personal use. Stilwell noted that 'Unfortunately he was not killed.' After realising that the track was blocked he decided to move across country, initially making northwards parallel to the railway. He now reckoned that his group would have to make for the Chindwin and, ultimately, India, so he chose to take a difficult and rarely used route mainly in order to avoid the struggling mass of desperate Indian and Burmese refugees. After many privations his group reached Indaw, where there was complete pandemonium, with Chinese soldiers looting everywhere and killing civilians who tried to stop them. At Indaw he had his last contact with the outside world. After commenting on the 'dumb Limeys sitting around', he referred scathingly to a report from the BBC in London: '"General Alexander, a bold and resourceful commander, has fought one of the great defensive battles of the war," and a lot of other crap about what the Limeys have been doing.'

After Indaw he led his party grimly forward, trying to keep ahead of the deluge of refugees. As the road petered out, all transport had to be abandoned and the heavy wireless destroyed. Final messages were sent to the American HQ in Delhi requesting that food and help should be sent to the area of Homalin, which they hoped eventually to reach.

Stilwell's whole philosophy in the military training he had given, from West Point and Fort Benning onwards, had emphasised the responsibility of the officer on the ground to lead his troops and to make decisions. Rarely can a full general of nearly sixty have been set such a severe practical test. He addressed the assembled group and gave clear orders. All food would be pooled and put under the charge of a senior American officer. Personal belongings were to be reduced to an absolute minimum. He told them that they faced a march of about 140 miles over daunting mountains, the formidable Chindwin river and through the most hostile terrain, with the imminent threat of monsoon. He calculated that they must cover fourteen miles a day if they were to reach their destination before the food ran out. He emphasised that the only way they could survive was through the discipline which he established, and he concluded with the observation that they would probably hate his guts but they would survive.

He set off and led the column personally, setting the pace and strictly controlling the time of daily marches. He was appalled at the poor physique and stamina of most of the westerners, and his disjointed jottings bring alive much of the tension and suffering. 'May 7 Start ordered for 5.00. Easy pace down river. Till 11.00. Holcombe out. Merrill out; heat exhaustion. Lee out. Sliney pooped. Nowakowski same. Christ but we are a poor lot. Hard going in the river all the way. Cooler. All packs reduced to ten pounds.' Always on the lookout for help for his people, he hired sixty carriers when they passed a friendly village, and on another occasion he took on a large team of mules under Chinese drivers.★

Stilwell's grimly determined leadership kept the party moving despite fatigue, sickness and suffering. Morale improved slightly when an aircraft appeared; this they at first assumed to be Japanese, but it turned out to be an RAF Dakota, which flew low over them and dropped food and medical supplies. The air drop kindled the hope that some messages had got through and that they might actually survive. On 10 May they reached the River Chindwin; here they obtained rafts to help them move down the river, which it was hoped would make travelling easier. They still had some of the mules, and these were sent on ahead under their Chinese muleteers. While the group assembled, the Burmese nurses put up matting roofs on the barges to shelter the sick and exhausted. On 10 May the first rafts were launched, but formidable problems still remained. 'Nice ride but too damn slow. Swim. Nap. At dark supper, then at 10.00 off again. All night poling and pushing.' After the encouragement of the air drop, the party had high hopes of finding help and relief at Homalin,

---

★ An admirable and vivid account of the suffering endured by the refugees, who travelled the same route at the same time as Stilwell, has recently been published (Stephen Brookes, *Through the Jungle of Death*, John Wiley, New York, 2000). It was written by a man whose parents were medical missionaries in Burma, and who as a boy went through the whole ghastly retreat and survived.

but when they reached the town it was deserted and morale fell to an all-time low. There was increasingly bitter criticism of Stilwell, but discipline held and on 14 May they were greeted by a British official from Imphal, who had organised food and medical supplies and a large number of mules. The help was welcome, but there remained five days of hard climbing and walking, although the sick were now able to ride on mules or ponies, and food was often available from friendly Naga villages. In one village the party arrived at a crowded camp where there were supplies of horses and mules and 200 bearers. Stilwell wrote, 'Soaked feet in brook. Rocky hillside in gorge. Tangkhuls squatting around their rice pots and fires. Lean-to shacks. What a picture, if only we had a movie camera. Thatched covered bridge. Chinese soldiers, Burmese girls, Americans and Limeys all in the brook washing and shaving and soaking feet.'

As the going got easier the party passed more villages, where they were greeted by the villagers with rice wine, red blankets, cider and chicken. Comments on Limeys continued to feature. On a day when they had covered twenty miles he noted, 'Two thirds of Limeys on ponies. None of our people.' On 22 May the group reached Imphal, and he commented tersely, 'Cordial reception by the Limeys.'

Stilwell was relatively fortunate to receive a cordial welcome at Imphal. When General Slim, who had brought his exhausted and emaciated troops up the Chindwin river and through the notoriously unhealthy Kabaw valley, reached Imphal the arrogant and abrasive Corps Commander, General Irwin, was extremely rude to him. When Slim complained, Irwin replied, 'I can't be rude. I am senior to you.' Similarly, General Punch Cowan, who had led 17 Indian Division through the retreat, was shown a bleak, empty hillside with monsoon rain pouring down it as the billet for his troops. Slim and Cowan protested most vigorously about their reception, and possibly their protests benefited Stilwell when he and his group arrived a few days later.

The reception accorded to retreating American and British units at Imphal and in the hill towns of northeast India, while deplorable, can be partially explained. These hill-stations were rather sleepy, provincial places full of generally well-to-do people, usually in the army or retired from the army. They had kept up their usual social life of dinner parties, dances, tennis and flirting, and they were almost completely unaware of the avalanche of sick and wounded military personnel and destitute refugees that was about to engulf them. Back in 1942 they were not able witness the day's military action on television in the evening. Even as far away as Ranchi, which was also deluged with wounded, Slim and Calvert, both of whom had survived the retreat, obtained the help of a formidable hospital matron. This lady made an announcement at the garrison's fancy dress ball, and help was immediately forthcoming.

Another grave problem arose at this time. For centuries, Burma and Assam had been suspicious of Chinese aggrandisement – as they still are in the twenty-first century – and when 38 Division under General Sun arrived near Imphal, the Indian authorities initially wished to disarm them. Stilwell sent one of his senior colleagues to resolve the problem. General Sun had been fortunate not to receive Chiang's order to move north to Fort Hertz, and by superb leadership he had brought his division out of Burma intact. Under vigorous pursuit by the Japanese, one of his regiments had conducted a classic rearguard action that won high praise from both Americans and British. Sun and his division demonstrated what the Chinese could have achieved with sound leadership.

While Stilwell was making his way to Imphal, the Chinese divisions left in Burma had mixed fortunes. As 38 Division moved up the Chindwin valley, having failed to receive Chiang's order, 22 Division and 96 Division from the now disintegrated Fifth Army moved slowly north towards Myitkyina and Fort Hertz. During July and August 1942, 22 Division and the remnants of 96 Division reached the area of Ledo, the northern terminus of the Assam railway, which later was to become the key to the supply of the entire British Fourteenth Army as well as the American and Chinese CBI forces. Valiant attempts were made to set up stores of food along the route taken by these divisions, and initially they and the refugees managed fairly well. They were also generously supplied by the hospitable Kachin tribesmen, but when supplies dried up looting began and the Chinese troops – particularly 96 Division – gained an appalling reputation for looting and for murdering refugees as well as local villagers and their families. In *Through the Jungle of Death* Brookes describes the suffering of the refugees, and also the menace of the marauding Chinese, through the area from Myitkyina and the Huckauwng valley. Despite its bad reputation, 96 Division left the area of Ledo, moved east and north to Fort Hertz and, showing remarkable powers of endurance, eventually reached China.

While the remnants of the Allied forces were arriving in Imphal, Ledo and Fort Hertz, there were still six Chinese divisions in eastern Burma, most of which were retreating before the Japanese advance. During May 1942 it appeared that the Japanese were going to launch a major attack up the Burma Road, thus cutting off China completely from western help. After the war Japanese officers denied that there were plans to advance so far up the Burma Road, but at the time Chiang and General Chennault, who commanded the American Volunteer Group of trained American pilots, prepared for a major attack. As part of the Japanese advance a strong force with tanks and motorised infantry did move up the Burma Road past Lashio and Lungling, but they were halted by Chinese forces at the Salween gorge, where the Burma Road crosses the Salween river.

The initial Japanese advance had been held up at Taunggyi by the stout resistance of the Chinese 200 Division. Determined to keep up the momentum of their advance towards Mandalay and the north, the Japanese more or less bypassed Taunggyi, and during May the Chinese started to move from there north towards Myitkyina. They reached Bhamo, but then turned east, and by using minor roads and tracks reached China without further major military action. In spite of the success of the Chinese in holding up the Japanese at the Salween gorge, Chiang remained extremely apprehensive about further advances by the Japanese. He therefore concentrated two divisions – 28 and 29 – which had not been involved in the main fighting and directed another army, the 71st, to move down the Burma Road from Yunnan. These forces engaged in some fierce fighting in and around Lungling, and the Japanese advanced no further.

Having reached Imphal on 22 May, Stilwell, after a very brief pause, went by road to the nearest airfield and flew to Delhi, arriving there on 24 May. He gave a memorable press conference, finishing with the words, 'I claim we got a hell of a beating. We got run out of Burma, and it is as humiliating as hell. I think we ought to find out what caused it, go back and retake it.' This admirably blunt statement, which was widely commended, was a necessary antidote to the wildly exaggerated claims that appeared in most American newspapers. Referring to a clash on the Burma Road, one paper claimed, 'Invading force crushed by Stilwell', when in fact Stilwell was just completing his weary march to Imphal. Providing slightly more detail on the causes of the defeat, Stilwell wrote: 'Hostile population; no air service; Jap initiative, inferior equipment (arty, tanks, machine guns, trench mortars), inadequate ammunition, inadequate transport (300 trucks mostly in the Fifth Army), no supply set up; improvised medical service; stupid gutless command; interference by Chiang Kai Shek; rotten communications; British defeatist attitude; vulnerable tactical situation; knew it was hopeless.'

By the middle of May 1942 the Japanese had won a remarkable victory. They had driven the British, American and Chinese forces out of the whole of Burma and were poised on the border of northeast India. They had cut the Burma Road, thus denying western supplies to Chiang, and were able to threaten the tenuous air link from India to Chungking. Calcutta, where most American and British supplies were now concentrated, was within easy bomber range. From their position in Burma they could attack either China or India. Their serious strategic plans included an advance into India, headed by the Indian National Army (which consisted of captured Indian soldiers, who were prepared to fight against the British). There was strong anti-British feeling across much of Bengal, and the Japanese assumed that their advance would spark off a major revolution that could overthrow the British Raj.

On 20 May, a couple of days before the end of his heroic trek, Stilwell wrote that it 'Rained all night'. As they struggled through the jungle he and his party had dreaded the onset of the monsoon, but it was the monsoon rain more than any American, British or Chinese forces that was responsible for halting the Japanese advance. So from May 1942 the focus of the war in Burma changed. Slim, who later was to lead the successful recapture of Burma by the Fourteenth Army, summed up Stilwell's performance during the retreat. Compared to Stilwell's view of the British it was a generous assessment.

> Stilwell had a dogged courage beyond praise ... He was constantly on the lookout for an aggressive counter-stroke, but his means could not match his spirit. He could not enforce his orders, nor could his inadequate staff keep in touch with his troops. When he saw his formations disintegrate under his eyes, no man could have done more, and few as much as Stilwell, by personal leadership and example, to hold the Chinese together, but once the rot had set in, the task was impossible.

CHAPTER 5

Taking Stock

With his arrival in Imphal in May 1942 and subsequent rapid moves to Delhi and then to Chungking, Stilwell left behind not only the daily struggle to survive in the retreat through the Burmese jungle but also the fierce struggle he had relentlessly pursued to force the Chinese divisions under his command to accept his orders and face the Japanese enemy. From June 1942 he was engaged in a different task. At the highest levels, in Delhi, Chungking and Washington, he fought his corner in the global strategic allocation of priorities and supplies to make possible the creation of effective fighting divisions from the Chinese troops who had retreated into India and were estimated to number between 9,000 and 13,000 men. He expected to lead these troops, retrained and re-armed, to achieve what had been, and remained, his unchanging goal – to recapture northern Burma and reopen the Burma Road. This in turn was to enable the Chinese to launch a major campaign to drive the Japanese out of southwest China and make possible the destruction of mainland Japan by American bombers based in the recaptured territory.

Even before the retreat Stilwell had drawn up a detailed plan, which he submitted to Chiang Kai-Shek in April 1942. His plan assumed that the Japanese advance could be stopped and contained somewhere in mid-Burma, and he proposed that 100,000 Chinese soldiers should be assembled in India. There they would be trained, equipped and formed into two corps each of three divisions. Chinese officers and NCOs, carefully selected by Chiang, would be given command up to regimental level, but higher commanders and staff officers would be American until Chinese with suitable ability, training and experience emerged. The plan intended to start moving the troops to India in the months after May 1942 to give them up to six months of intensive training, and then to launch a counterattack from the Indian base to recapture Burma. Chiang considered this plan and accepted it with certain modifications. He argued that half the senior commanders should be Chinese and insisted that Chinese troops must not be used to suppress civil disobedience in India. This was a wise precaution, for during the next two years the British military authorities had to deploy vast numbers of troops to protect military installations in Calcutta and across Bengal against the Congress campaign for independence. The writing on the wall was 'Jai Hind' – 'Get out of India'.

As soon as he reached India, Stilwell reported to Marshall and Stimson and urgently requested an American division to be placed under his command to spearhead the recapture of Burma. He argued strongly that an American division in India would be a major factor in the crucial issue of keeping China in the war. He strongly criticised the policy of allowing Chiang to distribute the American supplies across vast numbers of ineffective divisions instead of concentrating it on just a few. He was equally pungent in his criticism of senior Chinese officers who never went to the front, never undertook reconnaissance and never supervised their troops. In both Washington and Chungking he demanded that some of the Chinese army and divisional commanders should be shot for criminal incompetence during the retreat. He backed up this demand with the suggestion that all the American and Chinese forces should come under one commander in whom Chiang had confidence. Washington did not accept all these arguments, and in any event by June 1942 the whole situation had changed dramatically for the worse.

In the few brief days Stilwell spent in Delhi he wrote a short letter to his wife that illustrates his real feelings.

May 26 (7 A.M.), New Delhi: LETTER TO MRS. STILWELL Ole Pappy calling from India, and reporting in from Burma. Everything O.K. I'm a little underweight – to be quite truthful I look a good deal like the guy in the medical book with his skin off, showing the next layer of what have you. However, I'm eating is [*sic*] on again fast. I was damn glad to get my gang out of the jungle. Most of them now consider me more of a mean old s.o.b. than ever, because I made them all play ball. Rank or no rank. We had quite a trip, which I suppose will now be exaggerated, as usual, till it's unrecognisable.

Tomorrow or next day I'll be going back to report to the G-mo and I sure have an earful for him. He's going to hear stuff he never heard before and it's going to be interesting to see how he takes it.

I have hopes that someday we can step on these bastards (Japs) and end the war, and if I am lucky enough I can go back and have a few days at a place called Carmel, where there are a few people I know who will welcome a vulgar old man, even though he has proven a flop and has been kicked around by the Japs. Meanwhile the vulgar old man is trying to think up a scheme to kick *them* around.

On 29 May, within a week of emerging from the jungle at Imphal, Stilwell left for Chungking. He was close to complete exhaustion and his emaciated figure showed the ravages of dysentery and jaundice. He had lost 20 pounds in weight. His journey via Assam was delayed at Kunming for three days by bad weather – it was now the height of the monsoon – but because of his temperament these were days of frustration rather than rest or recuperation. He reached Chungking on 3 June after travelling over the Hump, the route that became synonymous with the massive American airlift of military supplies to Chiang that continued until the end of the war.

On arrival in Chungking he was taken to a large house that was to serve as his home and office until he returned to the USA. There were 29 servants, who he quickly realised were there to spy on him as well as look after him. He had fairly modest personal quarters, with a large, gloomy bedroom, a bathroom with antiquated plumbing and a small office, where he spent most of his time. His staff lived in other parts of the rambling house. Considering the disasters of the previous months, Stilwell received an immediate and cordial welcome from Chiang and Madame. He was given a quick medical check by the American embassy doctor, who confirmed serious jaundice, and he was then invited to spent the weekend with the Chiangs.

Chiang was angry – and with reason. As he saw it, his philosophy of not attacking, and of not involving his divisions too heavily, had been vindicated. He had given in to Stilwell's arguments and as a result had lost most of the Fifth Army, the only army with both artillery and transport. Chiang carefully quoted the great Chinese military thinker Sun Tsu who, in 400 BC, in *The Art of War*, laid down precepts which have rarely been bettered. Chiang seized on one of Sun Tsu's aphorisms, 'Ten victories is not the best. The best is to win without fighting', to justify his approach. Unfortunately Chiang misunderstood both this and almost all the rest of Sun Tsu's advice on waging war – with disastrous results.

In practical terms, whatever the argument or philosophy, Chiang had suffered cruel reverses. He had lost his best-trained army. The Japanese had blocked the Burma Road and cut him off from American supplies. In retaliation for the Doolittle air raid on Tokyo they had launched another attack on southwest China and were dangerously close to Chungking. By June 1942 Chiang realised that he was being excluded from top-level discussions with Roosevelt and Churchill, and this increased his hatred for the British, whom he increasingly saw as filching supplies that were rightly his. Chiang's view that he should be receiving as much backing as possible from America and the Allies, in the form of money and military supplies, was widely supported in Chungking. He wrote personally to Roosevelt threatening to pull out of the war. It was part of a deadly game of bluff. He threatened to pull out while at the same time calculating that he had to take sufficient action against the Japanese to keep American supplies flowing to his HQ. Chiang's two top priorities were to ensure that supplies continued to come over the Hump and to obtain more support for Chennault and the American Volunteer Group.

Stilwell and Chennault were to fight a long, deep and bitter feud, which was made worse by the lack of mutual understanding and almost complete contempt each felt for the policy of the other. Stilwell, with his passion for building up an effective Chinese army in order to counterattack and recapture north Burma, was openly contemptuous of Chennault's constant claim that with a few more wings of American bombers he could quickly knock Japan out of the war. Many of their disputes centred on the allocation of the supplies coming over the Hump, which was under Stilwell's control. During the Burma retreat Stilwell had been abrasively critical of Chiang, and their relationship remained stormy; he was, perhaps, unaware of the close, warm and long-standing link between Chennault and the Chiangs.

So far as fighting the Japanese went, by the summer of 1942 Chennault had admirable achievements to his credit. He had learnt to fly in 1917, but he missed the action on the western front. Having, as he said, 'tasted the air', he became a passionate supporter of flying, and during the 1920s and 1930s he organised air shows with his Flying Trapeze. All his aerobatics were designed with an eye to the development of future fighting aircraft. He watched apprehensively the huge Russian production of aircraft and the Nazi development of the Heinkel bomber and its use in the Spanish civil war.

Chennault had become deaf, and in 1939, doubting his prospects for further promotion in the USAAF, he retired and left for China to run an aviation school. By then China had suffered years of indiscriminate attacks by Japanese planes – notably the Mitsubishi Zero – against which it had no defence. Chennault had been personally invited to China by Madame Chiang Kai-Shek, and he witnessed a devastating Japanese air attack on Chungking. He was immediately plunged into fighting against the Japanese and was presented with his own plane by Madame. During 1940, with the example of the Battle of Britain fresh in his mind, Chennault went to Washington to lobby for American support for the air defence of China. Roosevelt gave some support to the idea of the American Volunteer Group, which Chennault organised, and which was allowed to recruit USAAF pilots with offers of generous bonuses. The first AVG units arrived in Chungking in 1941 armed with the Tomahawk P40, a strong aircraft with heavy fire power but less nimble than the Japanese Zero it was to face.

By the time of Pearl Harbor Chennault was commanding a force of more than eighty pilots in what became famous as the Flying Tigers. Early in 1941 the Flying Tigers were leased an airfield in southern Burma, and on 20 December 1941 they had their first successful clash with Japanese bombers. From then on the Flying Tigers were in constant and effective action against the waves of Japanese bombers that attacked Rangoon, and in February 1942 they shot down twenty-five enemy planes in one day. They co-operated with the RAF, but this had obsolete Buffalo fighters and was rapidly knocked out. Then the Flying Tigers, like all other units, were swept back by the Japanese advance, but they moved adroitly and managed to return to China intact while at the same time helping to halt the enemy advance at the Salween bridge on the Burma Road.

During 1942 the Flying Tigers were absorbed into the USAAF and Chennault became a major general. With very few casualties, and helped by his excellent training, the Flying Tigers destroyed nearly 300 Japanese aircraft. Madame observed that 'Chennault performed the impossible'. His achievement and his close, warm relationship with Chiang and Madame were significant factors in his long-standing feud with Stilwell. As the clash continued Chennault made more and more extravagant claims. It was unfortunate both for them and for China that these two brilliant, able and outstanding characters were from the start almost totally at loggerheads over the fundamental issue of whether to recapture northern Burma in order to open the Burma Road or whether to bomb Japan into submission from airfields in southwest China.

Stilwell took with him to this first meeting with Chiang and Madame a very detailed memorandum which set out his plans for reforming the Chinese army. He said that all available material should be concentrated on a few, dependable, well-equipped and well-supported divisions that should be brought fully up to strength. Junior officers and soldiers were willing, disciplined, inured to hardship and responsive to leadership, but the divisional and army commanders were the real problem. They were not efficient, seldom went to the front and rarely supervised the execution of their orders. They accepted reports from the front without checking them, and these were often exaggerated or entirely false. They ignored the need for reconnaissance and seemed to think that issuing orders from fifty miles behind the line was all that was required of them. Many were personally brave but lacked moral courage. He recommended a rigid purge of inefficient commanders.

For a man as blunt as Stilwell he treated the matter of Chiang's interference with marvellous delicacy:

> The system of command must be clarified and unity of command insisted upon. The Generalissimo must pick some one man in whom he has confidence, give him a general directive, and then let him handle the troops without interference from anyone. This man must not only control the tactical direction of the troops but also their transport, supply, communications and medical service. During the Burma campaign letters and instructions from various sources reached various commanders who, as a result, were confused as to their action. The Generalissimo himself writes to various commanders making suggestions based on his knowledge of the situation and giving advice as to courses of action in certain contingencies. These commanders, in their high regard for the Generalissimo's experience and ability, invariably interpret these suggestions and this advice as orders and act on them. (The Generalissimo gets unquestioned loyalty from his officers.)

The memorandum continued by recommending the complete reorganisation of transport, supply and medical services, prompt rewards for gallantry and prompt and ruthless punishment for offenders of any rank. The situation could only be saved by the vigorous and immediate overhaul of the entire organisation.

During the next ten days Stilwell was ill with jaundice, which medical treatment did little to help. As late as 17 June he wrote grimly, 'Two weeks of this goddam jaundice.' During his illness he had some conferences with his American colleagues, including Chennault, and also wrote to his wife:

> When I got here I was met by letters from you and it sure was good to have them. Your letters are the only bright spot in a drab existence, so send me one occasionally. I am enclosing a few photos taken at Dinjan just after I had gotten out of the jungle to prove to you that I am not nearly dead yet, although I am a bit skinny. Dorn and I dropped about 20 pounds apiece, but we'll get it all back. I didn't waste much time in India. Took three days to polish off the paper work at Delhi; then shoved off.

We are oppressed by the magnificence and grandiose style of the Delhi headquarters. Both American and British. The Limey layout is simply stupendous, you trip over lieutenant generals on every floor most of them doing captain's work or none at all. Came to Kunming in a bomber and then got stuck there for five days on account of bad weather here at Chungking. We finally got here on June 3, and next day I made a report to the Big Boy. I told him the whole truth, and it was like kicking an old lady in the stomach. However, as far as I can find out, *no one* else dares to tell him the truth, so it's up to me all the more. He has of course kept an eye on me all the time through certain agencies which I know are always present, but which I cannot identify very well. In fact, I pay no attention to them at all – just go ahead and let nature take its course. There are several things cooking now which will take a lot of talk: I hope some good will come of them, but my recommendations are so radical that it will be a wrench for him to put them into effect. Very cordial welcome from both him and Madame. Whether it means anything or not I of course don't know as yet.

For weeks, as he struggled to recover from his jaundice, Stilwell remained in Chungking and had frequent discussions with Chiang and Madame. These centred on three main issues: the reorganisation of the Chinese army, the provision of all the necessary military equipment, and the question of who should command the Chinese forces in India. Stilwell continued to argue that there was little point in providing expensive modern equipment unless the whole Chinese army was reorganised so that the supplies could be concentrated on a few good divisions and not scattered across the country to more than 300 divisions. He added that it was futile to give a tank or a modern gun to a peasant who had never handled anything more sophisticated than a wheelbarrow.

Madame, in some ways more forceful than her husband, supported General Tu's claim that he should command the Chinese forces in India. Stilwell, who had witnessed Tu's pitiful performance during the retreat from Burma, considered him to be absolutely useless and would not agree. In the end Stilwell accepted a compromise, and General Lo was appointed. During the discussions about a commander for the forces, Chiang sent a memorandum to Stilwell which goes some way to explain his habit of corresponding directly with the divisional commanders:

> There is a secret for the direction of Chinese troops unlike the direction of foreign troops. I am well aware of the fact that our senior officers do not possess enough education and sufficient capacity for work. Anticipating they will make mistakes I often write to them personally so that, timely warned, they might avoid them. Knowing their limited capacity I plan ahead for them. We have been carrying on the war of resistance for five years in such conditions ... If you are with me closely for a few months you will understand the psychology of Chinese officers, and I will tell you more about their peculiarities.

Stilwell considered this to be the usual crap.

The discussions on organisation for the CBI theatre were difficult enough, but they were soon to be overshadowed by complex extraneous strategic issues. By June 1942 Chiang had clearly realised that he was not going to be represented on the Combined Chiefs of Staff Council and, what was more significant for him, the Munitions Assignment Board, which allocated all American military supplies in overseas theatres. Chiang's powerful and scheming agent in Washington, T. V. Soong, determined to give maximum publicity to this issue and to keep it in the forefront of their demands. In the early part of 1942 nearly 150,000 tons of Lend–Lease material allocated to China had become stranded in America and another 45,000 tons in India. Soong agreed to the USA repossessing the 150,000 tons and in return accepted a promise of 5,000 tons of equipment per month to be supplied over the Hump. This would be controlled by Stilwell.

The figure of 5,000 tons a month remained central to the long and bitter in-fighting between Washington and Chungking and between Chiang and Stilwell. Five thousand tons was an easy round figure for negotiations at high level. In practice it was an almost impossible commitment. It took no account of the appalling flying conditions over the Hump. The monsoon storms, which started in mid-May, combined with the most formidable mountain barrier inflicted a very heavy toll on both men and machines. In the next two years more than 500 aircraft were lost making the trip over the Hump – an average of twelve planes every month, and more during the monsoon. The loss of aircraft was serious enough, but the loss of the experienced and intrepid air crews who worked valiantly to keep old and worn-out machines in the air in spite of grave shortages of spare parts was even more threatening to the enterprise. When an aircraft crashed very few of the crew made it back to base, and those who did brought tales of the whitened bones of crews lost earlier hanging in the trees.

It increasingly appeared to Chiang that he was being given specious promises which the American administration never intended to keep. The 23 American Pursuit Group of fighter aircraft had been promised but did not arrive. He and other Chinese leaders, supported and encouraged by Chennault, set the highest store on the provision of American air power to operate from the airfields in the approaches to Chungking.

The failure to provide promised aircraft caused a serious crisis in the relations between Chiang and America. The top-secret Doolittle air raid on Tokyo was carried out by bombers that set out from an aircraft carrier in the Pacific and landed on airfields in southwest China. Because of the notoriously lax Chinese security, the raid was kept secret until the last moment even from Chiang, and what appeared to the Americans as a brilliant blow against the Japanese only infuriated him. The immediate and angry Japanese response to the Doolittle raid was to send a major military force of more than fifty battalions to advance through Chenkiang province on the approach to Chungking to annihilate everyone in the area and to destroy the air bases.

This heightened the tension in Chungking. Chiang, encouraged by Soong in Washington, increasingly blamed Stilwell for the broken promises and for not producing all the supplies that had been pledged. Neither Chiang nor Stilwell fully realised that there were equally urgent demands in other theatres of war and that China was fairly low down on the list of strategic priorities. Stilwell pleaded with Marshall for more help, and Chiang wrote personally to Roosevelt, but few aircraft arrived. The main supply airfield in Assam was frequently jammed with aircraft that were grounded because of the lack of aircrew or spare parts. All these difficulties meant that, instead of the 5,000 tons a month that had been promised, about 100 tons a month were delivered. Soong kept up the pressure, sending letters and memoranda to Roosevelt, Churchill and many others. He threatened to withdraw China's support if a minimum supply programme was not maintained.

Despite the continuing clash over the whole question of supplies, during early June 1942 Stilwell had prolonged and fairly amicable talks with Chiang and Madame on many wider issues. When he argued for the urgent reorganisation of the Chinese army, Madame pointed out that her husband had many complex issues to consider. Stilwell understood that, but he added in his diary: 'With the U.S. on his side and backing him, the stupid little ass fails to grasp the big opportunity of his life.' He added that Chiang had frequently double-crossed him in Burma and never replied to any of his memos. 'The question now is what do I do next? Just sit here, or resign?' On 21 June events took place half a world away from Burma which high-lighted all of Chiang's and Stilwell's problems. In North Africa, Rommel and the Afrika Corps had won a series of battles, and on that day his troops captured Tobruk, taking 30,000 prisoners and capturing half a million gallons of petrol and three million rations. On the same day Churchill, in Washington with Roosevelt, heard the news. Later he said that it was the worst blow he had received during the war. To help Britain after the fall of Tobruk, with Rommel now poised to advance to the Suez canal, Roosevelt diverted Brereton and the promised bomber force from China to the Middle East. At the same time a large consignment of Hudson bombers was diverted from India to Cairo and 300 Sherman tanks were sent to Egypt. These decisions were made to meet a grave military crisis, but the effect on the Chinese, who were not even informed, was disastrous. On 26 June Stilwell went with senior American colleagues to see Chiang and Madame to pass on the news that Brereton's bomber force and the Hudson aircraft had been diverted to the Middle East.

Chiang was furious and demanded to know who could divert a force that had been authorised by the President. Of course, the answer was that Roosevelt himself had done it. Madame made fierce allegations of Stilwell's bad faith and argued that there was no point in China remaining in the war since China was not important to the rest of the Allies. Stilwell radioed Marshall with the main details of the crisis he faced, and Roosevelt replied to Chiang the next day but did not make any firm promises.

Roosevelt's reply did little to assuage Chiang's anger, and Stilwell received from the latter what became known as the Three Demands. These were that:

1. Three American divisions must be deployed to India by September to reopen the supply route up the Burma Road.
2. Five hundred war planes should be provided by August and subsequently kept up to strength.
3. Five thousand tons of supplies a month must be sent over the Hump from August.

Chiang accompanied these demands with the clear threat that China might pull out of the war if they were not met. When Madame insisted that Stilwell should forward the demands with his recommendation, he demurred. She was furious. 'Obviously mad as hell. She had cracked the whip and the stooge had not come across.'

The summer of 1942 was the lowest point of the war for the Allies. Rommel was threatening Egypt and the Suez canal. The Nazi drive to Stalingrad looked unstoppable, and it was feared that these two pincer movements might meet up in Syria and Iraq and cut off Allied access to all Middle East oil. It is no wonder that the situation in China appeared less urgent.

Although Stilwell had to bear the brunt of Chiang's anger and outrage, he was able to understand that side of the problem. On 25 June he wrote: 'Now what can I say to the G-mo? We fail in all our commitments and blithely tell him to just carry on old top. The A.V.G. is breaking up, our people are dead slow about replacing it, the radio operators don't arrive and our boys are brand new at the game.'

On the next day Madame spoke to him directly. 'Now I'm the villain. I sabotaged the transport grab … In general I'm an s.o.b, … I am afraid I am now suspect. Also, I am afraid the War Department is using me as a whipping boy. "In a jam, blame it on Stilwell." ' With deep and increasing bitterness Chiang and Madame began to blame Stilwell for all the failures in the supply system and for all the broken promises. This intense feeling gave birth in Chiang's mind to the idea that Stilwell should be removed.

Stilwell had been forced into an untenable position by events over which he had no control, and although he knew he could rely on the support of his old friend Marshall, he was less certain of the Washington administration as a whole. He therefore felt it necessary to clarify his situation and to spell out his various responsibilities. He was the American representative in China and commander of all US forces in the China–Burma–India theatre. This involved co-operation with the British in Burma and India. He was Chief of Staff to the Generalissimo and controller of all Lend–Lease supplies. He was responsible for military planning, for training – particularly of the Chinese troops in India – and for field operations, but he was *not* responsible for the procurement of supplies. He concluded, 'My only objective is the effective prosecution of the war.'

During the crisis it became clear that Soong in Washington had altered and toned down Roosevelt's reply to Chiang. When the truth emerged Soong's deviousness, or dishonesty, made Chiang extremely angry. Stilwell, referring to Soong, wrote, 'The damn fool: didn't he know he'd be caught. He should be called up, dressed down and thrown out. Imagine an official of his position suppressing a message of such importance from Frank to Peanut.'*

The doctoring of a message from the President of the United States was clearly a grave matter. Roosevelt took it very seriously indeed and sent a special envoy, Dr Currie, to Chungking. Currie, who arrived in July, was an experienced negotiator and understood the Chinese situation. He supported Stilwell's general strategy but was

* The Peanut, usually with the addition of adjectives, became Stilwell's normal way of referring to Chiang.

critical of some of his attitudes. He recommended the restoration of an airlift target of 3,500 tons a month, and it was agreed that all correspondence with the President should be copied to Stilwell. Currie took part in some of the long, detailed and difficult negotiations that Stilwell was conducting during this period, but, having witnessed the depth and intensity of the bitterness felt by Chiang and Madame, when he returned to Washington he recommended that Stilwell should be transferred to another theatre and that Soong be replaced as Chinese ambassador to Washington. At this stage Roosevelt, Stimson and Marshall saw clearly that Soong had caused the crisis and they remained loyal to Stilwell.

Some progress was finally achieved by the long and tortuous negotiations held through June and July 1942. The British, reluctantly, agreed to the Chinese troops being housed and trained at Ramgarh, a large camp some 200 miles west of Calcutta. Their main concern was the presence of 8,000 of these troops in Bengal, where the Congress independence movement was strongest. This was a remarkable achievement by Stilwell, who gained the agreement of the British to his control of training, equipment and supply while they housed, fed and paid the Chinese troops.

Stilwell, as an American patriot, believed passionately that because of the colossal American investment in both men and supplies he should have a controlling role in the strategy. He argued constantly in favour of the provision and training of thirty Chinese divisions in the Kunming area so that they would be ready and well placed for a major offensive against the Japanese. In contrast, Chiang had complex reasons for opposing this plan. He felt that the commander of thirty well-trained divisions could become a military and political threat to him. At the same time, many of his most loyal supporters were the commanders of the three hundred divisions scattered across China. He rarely deviated from his view that American supplies should be carefully conserved so that after the war, when the Allies had defeated the Japanese, he would be in a strong position to fight the Communists under Mao.

The general strategic plan, which Stilwell put forward in July 1942 and which was agreed and supported in principle by both Washington and Chungking, envisaged one American, three British and two Chinese divisions attacking the Japanese from the major British base at Imphal. Simultaneously, twelve Chinese divisions would advance down the Burma Road towards Lashio. The two prongs would then join up in the area of Mandalay and drive on rapidly to recapture Rangoon and continue further south through Thailand to Bangkok. Another group of nine Chinese divisions based near Kunming would advance due south from Kunming towards Hanoi in French Indo-China. This appeared to be a feasible and realistic plan, although most American commanders remained sceptical of Chinese determination and already suspected that Chiang would stockpile most of the weapons, aircraft and other material provided in response to his incessant demands for use against the Communists after the war. The depth of the scheming is illustrated by Soong, who in an unguarded moment suggested that when the war was over Chiang would be thrown out within six months.

Colonel Frank Dorn, a long-standing and loyal supporter of Stilwell, made a significant comment when he forwarded the plan to Washington. He stressed that all aid must be supplied 'on an ultimatum basis' dependent on Chiang's agreement to act. 'If he threatens to make peace tell him to go ahead.' Dorn added that across much of China there was substantial trade with the Japanese, and concluded: 'Until we re-take Burma, and re-open the port of Rangoon all talks and planning to aid China is utterly meaningless.'★

While high-level negotiations were going on, Stilwell concentrated on his other major responsibility of training his Chinese troops, especially those in India. In July 1942 he made an impressive broadcast on a Chinese radio station:

> Five years ago today I went to Wan Ping Hsien to find out what was going on in a clash between Japanese and Chinese troops reported there. I found that the Japanese were attacking the town and that, much to their surprise, the Chinese were putting up a spirited resistance. This

★ C. Romanus and R. Sunderland, *Stilwell's Mission to China*, Center of Military History, Washington, 1953, p. 183.

defence proved to be prophetic and symbolic; the Chinese defence has stood up, and now, after five years it is a privilege to be here and pay tribute to the man who has carried the burden and gone through the test of battle – the Chinese soldier. To me the Chinese soldier best exemplifies the greatness of the Chinese people – their indomitable spirit, their uncomplaining loyalty, their honesty of purpose, their steadfast perseverance. He endures untold privations without a whimper, he follows wherever he is led without question or hesitation, and it never occurs to his simple and straightforward mind that he is doing anything heroic. He asks for little and always stands ready to give all. I feel it is a great honour, as a representative of the U.S. Army to salute here today the Chinese soldier.

Although Dorn had dismissed the danger of Chiang doing a deal with the Japanese, Stilwell was less certain. The Japanese foreign minister had been active in Chungking and Peking, and Stilwell's intelligence service informed him that a senior Chinese official from Peking who was well known as a Japanese collaborator had come to see Chiang with peace feelers from the Japanese. Stilwell knew better than most the strong German influence in China during the 1930s, and among the Chinese under the virtually fascist rule of Chiang there was considerable sympathy for the Nazis. In the wider strategic context, Chiang was apprehensive about the future role of Russia in eastern Asia and the danger of its possible support for the Chinese Communists under Mao Tse-Tung. He calculated that if America transferred its main focus away from a second front in Europe to the Pacific, Japan would be defeated and Germany might then be able to defeat Russia.

As it became obvious that Chiang was trying to get rid of Stilwell the antipathy between them deepened. He headed a letter to his wife 'The Manure Pile'. He wrote, 'This is the most dreary type of manoeuvrings I've ever done, trying to guide and influence a stubborn, ignorant, prejudiced, conceited despot, who never hears the truth except from me, and finds it hard to believe.' Stilwell's continuing anger and resentment at the incessant Chinese demands, and the complete lack of gratitude for what they did receive, was now compounded by the problem of the exchange rate between the American and Chinese dollars. The rate had been fixed at one to twenty, but when Chiang simply printed more notes to cover his declining revenue and the cost of the war he created wild inflation, which brought the real exchange rate to closer to one to four hundred and meant that Americans had to pay about twenty times over for everything they bought.

In the latter part of July 1942, in an atmosphere of increasingly bitter tension, Chiang argued strongly that he could order Stilwell to obtain supplies. This Stilwell, backed by Washington, rejected. He continued to send Chiang memoranda on important issues, and these were rarely answered. The atmosphere was not improved when it became known how many lies Soong had spread about Stilwell. The first of August was a fairly typical day. He wrote, 'To office and worked through some poison. S.N.A.F.U.* with Peanut. No answer on anything. He's having a hell of a time with his face.'

Then he wrote to his wife:

'OFFICE OF THE COMMANDING GENERAL, AMERICAN ARMY FORCES, CBI: LETTER TO MRS STILWELL
Got some paper at last, so now you can see what a big shot I really am. Actually, it's all wind. This is just a side show, and I'm beginning to wonder if any life can ever be pumped into it. You can imagine the continuous struggle to overcome the inertia of centuries, and battle the jealousies of Chinese officialdom. That ought to be spelled Official-dumb. You know the type of gangster that gets to the top here, so I won't go further into my troubles. But it's a hell of a way to fight a war, from my point of view, and it makes me feel like a complete slacker. Now if I were in addition a slicker, I might make some headway.

This was the start of a period when Stilwell travelled constantly between Rangoon, Delhi, Chungking and Kunming, the main base for the supplies flown over the Hump. His personal aircraft was an aging DC3, and in this he flew over the Hump to the air bases in

* This acronym, well known to most British soldiers in Burma, meant 'situation normal, all fouled up'.

Assam and from there another thousand miles to Delhi. From Delhi he made frequent onward trips to the great base at Ramgarh, where over 8,000 Chinese soldiers were being trained and equipped for the reconquest of Burma. To carry out his multifarious responsibilities he also had to visit Karachi, the main port for military material brought by sea from the USA.

The training camp at Ramgarh, which lay about 40 miles from a major British base at Ranchi, brought Stilwell once more into close contact with Slim. Slim referred to 'our old friends the Chinese', remembering perhaps the help he had received from General Sun and 38 Division in the desperate fighting around Yenangyaung. Slim admired Stilwell's determination and his indomitable will. Few people – American, British or Chinese – really believed that an effective fighting force could be created from the Chinese troops at Ramgarh, but Stilwell was achieving it. Grave difficulties faced him. The Indian authorities were apprehensive about the presence of 8,000 Chinese troops in Bengal, and the Chinese leadership – notably Chiang and Chennault – continued to demand a massive build-up of aircraft for bases around Chunking and strongly opposed the priority given to the idea of the reconquest of northern Burma and the opening of the Burma Road. Stilwell bluntly refuted this argument by pointing out that occupying forces could only be driven out by ground troops and not by aircraft. Slim wrote:

> Stilwell was magnificent. He forced Chiang Kai-shek to provide the men; he persuaded India to accept a large Chinese force, and the British to pay for it, accommodate, feed, and clothe it. The American 'Ferry Command' then flew thirteen thousand Chinese from Kunming over 'The Hump', the great mountain range between Assam and China, to airfields in the Brahmaputra Valley, whence they came by rail to Ramgarh. This was the first large-scale troop movement by air in the theatre and was an outstanding achievement. The young American pilots of the Hump should be remembered with admiration and gratitude by their countrymen and their allies.*

* Slim, *Defeat into Victory*, p. 144.

To make his command effective, Stilwell kept his main HQ in Chungking, under Brigadier General Hearn, and a second HQ under General Sibert in Delhi. Brigadier General McCabe commanded the Ramgarh Training Centre, and Brigadier General Bissell, who had been in Chungking with Stilwell, commanded the Tenth Air Force. Despite a clear command structure, Stilwell still faced formidable problems – notably of supply. Most supplies came across the Pacific from Los Angeles. Bombay was the best port, but it was constantly clogged up with British shipping and war supplies. Calcutta was much closer both to Ramgarh and to the Hump airfields in Assam, but it too was clogged up and was under frequent threat of Japanese air raids. Karachi had advantages but was separated from Ramgarh by the whole width of India and a hopelessly inadequate railway system. The Indian railways were unable to cope with the huge volume of traffic needed to build up Stilwell's forces and the whole of the British Fourteenth Army.

One of Stilwell's really great achievements, and one that is often overlooked, was the astounding success of the training regime at Ramgarh which he personally set up and, initially, supervised. The two Chinese divisions that had escaped to Imphal – 38 and 22 – were reconstituted. The men were well fed in a well-organised camp, given medical care and received regular pay – something they had never before experienced. Under American instructors running a crash programme the Chinese soldiers made remarkable progress, particularly in the difficult process of converting from infantry to artillery. Slim noted that 'Everywhere was Stilwell, urging, leading, driving'.

During August 1942 Stilwell shuttled between Ramgarh and Delhi, constantly dealing with problems. Of necessity he had to make decisions while he was on the move between his different HQs, and this inevitably created some confusion and contributed to the criticism that he was not a good administrator. The arrest of Gandhi in Delhi on 9 August followed by serious riots highlighted the issue of internal security, as did the ominous first signs of the devastating famine in Bengal. In Ramgarh Stilwell drove things forward, but there were frequent clashes between Chinese and US instructors, who generally

disliked the posting to Ramgarh. Stilwell intervened and supported
the British when they insisted that the pay they provided should be
given directly to the soldiers. The Chinese custom had been for the
general commanding a division to receive all the pay for the division,
and this he rarely passed on to the troops.

While Stilwell was busy in Ramgarh and Delhi, serious discussions
took place between Roosevelt and Marshall. Currie had returned
to Washington, where he suggested that things would be easier if
Stilwell, with his abrasiveness, was removed. Roosevelt considered
the idea and sounded out Marshall. He was contemptuous of Currie
and resolutely backed Stilwell as the only person likely to gain any
effective military action from Chiang in return for the colossal
Lend–Lease supplies.

Stilwell's diary and letters for August 1942 continued to mix
serious comments with the trivial: he had to change his glasses; the
country was flooded by the monsoon rain; anti-British disturbances
made travel dangerous; he had had no letters for two months –
'perhaps they are going by sea via Russia'; and there were tigers on
the rifle range at Ramgarh. In a letter to his wife he wrote:

> I have now arrived at the pinnacle of social success, having been enter-
> tained at lunch by the Viceroy himself. I am all in a dither over it. I
> took Dorn along and he made some good remarks about it. Nobody
> dared to open his trap at the table so it was up to me and the Vicey to
> keep the conversation going. They must be after something because
> Wavell also had me to lunch. He was not at all upstage, but he's not
> what you call animated – in fact he impresses me as being a tired old
> man. Very cordial and probably tied down with instructions from
> London …
>
> Make the most of Carmel … If I could get some new teeth and
> eyes and some hair dye, I wouldn't look a day over seventy.

After his August activities in Ramgarh and the high-level discussions in Delhi, Stilwell flew to Chungking to report to Chiang.
He brought with him many photographs of Ramgarh, the camp and
the training activities. Chiang was impressed and the atmosphere was

cordial, but even so Stilwell could barely hide his frustration. 'He was much pleased with it. Why shouldn't he be, the little jackass. We are doing our damndest to help him and he makes his approval look like a tremendous concession.' Having gained Chiang's approval of the Ramgarh centre, Stilwell then had to gain agreement to the next part of his strategy – to fly large numbers of Chinese soldiers to Ramgarh using the empty aircraft that had brought supplies over the Hump to Kunming. Chiang agreed, and the first troops were flown down in October 1942. Thereafter the American air service returned over the Hump with an average of 500 men per day. This was one of the earliest large-scale troop movements by air and is a tribute to Stilwell's vision and determination.

During this visit, although he obtained Chiang's agreement to the large-scale transfer of Chinese troops for training at Ramgarh, he still had to fight hard on the wider – and as he saw it, crucial – issue of concentrating thirty effective, well-armed and well-trained divisions at Kunming as the nucleus of the Chinese forces ready to take part in the recapture of Burma and the reopening of the Burma Road. He was able to advance his side in the game of double-bluff by hinting that the American war department was seriously considering stopping all military supplies unless China actively pursued the thirty-division proposal. He even proposed specific units that he thought should be chosen for the training.

The background to the discussion of the thirty-division plan was the 300 divisions, or four million men, in the Kuomintang army. In practice these were mostly half-starved peasants with no equipment or training and who were badly led and not fit for military activity. Stilwell had witnessed this when he was military attaché in the 1930s, when he compared Chiang's troops adversely to the Communists. He had noted that for every battle casualty in the Kuomintang army, nine deserted or died of disease. The thirty-division plan was put forward even before Pearl Harbor, but Stilwell was aggressively determined to make it a reality. The real crux of the military situation in China was, to Stilwell's constant frustration, the ineptitude of Chiang's troops and the fact that he had almost no influence over the warlords and the 300 divisions they controlled. Chiang frequently made agreements with Stilwell or with Washington, but he rarely had any effective way of carrying them out. He made promises to one after another visiting American dignitary, who were taken in by his charm – and particularly Madame's – and went back to Washington wondering if part of the problem in Chungking was, perhaps, Stilwell.

Throughout September 1942 Stilwell continued to wrestle with the intractable issue of the thirty Chinese divisions. He had a lengthy discussion with senior Chinese General Liu Fei about the future role of the Chinese forces in Burma. Liu suggested that China would put between five and ten divisions into Burma provided that there were six British or American divisions. Then three Chinese armies would hold two Japanese divisions at Lashio while the Americans and British engaged the other eight Japanese divisions. He explained that the Chinese could not attack because they had no planes or guns, and that if they did attack the Japanese could send ten divisions and hundreds of aircraft and all would be lost. The Chinese would attack when the Japanese were heavily engaged elsewhere and only if they were sure to win. Liu argued further that one-third of all Kuomintang forces were needed to face the Communists in the north. This detailed discussion, which Stilwell dismissed as pure crap, does go some way to explaining the hopeless position Chiang felt he was in and why he appeared to renege on all his promises.

In these discussions Stilwell clashed once again with General Lo, who had been with him during the retreat from Burma and was to come under his command at Ramgarh. Lo brought up the issue of pay for the soldiers at Ramgarh, which was provided by the British, and argued strongly that all of the 450,000 rupees should be paid to him. This was bluntly refused. After discussion with another senior and influential Chinese commander, Stilwell wrote: 'He makes inaction a virtue by proving conclusively the impossibility of action.'

Towards the end of September, Stilwell received Washington's formal reply to the Three Demands. This agreed to increase the number of aircraft and the tonnage flown over the Hump, but it stated that no American divisions would be sent to Burma. Stilwell wrote, 'It amounts to doing *nothing* more than at present. I suppose I am to kid them into reorganising the Army.' The depth of Stilwell's frustration was shown by his final comment. Forces for Burma 'will be the Ramgarh detachment, the Tenth Air Force, the Yunnan mob and a limited British detachment. In other words, what we have got. How *very* generous. Oh yes, a guy from operations will come out and show us how to do it.'

At the end of September, after a gap of many weeks, the post from home turned up. Soldiers on active service, from privates to generals, long for letters from family and friends. Stilwell was overjoyed, but the mail did not bring good news for some. In a field hospital in Burma a wounded man received a letter from his wife saying that she had gone off with another man. He shot himself.

Stilwell replied to his wife. 'Just rereading the Feast of Letters. Boy did I get some letters. I've read it all three or four times already and it helps to offset the manure pile.' He replied with questions about his son Ben's fishing, his daughter Alison's art exhibition and his dog Garry. He felt that his letters must be as dull as dishwater, and merely remarked on the weather, but he passed on the news that Dorn, who the family knew, had been promoted to full colonel.

Occasionally Stilwell's diary contained several paragraphs on a particular topic, as if he wanted to clarify his thoughts. On 5 October 1942 he wrote, 'Troubles of a peanut dictator,' and outlined the serious problems which Chiang faced in his relations with the governors of the different Chinese provinces, who were also commanders in charge of the province and controllers of the local division. 'So the Peanut lays off and waits. The plain fact is that he doesn't dare to take vigorous action … Why doesn't the little dummy realise that his only hope is the 30-division plan, and the creation of a separate, efficient, well-equipped, and well-trained force.' When he wrote this Stilwell had just received a report on the effect of the Japanese retaliatory attack on southwest China after the Doolittle raid on Tokyo. He noted scathingly that the so-called reconquest of the area the Japanese had occupied was merely Chinese troops re-occupying it after the Japanese had left. They had wrecked the buildings, destroyed the paddy fields and carried off all metal, from railway lines to cooking pots. 'Peanut directed operations from Chungking with the usual brilliant results.'

Early in October Stilwell made some barbed comments about the visit of Senator Wendell Willkie, whom Roosevelt had defeated in the last election and was thought likely to be the next president. The Chiangs turned on all their charm, and Willkie was treated to a constant programme of visits and entertainment. He was even lodged in a Chinese house instead of the American embassy. 'Keep him well-insulated from pollution by the Americans. The idea is to get him so exhausted and keep him so torpid with food and drink that his faculties will be dulled and he'll be stuffed with the right doctrines.'

Willkie was renowned for his uncritical acceptance of prejudiced views, and Stilwell was forced to watch as brilliant military displays with guns, tanks and aircraft, with fit, well-equipped troops, were laid on for the visitor. Willkie was convinced that China was a noble and powerful military ally. He commented that militarily China was united under able generals and the army knew what it was fighting for. 'Crap', thought Stilwell. Willkie did not see the pathetic and emaciated men who were often sent from Kunming to Ramgarh.

Stilwell fumed at the sycophantic attentions the Chiangs paid Willkie. He realised that their motives were to gain support for Chennault's plan (and, incidentally, rid themselves of him, Stilwell) and to obtain ever larger supplies of American aircraft and crews. They hoped that their influence on Willkie would help to sidetrack Stilwell's firm resolve to reform the Chinese army. To Stilwell's disgust Willkie, who pointedly ignored him, clearly fell for Madame's charm and invited her to make a goodwill tour of the USA. He felt that Willkie was completely sold on Chiang Kai-Shek and Madame, and on 7 October he wrote: 'Willkie off thank God. Hardly spoke to me. Utterly indifferent.' Stilwell's future might well have been adversely affected when Willkie returned home and wrote a book, *One World*. Full of praise and admiration for the wonderful leadership of Chiang and Madame, it sold a million copies.

CHAPTER 6

Regrouping

When Stilwell and Slim reached the relative security of the British base at Imphal in May 1942 and Stilwell started his prolonged efforts to cajole Chiang Kai-Shek into taking effective action, both were assisted by the monsoon which, more than any military force, stopped the Japanese advance.

As early as June Slim took command of the British XV Corps at Barrackpore, a large military base near Calcutta. The Corps consisted of 14 Division, based at Chittagong, and 26 Division in the Barrackpore–Calcutta area. Slim was as eager as Stilwell to recreate an effective fighting force, but he had other responsibilities as well. The Japanese had advanced well into the Arakan north of Rangoon (see map on p. 48) and were close to Imphal and Kohima, so Slim's first priority was of necessity the defence of Bengal against further enemy advance. The combined Japanese naval and air forces had played a crucial role in the capture of Singapore and Malaya and the elimination of British naval power in the Bay of Bengal, and one of Slim's most urgent responsibilities was the defence of the Sunderbans – the mangrove forest-covered approaches to Calcutta on the Ganges delta – and Calcutta itself from likely Japanese attack.

While Stilwell continued his impatient criticism of the Limeys and their inadequacies, Slim faced mounting difficulties. In August 1942, Gandhi launched his so-called non-violent campaign to remove the British from India, a movement which, as has been seen, had the sneaking admiration of Stilwell, Chiang and others. The non-violent element was short-lived, and during 1942 Gandhi's followers made ferocious attacks on railways, bridges, signals, stations and trains. The widespread attacks on trains frequently resulted in all Europeans being taken off the train and hacked to death. Another racial element now appeared. A large percentage of railway staff were Anglo-Indian (i.e., people of mixed race) who were not popular with the average Indian, and they suffered disproportionately in the attacks. At this time Slim had to deploy 57 battalions – the equivalent of four or five divisions – on internal security, with much of that effort directed at defending the railways. He also had to consider whether the Indian campaign against the railways was linked to a further Japanese advance.

The danger to the Burma forces from the campaign of railway sabotage can be illustrated by the fragile rail link from Calcutta. This travelled northeastwards to Dimapur (the rail junction for Imphal) and on to Ledo, the rail centre for Stilwell's forces in north Burma and the supply base for the flights over the Hump to Chiang Kai-shek in China. From Calcutta the railway was normal gauge for 200 miles. Then all supplies had to be reloaded for transport on a one-metre gauge railway for the next 250 miles. At the end of this stretch of line the wagons were shunted on to barges to cross the River Brahmaputra and were then put back on the railway to travel 150 miles to Dimapur, and beyond that another 200 miles to Ledo. This was the precarious supply route for all the future operations to drive the Japanese out of Burma. In 1939 the railway could carry 600 tons a day; by the end of 1943 the capacity had been increased to 2,500 tons, and then six American railway battalions with highly trained staff and modern equipment raised it to well over 4,000 tons a day. Fortunately the Indian protesters did not realize the damage they could cause by sabotaging this particular line, and they were not in touch with the Japanese.

At the same time as the railway route was being built up, a substantial road construction programme was under way. The achievement of the Indian, British and American engineers in building three strategic roads have rightly received the highest praise. The first went eastwards into the Arakan where, because there was no stone, brick kilns were built to provide the base for the road; the second led up to Dimapur and then onwards past Kohima and Imphal to Tiddim; and, finally, the Americans were building a spur running north from Dimapur to Ledo and thence southwards to Myitkyina.

While the internal security crisis continued, Slim's XV Corps moved to Ranchi, close to Stilwell's training base at Ramgarh. The strength of Slim's forces gradually increased. The 70th Division, a tried and hardened fighting force, and 50 Armoured Brigade came under his command, followed by 7, 5 and 20 Indian Divisions. Slim was then able to carry out what was a revolution in infantry jungle training in order to overcome the low morale and defeatist attitudes that understandably influenced the troops after the Burma defeat. Thus, at Ramgarh and Ranchi, with Stilwell, General Sun and the Chinese, along with Slim's increasingly powerful and well-trained force, a feeling of confidence was slowly established. Plans were made for an attack in the spring of 1943, but Slim believed that it was more important to build up sufficient strength and confidence in new tactics to be certain of victory.

While sound co-operation continued between Stilwell and Slim on the ground, there were still complications at a high level. Wavell was under some pressure from the Viceroy of India, Lord Linlithgow, to put forward the realistic concern of the Indian government over the presence of so many Chinese troops in Bengal at a time when Gandhi's campaign was at its height. Stilwell fumed at the objections and was generally contemptuous of Wavell, whom he saw as a beaten man, but there was some reason behind the concern, for shortly afterwards a map was produced in Chungking that showed India and most of north Burma as belonging to China.

Stilwell went to Delhi in October 1942 for a conference with Wavell on the outstanding issues. He wrote:

> Wavell, a lot of bull and crying about this and that. He made it plain the Ramgarh Training Centre is not welcome. All sorts of difficulties – railroads, roads, water, food transport. Will hinder Indian Army development … Well, to hell with the old fool. We have just smoked them out. They don't want Chinese troops participating in the retaking of Burma. That's all. (It's O.K. for US troops to be in England though) … Limeys getting nasty about Ramgarh. Wavell must have a formal request – for the Viceroy. How many troops to come and what for? WHAT FOR? My God! I told them, to help our allies retake Burma.

After three days of conference there was a sudden change in the British attitude – the result, Stilwell assumed, of a cable from Washington or London. 'Everything is lovely again, so obviously George [Marshall] has turned on the heat.' The main result achieved by the conference was the agreement that any operation in the spring of 1943 must be of a limited nature and would be carried out by the British on the northern Arakan coast, with the possibility of an attack on the small port of Akyab. Stilwell proposed that the Chinese divisions should advance into Burma through Imphal, but Wavell, pointing out the inadequacy of the approach roads, assigned to the Chinese the northern sector based on the Hukawng valley. Stilwell accepted this and agreed that his mission should be to capture Myitkyina with its airfield, and from there to make contact with the Chinese divisions advancing from Yunnan. The Americans also undertook the task of building the road from Ledo down the Hukawng valley, eventually to join up with the Burma Road.

After the Delhi conference he briefly gave his impressions in a letter to his wife. 'I feel I have been through the wringer ... I am in no shape to write even a note. Our Limey friends are sometimes a bit difficult, but there are some good eggs among them. It is no fun bucking two nationalities to get at the Japs.' He described a party with Archie (Wavell). 'The British don't quite know how to take me. I catch them looking me over occasionally with a speculative glint in their eye. Some of them that I had thought most hidebound and icy prove to have a good deal of my point of view, and take delight in watching me stick the prod into the Most High.' He mentioned that he had asked for his son-in-law Colonel Ernest Easterbrook to join his staff, and a few weeks later his son, Colonel Joseph Stilwell Jr, also joined him. He described the success of training at Ramgarh: 'The Peanut is, I believe, quite impressed. Unless he is terribly dumb, he will want to go on with this kind of business.'

As soon as he returned to Chungking he had an important meeting, on 3 November 1942, with Chiang, Madame and T.V. Soong. It was quickly apparent that Soong had been dressed down in Washington, and now – scheming as ever – he obviously thought that China would obtain more Lend–Lease materials if he supported Stilwell. Stilwell immediately noticed the different atmosphere, and his diary for the day of the conference is unusually detailed – probably due to the need to jot down the main points of a long and gruelling discussion.

To his surprise Chiang agreed to the idea of preparing fifteen divisions in Yunnan, subsequently known as Yoke Force, for the drive to recapture northern Burma and for these to be ready by mid-February 1943. Chiang confirmed Stilwell's command at Ramgarh and gave him the authority to sack the egregious General Lo. There was some complex discussion about joint commands with the British in Burma, but no major snags arose. In this lengthy discussion Chiang, understandably, demanded British and American naval activity in the Indian Ocean and the Bay of Bengal to prevent Japanese reinforcements coming in through Rangoon. The day after the meeting Stilwell saw Soong again and commented: 'If he does half of what he promises [we] will get somewhere.' He added: 'What's the game? But who cares if we get going.'

The appearance of Soong certainly changed the atmosphere in Chungking, and Stilwell found a real enthusiasm among the Chinese commanders for the creation of an effective fighting force. He was determined to make the most of this opportunity, but he still harboured suspicions of the British – 'if we can keep a fire lit under Wavell'. These suspicions were shared by many senior Americans and have been repeated by Tuchman, who stated, inaccurately, that the British never ceased to oppose the prospect of the road from Ledo to join up with the Burma Road. There is no evidence for this. As usual in his diary, Stilwell mixed high strategy with personal comment. In November his son, Joe, arrived and brought family letters and knitted socks. 'The socks were delivered promptly and are gorgeous. If they prevent cold feet, you've done something for your country.' His fluent French had not been used for some time, but he referred – as an alternative to the 'manure pile' – to *affaires empoisonnantes*. The enthusiastic build-up of Yoke Force led to a serious clash with Chennault, who continued to demand a larger proportion of the equipment brought over the Hump. Stilwell remained highly suspicious of Chennault because he had the ear of Madame, who soon afterwards left for her tour of the USA, where she was even photographed in a car with Roosevelt.

Stilwell's optimistic phase did not last. By the end of November 1942 he was commenting: 'Ominous stuff from India. Limeys thinking on limited lines. Their objective is a joke.' The hopes of activity by the Royal Navy and RAF demanded by Chiang were dashed, and Stilwell was even furious with Marshall, who had sent a detailed assessment that amounted to nothing more than they already knew. 'I'll be God-damned if I can tell whether they are laughing at me, or whether they can possibly be that dumb.' After another dig at the Limeys he concluded, 'This is as lousy a job as was ever invented.' As if this was not enough, Soong came to warn him, in a friendly way, that he should not press Chiang too hard because he might resent it, feeling that he had already done a great deal.

During these prolonged discussions the British launched a small advance by 14 Division down the coast from Chittagong towards the important island of Akyab, from where the Japanese could bomb Calcutta. The operation was supervised from Eastern Army HQ by General Irwin, who had been so offensive to Slim when he got back to Imphal. Irwin had an old-style attitude and had learnt nothing from the recent disasters. The advance started fairly well and reached the small coastal town of Donbaik. Then, disastrously, it paused, giving the Japanese time to bring up reinforcements and build defensive bunkers. Irwin – ignoring the basic military precept that you do not reinforce failure – sent more and more troops to Donbaik, five brigades altogether. They failed to advance and suffered heavy casualties. Perhaps it was just as well that Stilwell did not comment on this debacle, so reminiscent of the dark days of the Burma retreat. Significantly, Slim, who was busy at Ranchi revolutionising the training of XV Corps and building up its confidence, played no part in the early stages of this disastrous expedition in the Arakan.

In the wider strategic context, November 1942 witnessed a major turning point of the war. In October, at El Alamein, Montgomery and the Eighth Army had decisively defeated Rommel and the Afrika Corps, thereby destroying the German plan for a huge pincer movement to grasp the Middle East oilfields. At the same time the heroic defence of Stalingrad halted the Nazi advance – the other arm of the pincer – and saw the start of the magnificent drive by the Russians that ended in Berlin. The significance of the German setbacks at El Alamein and Stalingrad was reinforced by large-scale American landings in North Africa, code named Operation Torch. General Patton, very much a blood and guts commander, led an expedition from the USA of over 35,000 troops in 100 ships and landed near Casablanca and at Oran and Algiers in November. These events cheered Stilwell, as they did all the Allies around the world, and he hoped that the improved strategic situation would increase his chances of receiving all the help and support he had been promised.

General Marshall wrote to Stilwell personally:

> You have far exceeded our expectations in securing authority for the reorganisation, which you are now rapidly putting into effect. We are doing everything in our power to find the ships to carry to you at least the bare essentials you so urgently require … To paraphrase Mr Churchill's famous statement, nowhere has so much been done with so little, as under your driving leadership.

Stilwell had vigorously pushed forward plans for limited offensives in Burma in the spring of 1943 to capture forward Japanese airfields, including Akyab, from which Calcutta was now being bombed, and to regain enough ground to reopen land communication with China. This last point went as far as the President since it brought the possibility of bombing Japan with aircraft based in the Kunming area. As happened so often with Stilwell, a period of high hopes was followed by frustration and disappointment. A naval attaché from Chungking, openly disloyal to and critical of Stilwell, passed on his view that he should be replaced by Chennault not only to Chiang but to Wavell as well.

Wavell called two conferences in December 1942. Stilwell stressed the urgent need for a road from Ledo to Myitkyina, and preferably continuing to the area of Bhamo, from where materials could be delivered to China by road. If this was achieved it would more than double the tonnage of Lend–Lease supplies available to the Chinese. Wavell opposed these proposals on the grounds that it would not be possible to supply and protect a huge workforce of road-builders during the 1943 monsoon, which started in May. Stilwell then continued his argument that the Chinese divisions trained at Ramgarh should attack southwards from Ledo while the main Chinese force – Yoke Force – advanced from Yunnan and the British from Imphal. These discussions included the Anakim proposal for an amphibious attack on Rangoon, which Chiang was keen on because he assumed that it would massively increase his supplies. Wavell, although he was concerned to keep the co-operation of the Chinese, had to make it clear that Britain would not be in a position to mount large forces east of the Chindwin river early in 1943; he also announced that, because of the North African landings and the need to supply aid to Russia, the Anakim project and the naval challenge to the Japanese in the Bay of Bengal would have to be postponed. It was left to Stilwell to pass this information on to Chiang.

Returning to Chungking, Stilwell noticed an immediate change from the positive enthusiasm of November. He soon discovered that Chiang, without informing him, had cabled Roosevelt to demand that the British should be forced to carry out the Anakim attack. Chiang was frequently to make major decisions that were cabled to Roosevelt and which Stilwell only heard about at second or third hand.

Stilwell's diary jottings covering the period of Christmas and New Year 1942–3 are the usual mixture of high strategy and personal grumbles: 'Wavell just whining about difficulties; no hope of Limey naval action in Bay of Bengal; Wavell can't supply boys during the monsoon; he didn't tell me about the advance to Akyab; seven division plan now down to three; typical Chinese tactics – deliberate delay, then plead lack of time as an excuse.' Stilwell badgered Chiang for weeks to appoint an effective general to command Yoke Force, only to discover that Chiang had made the appointment without telling him. 'Both Chinese and Limeys want to sit tight and let the Americans clean up the Japs.' During this period Stilwell frequently refers to T. V. Soong as Teevy; Soong still appeared to be giving him genuine support and was trying to push Chiang in the right direction. Stilwell made an interesting comparison between the Indians, whom he saw as poor, ragged, dirty and apathetic, and the Chinese – bright, cheerful, laughing, well-fed and clean. 'India is hopeless.'

On 8 January 1943 the diary entry is 'BLACK FRIDAY ... Peanut says he won't fight'. Significantly, this major decision was relayed by Soong to Colonel Dorn and not directly to Stilwell, who commented when he heard it, 'What a break for the Limeys. Just what they wanted. Now they will quit, the Chinese will quit, and the goddam Americans can go ahead and fight. Chennault's blatting has put us on the spot.' Stilwell had warned Marshall of the danger of Chiang pulling out and suggested a very robust American response should it happen. 'If they don't get tough we will put ourselves in Peanut's hands for good.' During this lengthy fracas Soong appeared genuinely to side with Stilwell in trying to force Chiang to take effective action, especially over the creation of Yoke Force. The wretched General Tu now reappeared and Stilwell commented, 'Maybe we will get our revenge on the little bastard after all.' Next, Madame cabled urgently from Washington for Soong to go and help her because she felt she had failed in her mission – whatever that was. On 16 January 1943: 'Dorn caught three guys at my desk yesterday.' Among these jottings are fairly frequent personal grumbles, often in a self-deprecating vein: 'The voice of one crying in the manure pile', or references to Old Pappy with his white hair and bent back. Sometimes he scribbled execrable verse:

> Pappy's done his bit,
> He's shovelled all the ———
> He's just a sap,
> He took a rap,
> The wringer got his tit.

As he did his best to cope with all the frustrations and duplicity in Chungking he was seriously heartened by a letter from Secretary of War Stimson which put his position and his achievement in proper perspective:

Although I have not written you as often as I should have liked to, I have been following your negotiations and actions with the deepest interest and confidence. There is hardly a step you take that is not talked over by Marshall and myself and I know that our feelings for you are similar and deep. You have been sorely tried and I hope you realise how thoroughly we appreciate what you have been through. It is a very real source of gratification to us both that you seem now to be successful in conquering all of the difficulties which have been thrown in your path.

Wherever it is possible, we have tried to smooth your way for we believe in the soundness of your judgment and the correctness of your strategic decisions. We realise the dangers and difficulties of the North Burma campaign which have apparently so disheartened Wavell and his staff, but we agree with you in thinking it is a necessary prerequisite to any thoroughly satisfactory line of communications to China. We hope that you will be successful in conquering the difficulties of the terrain and the dangers of malaria.

When I offered you this China mission I knew it would be a tough one but I confess I did not realise how very tough it would be; and I wish you to feel now my sympathy and congratulations for the surpassing fortitude, skill and courage which you have shown in carrying through. I hope that the New Year will give you a full measure of success and the satisfaction that will go with it.
Very sincerely your friend,

HENRY L. STIMSON
6 January 1943

Stilwell's overall frustration can be seen in his comment when Roosevelt replied to the news that Chiang had refused his support for a Chinese advance from Yunnan. 'F.D.R. comes back at Peanut. "Why didn't you wait. I told you I was about to dicker with Churchill. For Christ's sake hold your horses."'

CHAPTER 7

1943: More Frustration

During the Christmas break and into the New Year of 1943 Stilwell had a little time to ponder over the wider issues which were likely to impinge upon him. He knew that Madame was in Washington criticising him and supporting Chennault, and he knew that preparations were being made for a high-level conference early in the New Year – and he worried. Stuck in Chungking in the suffocating atmosphere of the manure pile, he eagerly sought news from the outside world.

After seeing a Russian war film with shots of Stalingrad he wrote:

> What a fight the Russians have made … Tough physique; unity of purpose; pride in their accomplishments; determination to win … Rugged young soldiers. Tough women. Every last man, woman and child in the war effort.
>
> Compare it with the Chinese cess-pool. A gang of thugs with one idea of perpetuating themselves. Money, influence, position, the only considerations. Intrigue, double-crossing; lying reports. Hands out for anything they can get; their only idea to let someone else do the fighting.

He went on by observing that the indifference, cowardice, ignorance and stupidity of the leaders continued because of the dumb compliance of the common people. And America supported 'this rotten regime and glorifies its figurehead, the all-wise great patriot and soldier – Peanut. My God.'

Madame had arrived in the USA in November 1942 where, urged on by the missionary and China lobby, she quickly created a wave of emotional and sentimental support. She stayed at the White House. She addressed Congress and emphasised that it was more important to defeat Japan than Germany and that it would be achieved by the two great allies together. Listening to her tough Congressmen were nearly reduced to tears, but the British ambassador was slightly concerned when, in the emotional atmosphere, she expressed the hope that after the war all the lost territory would be returned to China – including Hong Kong. She came from a patrician family and objected to the term 'Madame', knowing that it could refer to the manager of a brothel. Her hosts quickly reassured her that it was how Queen Elizabeth (the wife of George VI) was addressed. This she accepted, gulping down flattery as usual. However, her arrogant and autocratic attitude, hidden at first, gradually disenchanted her generous hosts, and after several months they were eager for her to leave, which she did in May 1943.*

The impact she made was useful to Roosevelt, who, at the end of 1942, was considering his global strategy before meeting Churchill at Casablanca in January 1943. Roosevelt based his policy on keeping China in the war and co-operating with her as one of the Big Four in the post-war world. Reflecting the deep American distrust of Communism, Roosevelt hoped that after the war Chiang Kai-Shek would be strong enough to defeat the Communists under Mao Tse-Tung and to curb any Russian intrusion in eastern Asia. In American eyes, Chiang was the only leader likely to be able to unite China and should in the future become a major ally of America in Asia and the Pacific. Roosevelt wanted to believe this and to some extent deluded himself since, apart from Stilwell's, there were other reports from China that painted a realistic picture of the corruption, graft and general rottenness of Chiang's Kuomintang regime.

The Casablanca Conference in January 1943 was one of the most significant of the wartime meetings between Roosevelt and Churchill, though today it is not so well remembered as as the film *Casablanca* with Humphrey Bogart and Ingrid Bergman, which was being made

---

* She continued her dramatic career until 2003, when, known as the dragon lady of Taiwan, she died in New York at the age of 106.

at the same time. The two leaders agreed on the demand for unconditional surrender from Germany and Japan, on a second-front attack
on fortress Europe in the summer of 1944 and on continuation of
the massive bombing of Germany.

After these decisions were made, attention centred on South East
Asia. In the high policy discussions there was strong support for
Anakim, the amphibious assault on Rangoon that was much favoured
by Chiang. Linked to this was the belief that if Japan could be
attacked from airfields in southwest China, and if that was backed up
by a large-scale Chinese military attack, this would be the most effective use of American power. Even Marshall went so far as to suggest
that, if Anakim did not go ahead, the USA might transfer its main
thrust away from Europe to the Far East. The change in the general
slant of top-level opinion boded ill for Stilwell and favoured Chennault.
It was embarrassing for the Washington administration that, although
Roosevelt saw China as one of the Big Four, Chiang was not present
at Casablanca.

To mollify Chiang, a very high powered delegation that included
General Hap Arnold and Field Marshal Sir John Dill left for
Chungking as soon as the Conference was over. They went first to
Delhi, where they met with Wavell and Stilwell. It was agreed that in
the proposed 1943 attack Stilwell's forces would initially come under
Wavell's command, but that when they linked up with Yoke Force –
which was to be led by Chiang himself – all Chinese troops would
come under his command. Before Stilwell came to this meeting he
had an interview with Chiang, of which he wrote: 'Date with G-mo
at 5. He was sour as a pickle. Never one word of gratitude to the U.S.
Just what he can get out of us.' Stilwell returned with the delegation
to Chungking. Chiang was difficult and withdrew to what Stilwell
called 'Peanut's Berchtesgaden'. He was pleased to record that Arnold
and Dill had had their eyes opened and said that he, Stilwell, should
be awarded a laurel wreath. Arnold promised Chiang a generous
increase in supplies over the Hump. Central to this issue was the fundamental clash between Stilwell and Chennault and Chiang's demand
for Chennault to be independent of Stilwell. The Chinese airforce
was in absolute chaos, yet Chiang and Chennault merely demanded

more and more supplies. Chiang's reaction to Arnold's promises was uncompromising. 'Tell your President that unless I get these things I cannot fight this war and he cannot count on me to have our army participate in the campaign.' Afterwards Arnold said to Stilwell, 'I'll be God-damned if I take any such message back to the President.' Stilwell too stepped up the tension when he asked Chiang whether he would attack with Yoke Force even if the naval forces he had stipulated were not available in the Bay of Bengal. Chiang was furious with Stilwell for embarrassing him publicly, but Stilwell merely wrote: 'He can go to hell. I have him on that point. Arnold and Dill got a faint idea of conditions here and it made them sick.'

After the visit by the top brass to Chungking, a further conference was held in Calcutta in February 1943, with Soong, Stilwell, Arnold, Wavell and Dill in attendance. This achieved little except for the agreement that a major campaign in north Burma – with the British advancing from Imphal, Stilwell and his Chinese divisions from Ledo and Yoke Force from Yunnan – would start in November. At the same time on the diplomatic front, agreements were published which dealt with old treaty rights and the recovery of China's lost territory. Chiang made much of this, claiming that it put China on an equal footing with the USA and Britain. Stilwell soon began to realise that these conferences had weakened his position and gave considerable encouragement to Chennault and those who supported him in Washington. Roosevelt tended to listen to highly coloured reports by people who had made a brief visit to Chungking, and he had been taken in by Madame's charm and determination. Some of the reports were highly critical of Stilwell as an old infantryman bogged down in outdated attitudes who could not conceive of the significance of air power. It was argued that he had committed America to a difficult and dangerous campaign of ground attack in Burma when there was a brilliant and easy option in the form of attack from the air under Chennault. It is not difficult to see which option would appeal to a politician.

In the lengthy discussions on China policy that were held at this time, although Marshall, Arnold and Stimson remained loyal to Stilwell, a pro-Chennault group, which included Wendell Willkie and

Roosevelt's adviser Harry Hopkins, had the ear of the President and he overruled the decision of his military advisers. In a lengthy letter of 19 February 1943 he maintained that Stilwell was tackling Chiang in the wrong way and that one could not speak sternly to the leader of 400 million people. The main thing to consider was the strategic significance of Chennault's air forces. Roosevelt insisted that Chennault should have complete control over his operations and tactics. Marshall replied to the President point by point and reiterated his faith in Stilwell's judgement. In particular he gave a serious warning that if Chennault's raiders really started to hurt the Japanese there would be swift retaliation from Japanese ground forces, who would quickly overrun the Chinese airfields, and the Chinese army – 'underfed, unpaid, untrained, neglected, and rotten with corruption' – would be powerless to stop them. These words had ominous significance for the future.

After the President's letter Stilwell's difficulties increased. The supplies transported over the Hump averaged 3,000 tons per month, and this led to constant disputes with Chennault. One achievement of this period was the establishment of artillery and infantry training schools and the appointment of General Chen to command Yoke Force. Even here the rivalry of local commanders could obstruct and sometimes sabotage progress, and when the schools were established the Chinese soldiers were in such a deplorable state that they could not undertake the training, divisional commanders sent only half the officers they had promised, and those officers who did attend rarely took the training seriously. The only progress during this period came in the construction of airfields, which Chiang gave vigorous support in the hope that his airforce would enjoy a rapid build-up.

As the wider strategic issues were considered, two significant statements were made in January 1943. Stilwell sent Chiang a memorandum stressing that there was now an opportunity to make China strong and safe and that it should be seized enthusiastically while the supply of American weapons was available. If the plan to equip and train thirty divisions went ahead successfully, it would provide the basis for a further request for another group of thirty. It should only take a few months to turn the first thirty divisions into an efficient field force.

Stilwell concluded that without such a scenario it would be difficult to ensure continuing support for the supply of weapons.* This general statement was backed up by detailed plans to step up the training of two divisions at Ramgarh; to prepare the base at Ledo and push on with the start of the road from there to Myitkyina; to establish training schools especially for artillery; and to hasten the establishment of Yoke Force.

While Stilwell was trying to build up the Chinese forces, Chiang sent a letter to Roosevelt which, essentially, undermined all Stilwell's efforts. While emphasising the importance of defeating Japan on the mainland of Asia, Chiang argued that a part of any attack by the Allies must be an amphibious assault on Rangoon, and he added significantly that 'if the navy is unable to control the Burma seas it would be better to wait a few months longer'. Knowing that there was growing support in Washington for Chennault's thesis – notably from Harry Hopkins – Chiang wrote of the significance of air power fitting in with the grand strategy of the United Nations.

While these discussions took place, and while Stilwell fulminated against the Chinese and the British for letting him down and pulling back from action, a small and hardly noticed event took place which ultimately was to impinge dramatically on Stilwell and the whole campaign in northern Burma. A few months previously a remarkable British officer, Colonel Orde Wingate, had put forward the idea of long-range penetration, a revolutionary idea that depended on control of the air in the battle area.

Wingate had arrived in Burma just before the retreat, and he had met Mike Calvert at the Bush Warfare School at Maymyo near Mandalay. This school had been established to train guerrilla fighters not for the British army, but to go into China and assist Chiang's fight against the Japanese. As the retreat started Wingate flew up to Chungking to discuss guerrilla issues with Chiang, and then he returned to GHQ in Delhi. Wingate was a brilliant but difficult and abrasive character who, before the war, while serving as a captain in Palestine, had antagonised much of the British army establishment by setting up

* Romanus and Sunderland, *Stilwell's Command Problems*, Vol. II, p. 266.

the Jewish Night Squads and passionately supporting the Zionist cause. After the war started, and strongly backed by Wavell, then commanding in the Middle East, Wingate was appointed to lead a guerrilla-type force in the campaign to restore Haile Selassie in Abyssinia. Wavell was then posted to India, and that was when he called Wingate, as a colonel, to organise guerrilla groups behind the Japanese lines.

Thus, in July 1942 at GHQ Delhi, Wingate addressed a conference of senior officers, including representatives of Chiang Kai-Shek and the Kuomintang, and put forward his theory of long-range penetration. The idea was simple: to infiltrate a unit of up to brigade strength behind Japanese lines and supply it entirely by air. The unit, organised in columns of about 200 men and operating independently, would range widely through the jungle destroying railways, roads, telegraph lines, stores and ammunition dumps and ambushing enemy transport. These units, later known as the Chindits, would have to be trained to a very high standard of physical fitness and jungle fighting and would need top class map-reading skills and wireless communication since their very existence would depend on accurate supply drops in the jungle.

Among the senior officers at GHQ a few thought Wingate was brilliant, most thought his scheme would not work, and some – nurturing their antagonism – said he was insane, but Wavell supported him, and in August 1942 a Chindit training base was established. We have seen how the plans to recapture north Burma fluctuated wildly depending on the influence of pressure groups in Washington or Chungking or on the capricious decisions of Chiang, but the basic plan remained: that at the earliest opportunity the British would advance from Imphal, Stilwell and his Chinese divisions would advance southwards from Ledo towards Myitkyina, and Yoke Force would move in from Yunnan. It was on this assumption that the first Chindit expedition was organised, so that as the Japanese faced three assaults from west, north and east their supplies and communications would be attacked and destroyed by the Chindits operating in an area up to 100 miles east of Imphal. Their main target would be the rail, road and telegraph communications running north to the Japanese divisions facing Ledo and those facing British positions in Imphal.

While final preparations were being made for the launch of the Chindit operation, code named Longcloth, Stilwell went through a period of acute frustration. He wrote almost despairingly about conditions in China. He believed that the Sixtieth Army, which would be crucial to Yoke Force, would not accept orders to move because the senior officers were heavily involved in the lucrative opium trade. To make matters worse, huge stocks of petrol, clothing and weapons were being hoarded or sold on a thriving black market, the Chinese Red Cross was just a racket, with rampant theft and sale of medicines, and thousands of soldiers were suffering from malnutrition because senior officers kept their pay and the money provided for their food. 'A pretty picture,' wrote Stilwell.

The first Chindit campaign may not appear directly relevant to Stilwell's situation, but the Chindits were later to feature largely in his final campaign, and the story of how they emerged from the jungle and were catapulted to the attention of Marshall and Arnold, the Joint Chiefs of Staff and the Trident Conference in Quebec is a colourful illustration of the amazing fortunes of war.

Wingate and his ideas were fiercely opposed by most establishment figures in the British and Indian armies, and especially at GHQ in Delhi. This did not deter him. He set up a fearsome training programme, such that one Chindit officer commented later that after Wingate's training the campaign was a piece of cake. Thus, in the face of immense difficulties Wingate had the Chindits ready for action by the end of 1942. He was supported by General Scoones, the corps commander at Imphal, and in January 1943 77 Brigade, personally commanded by Wingate, moved up to Imphal ready for operation.

On 5 February, when the Chindits were all keyed up and ready to go, Wavell went to see Wingate in Imphal to tell him that the British were not ready to advance from Imphal, Stilwell and his Chinese divisions were not ready in Ledo, and Chiang had announced that Yoke Force was not going to move. Wavell pointed out that if the Chindits went ahead with their operation the Japanese, instead of defending themselves against three large-scale attacks, would be able to bring their whole power to bear on destroying the Chindits. Wingate had brought his force to a high pitch of readiness and he knew that his detractors, sitting at their desks in Delhi, would be pleased if the whole thing was cancelled, and he therefore convinced Wavell that despite the increased danger the operation should go ahead. This was a good example of how high-level decision – or lack of it – can impact on troops in action. Fully aware of the considerable risk Wingate, supported by all his officers, completed his final preparations and on 13 February 1943 the first Chindit units infiltrated into the jungle, achieving almost total surprise.

In spite of their rigorous training, the Chindits were embarking on a totally new form of warfare and had to learn costly lessons. They had practised river crossing, but they were ill-prepared for rivers like the Chindwin and the Irrawaddy, which were nearly a mile wide. Their mules were inadequately trained, and the burden imposed by intelligence and signals was overwhelming. Two columns under Mike Calvert and Bernard Fergusson made successful attacks at Nankan and Bonchaung gorge, which destroyed the railway from Mandalay to Myitkyina. These attacks, together with others on roads and bridges and the ambush of military convoys, wrecked the supply line to the Japanese divisions that faced Stilwell in the north and those facing Imphal. In addition to these successes, the Chindits learnt valuable lessons about every aspect of long-range penetration and the problems of supplying large mobile units behind enemy lines in the jungle.

The Japanese took some time to realise what was happening, but then they were able to concentrate all their forces on the destruction of the Chindits. In March the Chindits crossed the Irrawaddy and moved eastwards, but there the supply problem became acute and, early in April, the whole force was ordered to return to base. Wingate and the Chindit leaders decided that their best hope of returning safely was to move in separate columns. Most columns retraced their main route; one went north towards Ledo and one went due east until they reached territory held by the Chinese. Here they were treated as heroes, taken to Kunming and given a lift in an empty aircraft that was returning after a trip over the Hump – accomplishing in a couple of hours what had taken weary weeks of walking.

By the end of April 1943 the surviving Chindits began to arrive back in Imphal, most of them sick, exhausted and emaciated, with many too shattered ever to serve again. Wingate, whose iron determination brought his group through the ordeal, wondered if, having lost about 1,000 of his 3,000 men, he might face a court martial. In May 1943 he was taken to Delhi and on the 20th gave a press conference, at which he claimed the expedition had been a success. The western media, hungry for any success among the dismal record of failure and defeat in Burma, seized on the Chindits' achievement. Reuters wrote: 'Led by a relative of Lawrence of Arabia, a British ghost army made sabotage sorties from the depths of the Burmese jungle … The Japanese were harassed, killed, bamboozled and bewildered.' Louis Allen wrote that Wingate had infused a new spirit into the services, claiming that his first expedition 'had panache, it had glamour, it had cheek. It had everything the successive Arakan failures lacked.'* GHQ Delhi did not share this euphoria, but then an unexpected element appeared.

On 4 August 1943 Wingate was called to London to see Churchill. There followed a succession of events that would be too far-fetched to appear in fiction. Churchill, who intended to give Wingate no more than a pat on the back, invited him to dinner and asked him to outline his theory of long-range penetration. Churchill was so impressed that he decided to take Wingate with him when he left next day to travel on the *Queen Mary* from Glasgow to attend the Quadrant Conference in Quebec with Roosevelt, Marshall, Arnold and the Joint Chiefs of Staff. Wingate looked crestfallen and explained that he had hoped to see his wife Lorna while in Britain. She was travelling overnight from Aberdeen, so Churchill had the train stopped, Lorna Wingate was taken off, and she too travelled on the *Queen Mary* to Quebec. She had a son, born after Wingate was killed, who was clearly conceived on the *Queen Mary*.

While these dramatic events were taking place, Stilwell went through a dismal and worrying period coping with all the frustrations of life in the manure pile in Chungking and the almost endless

* L. Allen, *Burma: The Longest War, 1941–1945*, Dent, London, 1984, p. 118.

stream of promises and broken promises that flitted between Washington, Chungking and Delhi. Stilwell's warning of the danger of a Japanese attack if they were provoked appeared to be supported when they made a strong foray with five divisions on the upper Yangtze river. The attack put Chiang in a panic, and crucial troops and weapons were withdrawn from Yoke Force. When the Japanese withdrew down the river with ships and loot it was hailed as a great Chinese victory. More significantly, it was presented as such to Roosevelt in an attempt to prove that Chinese forces could handle any ground attacks made against them. This false claim was to have disastrous consequences. At the same time Stilwell flew to Ramgarh, where the training was proceeding well but where he had frequent and prolonged disputes with Wavell over supplies for the Chinese troops and dates for a possible attack in Burma. Stilwell wrote: '"Can't" is his best word. Everything else is so goddam "difficult".'

He had become increasingly concerned at the apparent impact on the American administration of Chiang's support for the Chennault thesis and the suggestion that Chennault should go to Washington to put his case to Roosevelt. Marshall and Stimson continued to back Stilwell firmly against the increasingly fanciful claims of Chennault, and because of their stand both Stilwell and Chennault were called to Washington in May 1943 to attend what became known as the Trident Conference. Chennault saw Roosevelt first, and he developed his plan to drive out the Japanese in six months if he received 10,000 tons of supplies over the Hump. This he claimed would enable him to sink one million tons of Japanese shipping. Roosevelt appeared to be impressed with the idea and, at the interview, gave Chennault permission to correspond with him direct without informing Marshall or Stilwell. Churchill was later to give this same dangerous privilege to Wingate.

In preparation for the Trident Conference Stilwell produced a memorandum which summed up the China situation. In it he claimed that Roosevelt had a total misapprehension of the character, intentions, authority and ability of Chiang Kai-Shek. He repeated the argument that if Chennault began to damage the Japanese by bombing raids, they would advance rapidly and destroy the air bases – as indeed they had already done. Without effective Chinese ground troops there would be nothing to stop them. He warned, ominously, that Chiang wanted to get rid of him and replace him with a 'yes' man. Stilwell's answer to these problems was clear and blunt. He proposed that all dealings with China should be through military channels, that the back door to the White House should be closed, that he should be able to bargain with Chiang, that he should be the President's representative and that the Willkies and his like should be kept at home. A clear strategic plan should be made, complete with dates, and Chiang should be held to it.

As President of the United States Roosevelt wanted to see China as a major world power, and he reminded Stilwell that you cannot talk severely to the leader of 400 million people. Despite the almost contemptuous view of Roosevelt that appears in his diaries, when it came to his turn with the President Stilwell appeared to be almost overcome, and he failed totally to present his case effectively. Roosevelt even asked if he was ill, and whether he should perhaps be relieved of his command. Afterwards Marshall appeared to think that Stilwell had let him down, but he continued to give him strong support because he believed that the Chennault policy was dangerously and absolutely wrong. Marshall and Stimson's firm stand behind Stilwell caused a serious rift with Roosevelt and Hopkins. As the conference continued the Chinese realised that things were going in their favour, and Soong went so far as to tell the Chiefs of Staff that China would make a separate peace unless supplies over the Hump were increased substantially. Stilwell believed that Churchill had Roosevelt in his pocket, and he was sneeringly dismissive of a gushing final tribute from Churchill to Roosevelt – 'Frank lapped it up.' In contrast to his meeting with the President he had a successful interview with Churchill, and on his way back to China after a brief leave at his beloved Carmel he travelled via London and was feted by the British government. When he reached Chungking he wrote: 'Back again on the manure pile after that wonderful trip home ... Back to find Chiang the same as ever – a grasping, bigoted, ungrateful little rattlesnake.'

The Trident decision of May 1943 to give Chennault priority had other dangerous repercussions. The vital American construction companies had to be switched from building the Ledo road to constructing forward airfields in order to meet the July deadline of four new airfields with twenty hard standings on each. Stilwell found building operations on the road at a complete stop, and in the period March to August 1943 only three miles were built.

In the period after the Trident Conference not only did Stilwell feel the President had let him down but it also became increasingly obvious that Chiang intended to take advantage of the situation. In addition, Chinese internal problems threatened to wreck the tenuous provisions for Yoke Force. The promised new divisions never came because the local warlords ignored Chiang or because they were needed to guard the rice trains. Weapons that had been assembled for Yoke Force were even scattered among divisions facing the Communists in the north. It appeared that Chiang was sabotaging the creation of an effective army because its commander would be a threat to him. In addition, nearly 70 per cent of the so-called 'picked reserves' for Yoke Force were rejected because of trachoma or other diseases. Stilwell commented bitterly, and with shrewd prescience: 'With whom did the Peanut take counsel? With the cook perchance, or with his old pal God ... The little squirt, on his own initiative will decide the fate of nations.'

The Allied plan to attack Burma, known as 'Saucy', was submitted to Chiang, but he delayed and criticised and demanded details of naval preparations in the Bay of Bengal. At this Stilwell gave vent to his real feelings about the Generalissimo, uncovering the depth of his antagonism that was, in the end, to cause his downfall:

> This insect, this stink in the nostrils, superciliously inquired what we will do, who are breaking our backs to help him, supplying everything – troops, equipment, planes, medical, signal, motor services, setting up his goddam SOS, training his lousy troops, bucking his bastardly Chief of Staff, and he the Jovian Dictator who starves his troops and who is the world's greatest ignoramus, picks flaws in our preparations and hems and haws about the Navy, God save us.

He also wondered whether Chiang was going to use his increasing involvement with the Communists in north China as an excuse to pull out of the Burma operation altogether, but then on 12 July 1943 Chiang agreed to take part. Stilwell commented: 'What corruption, intrigue, obstruction, delay, double crossing, hate, jealousy, skullduggery, we have to wade through. What a cesspool. What bigotry and ignorance and black ingratitude. Holy Christ, I was just about at the end of my rope.'

Following fairly closely on Chiang's tentative agreement in July 1943 to go ahead with the attack in north Burma, Roosevelt and Churchill met once more – again without the Kuomintang leader – in Quebec in August 1943. Wingate, who had carefully prepared his brief during the voyage on the *Queen Mary*, was invited to present his proposals for long-range penetration to the President, the Prime Minister and the Joint Chiefs of Staff.

Unlike Stilwell, who stumbled in the presence of Roosevelt, Wingate – not at all overawed by the occasion – produced a brilliant and lucid plan. He proposed that three groups of Chindits should operate in Burma: one to link up with the advance of Stilwell and the Chinese division from Ledo; a second to back up the planned attack by Yoke Force from Yunnan; and the third to concentrate on the area of Indaw, which was the main communications centre for road, rail and river traffic taking supplies and reinforcements to the Japanese divisions facing Stilwell in the north and those facing the British in Imphal and Kohima. Wingate's impressive presentation convinced the Chiefs of Staff, and more importantly Marshall and Hap Arnold, who had so recently been involved in the discussions with Stilwell and Chiang. Reflecting to some extent Stilwell's jaundiced view of the British, they decided to support Wingate because 'here was a Limey who actually wanted to fight the Japanese'. Arnold added another significant dimension. Convinced of the effectiveness of Wingate's plans, he offered him the support of 1st Air Commando under the command of two outstanding young USAAF colonels – Cochran and Alison. The Commando was a large force: 100 gliders, 100 Sentinels, the brilliant light aircraft so vital for landing and taking off from jungle strips, thirty Mustangs, twenty-five Mitchells, twenty Dakotas and twelve larger transport aircraft. This amazingly generous offer meant that the Chindits could fly into the jungle and be supported by air throughout their next campaign. Arnold wrote of Wingate, 'You took one look at that face, like the face of a pale Indian chief, topping the uniform still smelling of jungle and sweat and war, and you thought, "Hell, this man is serious."'

Churchill's spur of the moment decision to take him to the Quadrant Conference certainly paid dividends for Wingate, and this, with other decisions taken at Quebec, was to affect Stilwell's position dramatically. All the commanders at Quebec agreed (though in milder language than Stilwell's) that Wavell was played out, and they agreed that the command structure in South East Asia needed a drastic overhaul. The names of some very senior army, naval and RAF commanders were suggested, but all were for sound reasons rejected. At that stage Churchill proposed Admiral Lord Louis Mountbatten. He was young, ambitious, impetuous and imprudent, but he had flair and charisma, and most of the Americans welcomed the suggestion. Marshall was delighted, but some considered it a deliberate move to keep out General Douglas MacArthur. Roosevelt agreed to the setting up of South East Asia Command (SEAC), but privately he still suspected Britain of wanting to recapture her pre-war possessions.* Thus SEAC was created with Admiral Mountbatten as Supreme Commander and Stilwell as Deputy Supreme Commander. The image of defeat and lethargy in India even prompted Churchill to signal Field Marshall Alan Brooke (later Lord Alanbrooke), the Chief of Imperial General Staff, from Quebec to suggest that Wingate should replace Slim – a proposal for which the British military establishment never forgave Churchill.

Quebec brought together many of the tangled skeins of the Burma campaign, and another decision – attributed to Marshall – was to affect Stilwell directly. The enthusiasm for Wingate's idea of long-range penetration resulted in a decision to call for volunteers for an American long-range penetration group under the name Galahad, also to be supported by 1st Air Commando. Dogged by an unfortunate official

---

* Philip Ziegler, *Mountbatten*, Collins, London, 1985, p. 260.

title – 5307th Composite Unit (Provisional) – they were later universally known as Merrill's Marauders.

Stilwell heard of the Quebec decisions in August 1943 and made just a brief comment:

> East Asia Command is set up. India, Burma, Singapore, Malaya, Sumatra and Ceylon with Lord Louis Mountbatten at the top. I am deputy and have to kid the Peanut into using the boys. But George is leaving me in command of all U.S. troops, air and ground. The command set-up is a Chinese puzzle, with Wavell, Auk,★ Mountbatten, Peanut and me interwoven and mixed beyond recognition … George has read the riot act to Soong and maybe Peanut will come across.

Stilwell retained his deep suspicion of the Limeys, but he was soon to discover an unexpected ally.

In the weeks before Mountbatten's visit, Stilwell noticed a substantial change in the atmosphere in Chungking. He was approached by Madame and her equally formidable sister, who was the wife of the Chinese prime minister. He subsequently referred to them as May and Ella. In mid-September he had lunch with May who, referring to a senior Chinese general, said, 'Why in God's name, that goddam old fool doesn't do something, I don't know.' Stilwell did not entirely understand this sudden change but went along with it, thinking that it might have been the result of Marshall's showdown with Soong. Early in October he flew to Delhi for an initial brief meeting with Mountbatten and recorded, 'Louis is a good egg … full of enthusiasm and also of disgust with inertia and conservatism.'

Mountbatten, catapulted over the heads of many senior commanders, had serious and acrimonious clashes with many of them – 'cantankerous old bugger' and 'young whipper snapper' were just two of the phrases that were bandied about. Mountbatten, whose biographer refers to Stilwell as 'an acidulous misanthrope', knew of Stilwell's reputation and expected serious trouble, but surprisingly the two men achieved a considerable rapport. As one of his first tasks as

★ Auchinleck, who was about to succeed Wavell, who became Viceroy.

Supreme Commander, Mountbatten went to Chungking in October 1943 to visit Chiang and improve relations after Wavell's previous blunders. Mountbatten was immediately drawn into the complex and dubious political machinations of Chiang's court, and his arrival coincided with the climax of Chiang's attempt to get rid of Stilwell. He had been well briefed before his visit and, with his royal connections, was more easily able to cope with the stuffy and face-saving etiquette of the Chinese court. He was amazed at the 'awesome reverence' for Chiang, but at the same time – with his own background in the louche, upper-class bed-hopping set of the 1930s – he recorded that Madame 'had the most lovely legs imaginable'.

Even before he met the Chiangs, Mountbatten had been told by Soong that Stilwell had to go. As Stilwell was now Deputy Supreme Commander this was clearly an embarrassment. It is not certain whether Mountbatten played a decisive part, but shortly afterwards the decision was reversed and Stilwell's position was confirmed.

The reversal was, in fact, the result of a serious power struggle involving Chiang, the two sisters May and Ella and various senior Chinese generals. May and Ella arranged what was an extremely tense meeting between Chiang and Stilwell, who had to repeat that he sought only the good of China and regretted any misunderstandings. All may have appeared well, but for Chiang it was a grave loss of face which he was unlikely to forget, and Stilwell lost any last shred of respect for the Generalissimo. Mountbatten and the Chiangs exchanged lavish gifts, and when he left he felt that he had made real friends, a feeling that was reciprocated. Roosevelt was pleased at the greatly improved atmosphere.

On 21 October 1943 Stilwell wrote to his wife and uncovered his feelings: 'It has been a nasty damn experience, and I was on the point of telling them to go to hell.' He referred discreetly to the settlement, which included Chiang's agreement to Stilwell's command of all Chinese forces in Burma, including Yoke Force, and a promise that these forces would be ready by January 1944.

He soon left for Delhi and SEAC headquarters. He wrote: 'How do you like our stationery. It's about all we've got so far.' His hatred of bull quickly emerged:

Everyone is 'conferring', looking serious and important and thinking in big numbers ... What gets me is the enormous set-up considered necessary to launch a relatively small operation and the tremendous fuss and blah that is going on ... My trouble is that I can't say 2 and 2 are 4 in a sufficiently ponderous and pontifical manner and can't think up a thousand words to use in saying it. I'm just fed up to the gills with delay, pretence, inaction, dumbness. Also with intrigue, manoeuvring, double-crossing and obstruction. I will be happy when the real shooting starts: it will be a welcome relief from bickering and recrimination and throat cutting.

Although Stilwell sounded disenchanted, Mountbatten's visit and the rumpus in Chungking improved the situation and strengthened his hand. He had received solid support from Mountbatten and Roosevelt's agent General Brehon B. Somervell, and he received personal letters of gratitude from Marshall and Stimson. The latter wrote saying he felt that in fairness Stilwell should be given some less impossible task, but that whatever bludgeonings of fate he suffered there was confidence, always, in his courage and ability.

In India the decisions taken at the Quebec Conference began to take effect. The Allies set out to implement the plan to launch a campaign in north Burma, the main purpose of which was to reopen the land route to China to keep the country in the war and to allow the build-up of massive support for the increasing air attacks on Japan and Japanese shipping. A crucial part of the land attack was an advance from Ledo down the Hukawng and Mogaung valleys towards Myitkyina. This was Stilwell's constant theme, and it is greatly to his credit that it now emerged as Allied policy.

It had been realised at the Conference that drastic changes would have to be made to the supply system both to Ledo and for the increasing traffic over the Hump. The Indian authorities agreed to American railway units taking over and operating several parts of the tenuous Assam railway where the bottlenecks were worst. Army units also took over the operation of barges and ferry boats on the Brahmaputra river where the Ledo traffic crossed. At the same time, driven on by American vigour and determination, work started on an oil pipeline to take fuel from Calcutta to Kunming.

After the decision at Quebec to create an American long–range penetration unit based on Wingate's Chindits, Roosevelt sent out a presidential request for volunteers with experience of jungle fighting. Nearly one thousand veterans of the fighting in Guadalcanal and New Guinea came forward and another two thousand from the jungle warfare training camps in the USA and the Caribbean. By October 1943, 3,000 men under the command of the admirable Colonel Charles N. Hunter, a regular West Point graduate, had landed at Bombay and started training at a camp in central India, which was dry and arid and bore little relation to the conditions of the jungle in which they were to fight. Here, initially, they came under the command of Wingate, and they certainly came under his rigorous Chindit training regime.

The decisions made at Quebec had a direct effect on Stilwell and the situation in Burma and South East Asia, but before the frustrating year 1943 was over he was to become deeply involved with preparations for an even more momentous occasion – the Cairo Conference, where, at last, Chiang would appear as the equal of Roosevelt and Churchill. There was still the question of Stalin, who was not at that time involved in the war against Japan. There was serious doubt about the role of Russia in the Far East, so it was tactfully planned that Chiang would meet with Roosevelt and Churchill at Cairo, after which they – without him – would go on to confer with Stalin at Teheran.

Stilwell – the 'shirt-sleeved general' – watches American sergeants at Ramgarh instructing Chinese troops in weapon training. These soldiers, led by Stilwell, drove down the Huckawng valley and inflicted a major defeat on the Japanese. *Below*, Merrill's Marauders clean their rifles and light machine guns, while their mules – a crucial element in their success – stand nearby. Every infantry-man knew that his weapon had to be 'clean, dry and slightly oiled'

Madame Chiang Kai-Shek at an NBC studio doing what she liked best – bamboozling the American people

General Orde Wingate, the charismatic and abrasive leader of the Chindits, climbs into a Dakota – the plane Mountbatten said was a key factor for military success in Burma. Wingate was killed soon after this picture was taken. *Below*, Brigadier Mike Calvert (foreground), the Chindit commander whose intrepid leadership led to the capture of Mogaung, surveys the devastation in the town. This photograph was taken shortly before his dramatic interview with Stilwell

A Dakota releases supplies by parachute. Dropping supplies with pinpoint accuracy was a lifeline to both Merrill's Marauders and the Chindits, demanding accurate map-reading and clear signals

ick's Pike Life Line. General Pick was the brilliant engineer who drove forward the road from Ledo to link up with the Burma Road. He used large numbers of well-disciplined black troops and his units worked round the clock. He deserves almost as much credit for the success of this project as Stilwell. Pick accompanied the first convoy to reach Kunming. *Below*, the Burma Road, showing the hostile terrain with small camps clustered beside the road

The Cairo Conference. Roosevelt and Churchill are seated, with Chiang Kai-Shek and Madame on either side. Stilwell, hatless, stands behind Roosevelt. There were high expectations from this conference, but it ended in bitterness and recrimination. *Below*, Chinese and American soldiers view a Buddha – a reminder of the permanence of Burmese life against the ephemera of war – in Nankan, a crucial town for the link to the Burma Road

Chiang Kai-Shek and Madame with General Claire Chennault who, with the Flying Tigers, supported the Kuomintang from the earliest days of Japanese attack. He had a very close relationship with Madame – some thought too close. *Below*, American tanks with Chinese crews en route for Myitkyina pass the more normal form of transport in north Burma

Doctor Gordon Seagrave, who ran a mission hospital in northern Burma and accompanied Stilwell during the retreat. Here he is being welcomed back after the Japanese were driven out. *Below*, Stilwell, seen here with his son, in pensive mood after his promotion to four-star general

CHAPTER 8

The Sextant Conference in Cairo

Stilwell was accustomed to the sudden and violent changes in Chiang Kai-Shek's moods, but he was nevertheless surprised when in November 1943 the atmosphere suddenly became sunny and co-operative. He commented, 'Rattlesnake [Chiang] as affable as hell.' The cause of the change – of which initially Stilwell was unaware – was the agreement in October in Moscow at a conference of foreign ministers, reached in spite of some opposition from Stalin, that Chiang should be invited to the next major conference to represent China as one of the Big Four. It fell to Stilwell to produce the Chinese plan to be presented at the conference and, to help matters along, Chiang made all sorts of promises about supplies, weapons and troops. Roosevelt sent another representative, Brigadier General Patrick Hurley, to prepare the ground for the conference. At first he appeared as a breath of fresh air, but he overdid the flattery. He called Stilwell 'the saviour of China' and compared him to Marshal Ney. 'My God did I squirm,' wrote Stilwell. Hurley warned him that Mountbatten was now more in favour of the Chennault plan and was after Stilwell's scalp. Stilwell took Hurley to dinner with Chiang, where they confirmed their opposition to imperialism, expressed support for an attack on the Japanese homeland rather than Singapore and reaffirmed their faith in a strong, free, democratic China, predominant in Asia.

In his preparations for the Cairo Conference, known as Sextant, Stilwell had serious discussions with some senior Chinese generals, who agreed that grandiose plans would never work because Chiang's authority was shaky or non-existent outside Chungking. They also repeated the view that within six months of the end of the war Chiang

137

could be thrown out. Despite this Stilwell hammered out a plan, to which Chiang agreed, for China to produce ninety divisions for the recapture of Burma. The divisions were to be raised in three groups, the first to be combat-ready by January 1944 and the second by the following August. After that was achieved, there would be a land and sea attack on the Canton–Hong Kong area to restore sea-borne supplies. In return the Allies would mount a strong effort with naval, army and air attacks, and for the planned operation against Canton the Americans would provide ten infantry and three armoured divisions.

Stilwell left Chungking for the conference on 15 November 1943 and arrived in Cairo on the 20th. He commented on the River Tigris at Basra, on the aerial view of Jerusalem, on a duck dinner with wonderful French fried potatoes, and, in Cairo, on a visit to Shepheards Hotel for a haircut. He noted masses of barbed wire everywhere, concluding that it was 'the Limeys protecting Louis'.

CHAMPION, the plan SEAC had produced for the Burma offensive, had serious drawbacks to which Stilwell had drawn attention, but in spite of his comments the plan was put forward at Cairo as the main Allied proposal. The CHAMPION plan proposed the advance of the Chinese 38 and 22 Divisions from Ledo, an operation that was already under way; the advance into the Arakan of the British XV Corps, starting in mid-January 1944; and, if possible, the advance of IV Corps to Sittaung and beyond. In addition, long-range penetration groups would operate in February, an airborne attack would capture and hold Indaw, and a major amphibious operation would take place in the Bay of Bengal. All these operations were to be concluded by the end of April 1944 when the monsoon broke.

Chiang Kai-Shek started by openly criticising this plan, claiming that XV Corps and IV Corps should advance at least as far as Mandalay and demanding that, whatever air operations took place in Burma, the amount of material lifted over the Hump must not fall below 10,000 tons a month. The Cairo Conference brought bitterness and vicious wrangles, with few participants willing or able to see the picture as a whole. Chennault, for example, demanded 10,000 tons a month for the air forces in China but offered no reply to the question of what the ground forces would get. Wrangling continued

– between the Americans themselves, between Americans and British, and between both and the Chinese. Chiang remained the greatest problem. All of this Stilwell captured vividly:

> 2.30. To preliminary meeting. G-mo phoned, 'Do not present proposals.' Message that G-mo would come. Then he wouldn't. Then he would. Christ. Brooke got nasty and King got good and sore. King almost climbed over the table at Brooke. God, he was mad. I wish he had socked him. 3.30. Chinese came. Terrible performance. They couldn't ask a question. Brooke was insulting. I helped them out. They were asked about Yoke and I had to reply. Brooke fired questions and I batted them back.

The next day Stilwell and Chiang attended a major conference with General Marshall. 'George laying it on the line about U.S. planes, U.S. pilots, U.S. dough etc. A grand speech for the G-mo to hear and incidentally for the Limeys. Louis told to go and fix it with the G-mo. Welcome change from telling me to fix it up.'

Stilwell had been reprimanded the previous day about Chiang and especially for calling him Peanut, but he continues gaily, 'Louis in at 11.00 to spill the dope. He is fed up on Peanut. As who is not?'

On 25 November Marshall accompanied Stilwell to see Roosevelt. At the meeting Stilwell's main theme was that unless something was done about the Chinese high command, and if the effective troops were not placed under a US command with real power, all other effort would be wasted. The President appeared to give him little attention and, in reply to his request for US combat troops, suggested vaguely that a brigade of marines go to Chungking. However, the President did promise that America would equip ninety Chinese divisions and that with these divisions the Chinese would help in the occupation of Japan.

After the Cairo Conference Stilwell scored a line through the detailed notes he had prepared and wrote, 'F.D.R. is not interested.' Some of the bitter frustration that had dominated Stilwell's life in Chungking was brought home to his superiors in Cairo when Chiang, having agreed the CHAMPION plan with Churchill and

Mountbatten, refused it on every point the very same evening. Mountbatten attempted to save the situation, but Chiang remained adamant. Stilwell, knowing the value of using Madame Chiang as an intermediary, suggested that Roosevelt and Churchill try this ploy, and after a meeting with the couple over tea the two leaders gained Chiang's consent once again. Mountbatten commented that Chiang had driven them absolutely mad and he hoped that he would have more sympathy from the top when dealing with him in the future.

Churchill and Roosevelt left Cairo to go on to the great Teheran Conference with Stalin, and the next day Mountbatten called the other SEAC commanders together to get to work on the details of CHAMPION. He was staggered when Stilwell reported that just before Chiang left he rejected all the agreements he had made and that he would only give his agreement if there was an airborne assault on Mandalay and, of course, an undertaking to send 10,000 tons of supplies a month over the Hump. Mountbatten, who was to accompany Chiang on an inspection of the training camp at Ramgarh in a few days time, pretended he had not received this information in the hope that he could secure at least some agreement during their joint visit.

As a break from the tensions and frustrations of the conference, Stilwell and some friends flew up to Jerusalem, and this he described in a letter to his wife. He was shocked to learn that Jerusalem had been destroyed thirty-two times and that the streets from the time of Christ were probably thirty or more feet below ground level. 'The old surroundings have disappeared entirely and all that is needed to make you believe you are at Coney Island is a hot dog stand.' He commented grimly that, being the Holy City of Christians, Jews and Mohammedans, they had been fighting over it and tearing it to pieces for two thousand years. In contrast, he was tremendously impressed by the simple grandeur of the pyramids, and above all by Luxor and the great tombs, including Tutankhamen's. 'I am all smoked up over Egypt. I am a sucker for antiquities and this is where they are. I could spend months wandering around here, and hope to come back and do it some time … We shove off in a couple of days back to the manure pile. I wanted you to know what a grand interlude this has been.'

The British and Americans may have found Chiang infuriating, but the varied and confusing plans that were put forward at the Cairo Conference gave the Chinese leader some grounds for genuine doubt about what had been promised or agreed. He had consistently demanded an amphibious operation in the Bay of Bengal, and this produced a serious clash between Roosevelt and Churchill. To accede to Chiang's demands the Americans agreed to BUCCANEER, a plan to invade the Andaman Islands. Lying 400 miles south of Rangoon, the islands would provide a valuable base for bombing the Japanese in Burma and for attacks on Japanese shipping on its way to Rangoon harbour. In contrast, Churchill argued for an attack on Sumatra (Indonesia), which was close to Singapore. This aroused the deeply held suspicion of most Americans that the British wanted their help to recover the pre-war British Empire. By the end of the Conference there was a commitment to launch BUCCANEER – but then Roosevelt and Churchill went to meet Stalin in Teheran. Stalin argued forcibly for a second front, OVERLORD, with landings across the English Channel and in the south of France, and Roosevelt gave the plan his backing. This forced Churchill to agree. OVER-LORD, however, would generate an almost insatiable demand for ships and landing craft, so Churchill demanded the cancellation of BUCCANEER because of the overall shortage of landing craft. He reasoned that if Russia joined in the war against Japan once Germany was defeated it would lessen the need for a major effort in Burma and China. That might have been the case, but in the short term it gave Chiang another excuse to renege on his promises.

The Cairo Conference, which had been built up into a tremendously significant occasion, with the presence for the first time of Chiang at top level, in fact had little effect on the Burma situation. It was one of the most acrimonious conferences of the war and aroused very strong antagonisms between the American and British leaders. Barbara Tuchman, describing the conference in *Sand against the Wind*, after referring to Madame's feminine wiles and 'glimpses through the slit skirt of a shapely leg', wrote of Brooke as 'the type of Englishman who considered a foreigner something to be snubbed, and if non-white, to be stepped on'.

At Teheran, Roosevelt was still apprehensive about the possibility of China backing out of the war and freeing up thousands of Japanese troops to oppose the American advance in the Pacific. He was partly reassured by Stalin, who agreed to join in the war against Japan as soon as Germany was defeated, but he was scathingly critical of the fighting prowess of the Chinese army. Stalin's determined, powerful and forthright approach, which was such a contrast to Chiang's dithering, prompted Roosevelt to reflect whether Russia might be a more useful ally in the Far East in the post-war world. As a result of the Cairo and Teheran conferences Chiang was increasingly mistrusted in the west and, rather than being enhanced to the stature of a world statesman, his position was seriously undermined.

When Stilwell realised that BUCCANEER was likely to be cancelled, he saw the President again to seek advice on what approach to take when Chiang was given the news. Instead of offering practical advice, Roosevelt waffled on about the historic links between America and China, the achievements of the missionaries and the prospect of billions of dollars in loans after the war. He even discussed the possibility that Chiang might be overthrown. Both Roosevelt and Stilwell wished passionately to do their best for China but, tragically, they were almost totally at loggerheads. After their meeting Stilwell wrote, 'The man is a flighty fool.'

Back in Chungking, Chiang, enjoying his new eminence, had hardly announced the Cairo decision to launch BUCCANEER when he heard that it had been cancelled. The extent of his humiliation is shown in his immediate and exorbitant demands for a loan of a billion dollars, twice the number of aircraft and a doubling of the tonnage coming over the Hump. At the same time he emphasised the real danger of the collapse of the Chinese economy and China dropping out of the war. Fortunately for America, advisers other than Stilwell stated clearly that no loans should be made because the Chinese economy and its finances were totally chaotic. This realistic view was backed up by increasing disenchantment in Washington with the corruption, dishonesty and incompetence of every aspect of Chinese financial activity.

When Stilwell returned to Chungking he witnessed Chiang's fury at close quarters, but he bided his time, trying always to focus attention back on the campaign in Burma. In this he found that Chiang's attitude had hardly changed since the frustrating times of the retreat from Burma. Chiang argued that the Japanese were still too strong and therefore it was best to stay on the defensive because he could not risk the effect on the Chinese people of another defeat.

During early December 1943 Stilwell found time to write down some more considered thoughts. His critics have long maintained that he was acutely oversensitive and had such a chip on his shoulder that it warped his judgement. Some of his jottings at this time appear to confirm this. He wrote admiringly of Stalin, who had kidded Churchill that he should execute 50,000 German officers, saying that 'It was like a blood transfusion to see Stalin put backbone into our gasbags.' Shortly afterwards, however, he referred to 'Bloody Joe' and suggested that the western leaders were lucky to get away with their shirts in Teheran.

These comments were followed by a long memo headed 'DECK HAND DIPLOMAT. A brief experience with international politics confirms me in my preference for driving a garbage truck.' He followed this with a scathing indictment of diplomacy and the stuffed-shirt diplomat who thinks he guides the ship of state with lightning intellect and unerring precision and ends up without his shirt. 'Or rather our shirt … It is very confusing to a deck-hand to be pitch-forked in among this class of people, especially if he is a military deck-hand.' He argued that, in war, the military aspect should be of primary importance, but it is not allowed 'to infringe on the Sacred Cow of Diplomacy'. Taking a general swipe at incompetent people in senior positions, he wrote, 'As long as we go on paying off political debts with top posts, we handicap ourselves out of the race.' He stressed that the richest nation in the world was a standing temptation to chisellers. Again he referred admiringly to the Russians, who settled a problem in Manchuria by saying to the Japanese, 'If you Japs don't keep your pig's snouts out of our garden it will be too bad.' In his view 'The Japs needed no interpretation by the protocol boys to tell them just where they stood.' He advocated a mental attitude based on

realism and mused, gloomily, that international politics was like playing poker. All that was needed among a group of contestants was 'one
sucker, especially if he has plenty of dough'.

On 14 December 1943, after receiving mail and Christmas cards
marked 'Don't open till Christmas', he wrote to his wife: 'Like hell.
Where will I be by Christmas?' but then 'I came nearer to crying than
at any time since I saw you' – so perhaps he did have a sensitive nature.
He quickly reverted to the question of Roosevelt. 'Our Big boy
doesn't seem interested in us … The day of the giants is gone and
most of the bigger statues have clay feet. I don't care for a guy who
greets me as "Joe" and reaches for a knife when I turn round.' He then
made the first mention of going back into Burma, saying that his
Chinese divisions had done well at Ledo, and he also praised the
young pilots who kept the traffic going over the Hump. He ended on
a lighter note: 'I found out what Carmel means. In a guide book of
Palestine it means "Vineyard of the Lord". And ain't that the truth.'

The issues that were side-tracked, fudged or reversed at Cairo and
Teheran came back to haunt Stilwell in Chungking. Chiang, still
smarting from the cancellation of BUCCANEER, refused to commit
Yoke Force to firm action unless the Allies made a major landing in
Burma. Stilwell argued powerfully, but Chiang remained adamant.
He did, however, concede one significant point by giving Stilwell
complete control of the Chinese divisions that had been trained at
Ramgarh. Illustrating the highly volatile situation he was in, but also
his grim determination to prove that he believed in the Chinese
soldier, he wrote after Chiang gave him command: 'Apparently confidence has been established. A month or so ago I was to be fired and
now he gives me a blank cheque. If the bastards will only fight, we
can make a dent in the Japs. There is a chance for us to work down
to Myitkyina, block off Mogaung and actually make the junction,
even with Yoke sitting on its tukas. This may be wishful thinking in
a big way, but it *could* be.'

During this hectic week in Chungking, Stilwell touched briefly
on an issue that was to prove substantially more significant than the
defeat of the Japanese. On 15 December 1943 he wrote, 'The Reds
are no longer afraid of Chiang. The Central Government men desert

to them. One whole company deserted and the Reds sent the rifles back. "We can't force the men to return, but here are the rifles." More troops move up to contain the Reds, but their propaganda is working. They feel Chiang's position is weak.'

This small incident, illustrating the confidence of Mao's troops and their contemptuous attitude to the forces of Chiang and the Kuomintang, was indicative of major future developments in China. In the 1930s, although Chiang drove out Mao and the Communists on the Long March, Stilwell as military attaché compared Chiang's troops unfavourably with the Communists. Now, in a significant moment in December 1943, when Stilwell was about to give up the struggle with Chiang in Chungking and return to command his troops in Burma, an opportunity was lost that could have changed the course of China's history.

By 1943 Mao Tse-Tung had established himself as a tough and successful guerrilla leader. His success was based on a clear grasp of the principles of guerrilla war, as well as of the relationship between the guerrilla and the community, but at that time he was still in his remote fastness at Yan'an in northwest China. A few brief examples from his thesis on guerrilla war show at once the difference between him and Chiang. Mao wrote that guerrilla hostilities were the university of war and that military action was the way to attain a political goal; he even used humour, saying that 'we must become good at running away because we do it so often'. His basic but brilliant guerrilla theories laid the foundations for military success, but when Hiroshima ended the war against Japan in August 1945 he was still in a relatively weak position.

We can now consider one of the great 'what ifs' of history. Stilwell fought consistently for the creation of a strong and effective Chinese army. When Roosevelt was preparing for the Casablanca Conference, he stated clearly that the American aim was for Chiang to be strong enough to defeat the Communists and at the same time to curb Russian strength in the Far East. Stilwell backed this up with a strongly worded memo urging Chiang to seize the opportunity to make China strong and safe while the generous offer of American money, weapons, aircraft and supplies was available. Initially Stilwell had gained agreement for the supply and training of thirty divisions. As negotiations proceeded this number was raised to sixty and then to ninety. Stilwell, always the passionate American patriot who wanted his country's huge investment to be used effectively and honestly, developed a policy and a philosophy which, if implemented, would have changed the outcome of the Chinese civil war and, with it, the post-war history of China. Stilwell was strongly supported by his old friend and colleague George Marshall. If Chiang had only played straight with Stilwell and worked to build up his army with the help of American munificence, he would by 1945 have been well on the way to having ninety trained and effective divisions armed with modern American weapons.

Marshall was later to give his name to the Marshall Plan, in which America poured billions of dollars into the effort to rebuild Europe and save it from Communism. How much more enthusiastic Marshall and the American people would have been if, in 1945, they had been able to witness the triumphant advance of ninety divisions led by Chiang against the Communists, knowing that it was the outcome of American leadership and generosity and of the courage and leadership of their hero, Vinegar Joe Stilwell.

On 18 December 1943 this dazzling prospect was all but extinguished when Stilwell left the manure pile. He did note on that day that 'for the first time in history a foreigner was given command of Chinese troops with full control over all officers and no strings attached. Can you believe it?' He concluded with his usual down-to-earth view:

> I've had word from Peanut that I can get away from this dump tomorrow. That means I'll spend Christmas with the Confucianists in the jungle. 'Jungle Bells, Jungle Bells, jungle all the way, Oh, what fun it is to ride in a jeep on Christmas Day.' Until this mess is cleared up, I wouldn't want to be doing anything but working at it, and you wouldn't want me to either, thank God.

He actually left two days later, saying, 'Off for Burma again ... CAN WE PUT IT OVER?'

CHAPTER 9

Back to Burma

Stilwell arrived back in Burma in mid-December 1943 and went at once to the front-line HQ of General Sun's advancing 38 Division. Clearly the best of the Chinese divisional commanders, Sun was none-theless timorous when facing Japanese troops. Stilwell was driven on by his determination to prove that when well fed, well trained and well armed the Chinese soldier was as good as any, and he believed – correctly – that the only way of achieving this was to lead them personally. For this he has been seriously criticised, particularly by American military commentators, who ridiculed the idea that the Deputy Supreme Commander, a general, should fill the role of a battalion commander. Yet he had done that at Taungoo during the retreat and was to do it again in the fighting down the Hukawng valley. It does appear that he was not popular with other American commanders, and Mountbatten recorded that 90 per cent of them hated his guts, while among his own staff he was feared and disliked by many. This was to become a serious issue during the advance to Myitkyina, when it frequently appeared that his staff became syco-phantic and told him only what they thought he wanted to hear.

In spite of all criticism, Stilwell never wavered in his fundamental determination to ensure that, as an American patriot, he would do his best to see that the vast American investment in the Chinese cause was used honestly and effectively. He remained convinced that the best way to assist China was to drive forward in north Burma and re-establish a road link with the old Burma Road and that this should be achieved through positive leadership of the Chinese divisions trained at Ramgarh. The key to all this would be the capture of the town of Myitkyina and its airfield, from which Japanese aircraft were able to make damaging attacks on the airfields in northern India used by the planes taking supplies over the Hump and on the constant air traffic over the Hump itself.

These ideas were foremost in Stilwell's mind when he returned to Burma and set up his headquarters at Shingbwiyang, which, after slow and laborious progress, the road from Ledo had finally reached. Shingbwiyang lay just north of Yubang Ga, where Sun's advance troops were held up by a defensive position that was firmly occupied by Japanese troops of General Tanaka's 18 Division. Stilwell's forces were to discover, as did the advancing units of Slim's Fourteenth Army, that the Japanese defenders were rarely knocked out by an artillery barrage because they dug tunnels and constructed cover over their slit-trenches, and they were ready to defend their positions to the death.

To the Chinese troops who faced Tanaka, Stilwell not only gave strong tactical leadership but his presence among them and his well-known concern for their welfare also improved their morale dramatically. They were immensely impressed that a very senior American officer spoke their language, shared their front-line conditions and rations, distributed his own cigarettes and made sure that if they were wounded they would be flown out to hospital and not just left to die.

When Stilwell arrived at Shingbwiyang, Sun's leading units were in a bad way, having been surrounded at Yubang Ga by a Japanese counterattack. This was not as dangerous as it might have been because valuable lessons had been learnt from the first Chindit expedition, and supplies were airlifted in. Stilwell, after discussion with Sun, quickly organised another attack on Yubang Ga, which started on 24 December. The advancing Chinese units followed a creeping artillery barrage, but when the barrage lifted they hesitated for a few crucial minutes before going in to the attack, and as they tried to overcome the mines, barbed wire and trenches in front of the Japanese positions they were met by devastating Japanese machine-gun and mortar fire.

This was the start of a prolonged battle at Yubang Ga that lasted nearly a week but at the end of which the Chinese for the first time defeated a strong Japanese unit holding a prepared defensive position.

The victory was won at heavy cost – with more than 300 killed and 400 wounded – but it had a significant effect on the morale of all Chinese troops.

Stilwell's own jottings give a vivid impression of the battle. After the first day's fighting he wrote, 'All things considered the Chinese did a good job. The men are fearless and the junior commanders are O.K. Very tough going to get Japs out of this jungle.' The next day – Christmas Day 1943 – he noted that the Japanese who were left in a pocket that had been overrun had killed themselves with hand grenades. He did his best to encourage Sun, who 'swears they are trying to do a good job for the *lao hsien sheng* [the old gentleman, meaning Stilwell]. The troops are all bucked up to have me with them, but commanders are uneasy for fear I get hit and they be held responsible. Insistent that I stay back and let them do it.' By 29 December the Japanese had been driven back and seven Japanese officers had been captured. 'Good work by Chinese: aggressive attack, good fire control, quick action. They are full of beans and are tickled to death at beating the Japs.' These brief comments on the battle were frequently interspersed with details of what he had for breakfast – e.g., 'Breakfast oatmeal, hot cakes, bacon, coffee, jam and butter', and on 31 December his only diary entry was 'Turkey for supper, no fooling, with cranberry sauce and sweet potatoes. Last day of 1943. R.I.P.'

Clearly, it was Stilwell's leadership that brought the victory, but his isolation at the front line in the jungle meant that the flood of 'urgent' and 'top-priority' messages from Delhi and Chungking could not reach him. His able deputy in Delhi, Lieutenant General Daniel Sultan, did his best, but there were always issues on which Stilwell alone could decide. One such matter arose out of the need to determine SEAC's complicated command structure, which demanded his presence in Delhi. The problems were severe enough, but Stilwell's varied roles as Deputy Supreme Commander SEAC, Chief of Staff to Chiang Kai-Shek and commander of the American–Chinese forces added to the difficulty. This was exacerbated by Stilwell's antipathy to the British General Sir George Giffard, who commanded SEAC ground forces. Giffard was respected by his British colleagues, but to

Stilwell he appeared as the epitome of the Limeys who did not want
to fight. SEAC had proposed that Stilwell with his two Chinese
divisions, along with Slim and the Fourteenth Army, should come
under Giffard's overall command.

When the proposal was discussed at a conference chaired by
Mountbatten, Stilwell used every possible ploy to oppose it. He claimed
that, under his orders from the President, he could not put his troops
under a commander from another country. Then he claimed that as
Deputy Supreme Commander he could not be placed under the
authority of a lesser commander. Mountbatten tried desperately to
solve the problem. Slim, who was present, commented that Stilwell
fell back on a surly obstinacy that showed him at his worst. As
Supreme Commander Mountbatten could, ultimately, have removed
any senior officer, but to remove Stilwell in that situation was
unthinkable. Then, to everyone's amazement, when there appeared to
be total impasse Stilwell said he would serve under Slim until the
Chinese forces reached Kamaing in the Mogaung valley. Stilwell and
Slim then left the conference and went straight to the former's HQ
in Delhi to hammer out the details of how this almost Gilbertian
situation might be made to work. Fortunately the two leaders agreed
on their next move, which was to provide maximum support for the
Chinese who were advancing from Ledo towards Myitkyina against
Tanaka's 18 Division, and to use the Chindits to assist in that plan.
After describing this incident Slim explained that, based on his experience of Stilwell during the retreat from Burma he would send him
as few written directions as possible, and that when a serious matter
was to be discussed he visited him in person: 'Stilwell, talking things
over quietly with no one else present, was a much easier and [more]
likeable person than Vinegar Joe with an audience. Alone, I never
found him unreasonable or obstructive.'

Back in the jungle Stilwell had his first meeting with Wingate,
who had gone up to the HQ at Shingbwiyang – known familiarly as
Shing – to discuss co-operation between Stilwell's forces and the
Chindits. The plans for the 1944 attack in north Burma included a
Chindit brigade marching south from Ledo to attack the Japanese
base at Indaw. Wingate had chosen 16 Brigade, commanded by

Bernard Fergusson, for the task. Fergusson (later Lord Ballantrae) wrote two excellent books describing the first and second Chindit expeditions, respectively.* In one he recorded the significant moment when the two men met:

> Wingate heavy-browed, broad and powerful; Stilwell, with his steel-rimmed spectacles, tallish, wiry and gaunt. Both had determined faces, with deep furrows about their mouths; both could display the characteristics of prophets: vision, intolerance, energy, ruthlessness, courage and powers of denunciation to scorch like a forest fire. I stifled a desire to hear them quarrel, and listened attentively to the terms of the bargain which they had struck.†

In return for American help, when he set off from Ledo and moved southwards towards Indaw, Wingate would send off two columns to capture the Japanese base at Lonkin, some 30 miles northwest of Kamaing. This would deal a serious blow to the Japanese as Stilwell's forces advanced. Stilwell discussed the details and agreed the plan with Fergusson, whose background was Eton, Sandhurst the Black Watch and a period as ADC to Wavell. In addition, because of an eye injury he wore a monocle, so he appeared to be just the type of Limey officer who instantly repelled Stilwell. However, he was to learn later that Stilwell had written to Boatner, his chief of staff: 'Help this guy. He looks a dude but I think he's a soldier.' Fergusson, who was pleased with this comment and reproduced it in *The Wild Green Earth*, lived up to expectations and captured Lonkin. Unfortunately, this was to have little effect on the American advance, and the diversion of the two Chindit columns to Lonkin seriously weakened 16 Brigade, which failed in its main task at Indaw.

From January 1944, Stilwell was to have increasingly close relationships both with the Chindits and with his own long-range penetration units, Merrill's Marauders. The Marauders had been recruited and

* B. Fergusson, *Beyond the Chindwin*, Collins, London, 1945; and *The Wild Green Earth*, Collins, London, 1946.
† Fergusson, *Wild Green Earth*, p. 22.

trained with remarkable speed. They were brought by ship to Bombay and immediately started training under the Chindit regime. Colonel Hunter was involved from the start, and early in January 1944 General Merrill arrived to take over command. The Marauders were organised in three battalions, with each battalion divided into two combat teams of nearly 500 men under eighteen officers – nearly twice the size of a Chindit column. Like the Chindits they had no artillery or tanks, but they were effectively organised for their particular role, with special sections for pioneer, demolition, intelligence and reconnaissance work. Their weapons included carbines, sub-machine guns, light machine guns, heavy machine guns, mortars and rocket launchers. These weapons and their ammunition meant that each combat team needed a large number of mules.

When Merrill arrived, Mountbatten finally agreed to Stilwell's insistent demand that the Marauders should come under his direct command and not Wingate's. Merrill was an able graduate who had come up through the ranks and had been assistant military attaché in Tokyo, where he acquired a fair knowledge of the Japanese. Cheerful and self-confident, he did not immediately impress Stilwell, who, when told that the Marauders would move off in three weeks, wrote, 'My God, what speed.' Merrill used his knowledge of Japanese to gain maximum benefit from the Nisei, the Japanese-speaking Americans who were used for all aspects of intelligence work. Well before the Marauders arrived, the Office of Strategic Services (OSS) had established a framework of intelligence gatherers with the local Kachin hill people. Small groups of Kachins with American and British officers provided valuable information about Japanese units and their movements.

Nineteen forty-three had been a period of intense frustration for Stilwell, but in January 1944 the situation in north Burma clarified, albeit with top-level strategic plans and different code names still being tossed about. On the ground the road from Ledo had already advanced more than 70 miles through the formidable jungle-covered Patkai mountain range, which rose to over 10,000 feet. The two Chinese divisions, 38 and 22, whose fighting had made possible the advance of the road, were now poised at the heads of two important valleys – the upper Chindwin and the Hukawng – which led south along Stilwell's proposed route to Mogaung and Myitkyina. Merrill's Marauders were assembling rapidly, and the Chindit brigade under Fergusson was about to start its long march towards Indaw.

Stilwell's own comments during January are fairly brief and non-committal. He continued to grumble that the Limeys and the G-mo were reneging on their agreements, and he expressed concern that even Sun, the divisional commander in whom he had the greatest confidence, was timorous in the face of Japanese opposition. In a letter home he wrote that he expected to meet Tarzan any day, and, more seriously:

> This experience is different from the last time. Now we have aviation and ammunition and artillery and a certain amount of training, so we don't have to take it on the nose as we used to, with no chance of answering. The Chinese soldier is doing his stuff, as I knew he would if he had half a chance. It's only the higher-ups who are weak and they are still pretty terrible. The Americans are all doing a good job and they all enjoy the life. If I could just have a couple of U.S. divisions. But the Brain Trust won't turn them over, so I've got to go on struggling with my shoestring. The Glamour boy [Mountbatten] is just about that. He doesn't wear well and I begin to wonder if he knows his stuff. Enormous staff, endless walla-walla, but damn little fighting. And of course the Peanut is unchanged. The jungle is a refuge from them both.

His diary records fairly frequent efforts to bolster up Sun and make him more aggressive, but it also notes the devastation caused to Japanese positions by the accurate fire of the mortars. Several hundred Japanese dead were found in one captured strongpoint.

On 30 January 1944 Stilwell, straight from the front line in the jungle, attended a brief and bad-tempered conference in Delhi. He was to find that Chennault, together with General Wedemeyer, his own assistant, who later was to succeed him and whom he considered an arrogant and conceited young man, were increasingly critical of his policy and campaign in north Burma. At the conference Stilwell argued his case bluntly and forcefully. Referring obliquely to the thousands of staff at SEAC headquarters, he reminded them that Clive had captured India with 123 men. The conference discussed Mountbatten's proposal for AXIOM, a plan which returned to the idea of amphibious attacks with the corollary of the withdrawal of support for a major effort in north Burma. Stilwell's diary entry for this conference was merely 'The Limeys are welching' and 'Big walla-walla', but he realised the seriousness of the situation. He had learned that Mountbatten was sending a delegation to Washington to support the AXIOM proposal. The delegation included Wedemeyer, who was to argue the cause of the increasingly bitter anti-Stilwell group in Chungking. They alleged that he was arrogantly courting disaster, marching through a trackless waste, and that this could result in a serious defeat which would knock China out of the war. Stilwell realised the danger of this approach, which appeared to have the support of Churchill – who as ever was more interested in the recapture of Singapore and Hong Kong.

Stilwell returned to the jungle, but then, without informing Mountbatten, sent his own delegation to Washington ahead of the official group. He appointed Brigadier General Haydon Boatner, who was to become very close to him in the dramatic remaining months of the campaign, to lead his delegation. There followed one of the odd quirks of war – rather like Wingate's dinner with Churchill in Downing Street. Boatner, to his amazement, was invited to see Roosevelt alone to present the case for supporting Stilwell. The President even encouraged him to draft an appeal to Churchill to order Indian Command to help Stilwell and not to hinder him. To encourage Stilwell and Chiang, Roosevelt added the message that if Chiang co-operated fully he could take over French Indo-China at the end of the war. However, in spite of the high hopes and tensions engendered by these encounters, it all came to nought. The Joint Chiefs of Staff rejected the AXIOM proposals and Churchill refused Roosevelt's request. There was one significant result. Mountbatten was furious with Stilwell and considered his action in sending a separate delegation to Washington to be out of order and dangerously disloyal.

Back in the jungle the arrival of Merrill's Marauders gave a boost to Stilwell's hopes, but it also produced some difficulties. The Marauders were not all the tough, well-disciplined, experienced fighters for which the initial appeal had hoped. Rather, there were many unfit men with all sorts of problems. As often happens in war in response to a general appeal, units took the opportunity to offload their most difficult characters. During training many had reacted adversely to the severe Chindit discipline and, as they saw it, inadequate British rations. During their journey across India they had created severe problems by shooting from the train at cows – sacred to Hindus – in the fields and even at Indian peasants.

By the beginning of February 1944 Stilwell was able to clarify his plans. Because Chiang had once again refused to advance with Yoke Force, Stilwell brought Merrill's Marauders – code named Galahad – into the attack on the Japanese in the Hukawng valley. Originally they had been designated to operate with Yoke Force. During January, by dint of personal example, bravery, threats to shoot useless commanders and rewards for successful effort, Stilwell had badgered and cajoled the Chinese forces to advance against the Japanese. As part of this advance, 22 Division broke through the mountains and captured the Japanese base at Taro in the centre of the Taro plain on the upper Chindwin. Stilwell was opposed by General Tanaka, who had been instructed by Mutaguchi, the overall Japanese commander in Burma, to concentrate on delaying Stilwell's advance down the Hukawng valley and, as the ultimate priority, to hold the town of Kamaing at all costs.

Stilwell was still suspicious of interference from SEAC, and even from Slim – under whom he had agreed to serve – and the Fourteenth Army, and he therefore set up the Northern Combat Area Command (NCAC) to keep the Chinese divisions and Merrill's Marauders under his own direct control and to ensure his control over their supplies.

From this situation Stilwell planned for 22 Division to lead the advance down the dry-weather road towards Maingkwan and Walawbum. They were to be supported by the 1st Provisional Chinese Tank Group under an American commander, Colonel Rothwell Brown. The 38th Division, which had suffered heavy casualties in the

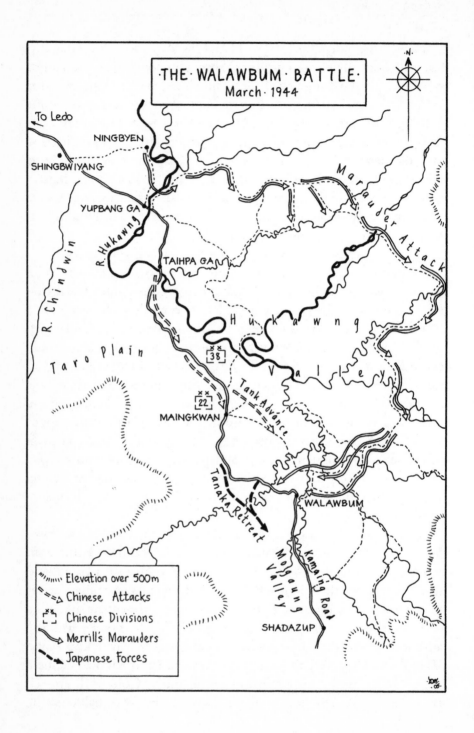

·THE·WALAWBUM·BATTLE·
March·1944

N

To Ledo

SHINGBWIYANG

NINGBYEN

Marauder Attack

YUPBANG GA

R. Hukawng

R. Chindwin

TAIHPA GA

Hukawng

Taro Plain

Valley

38

22

MAINGKWAN

Tank Advance

Tanaka Retreat

WALAWBUM

Mogaung Valley

Kamaing Road

SHADAZUP

"""""" Elevation over 500m
===△ Chinese Attacks
[¨] Chinese Divisions
⟋ Merrill's Marauders
- -➤ Japanese Forces

January fighting, would be used to clear the area to the east of the road, while in their first action the Marauders were sent on a wide sweep along the eastern fringe of the Hukawng valley. They aimed to reach Walawbum and cut off Tanaka's 18 Division before it could withdraw southwards. This very sound tactical plan posed a serious problem for Tanaka, who had to decide whether to stand firm at Maingkwan, where he would be in danger of being cut off when the Marauders reached Walawbum. This plan also illustrated a significant difference between Wingate's long-range penetration plans for the Chindits – a difference that was to be dramatically demonstrated early in March in the second Chindit operation – and Stilwell's tactics of using the Marauders in much closer support for the advancing Chinese divisions. Stilwell's approach had been commended by Brooke, the CIGS, who like most of the British top brass did not accept Wingate's precepts.

The Marauders set off on 21 February on their wide sweep east of the Kamaing road. They sent reconnaissance patrols to ascertain the boundaries of the Japanese positions, and there were some fire fights with enemy defenders, but the main body of the Marauders completed the operation, with three battalions approaching Walawbum by 3 March. During this first operation the Marauders received considerable help from Kachin guides and from a British officer who had been a colonial official and lived among the Kachin before the war. With their local knowledge, the Kachins gave crucial help to the Marauders, who normally operated in thick, unmapped jungle away from any roads.

When the Marauders approached Walawbum, 3 Battalion was deployed close to the town on high ground overlooking the road and the river. The 2nd Battalion advanced to the north of the town ready to cut the road up to Maingkwan. The 1st Battalion operated between the two wings and acted as a reserve to be called on when needed. It was planned that the Marauders would attack and hold their positions around Walawbum until 22 Division and the tanks arrived. When they took up their positions, they discovered the main Japanese telephone line from Tanaka's headquarters to the HQ at Kamaing, and one of their Nisei operators was able to intercept all the orders and communications affecting Tanaka's moves. Because of a breakdown in Japanese communication, Tanaka – although there had been some clashes with the Marauders' reconnaissance patrols – remained unaware that a substantial and effective American unit was approaching Walawbum and was blocking his escape route to the south. A tough and experienced commander, he did not appear to be too worried by the enemy presence at Walawbum. He still held a poor opinion of Chinese fighting troops and assumed that they would advance very slowly. He therefore left some defensive screens to impede their advance and decided to concentrate on destroying the Marauders at Walawbum.

The attack on the Marauders started as early as 4 March. In fluid and confused fighting the Japanese suffered heavy casualties and discovered that they were now facing a formidable enemy. In the close-combat jungle fighting the Marauders used the Thompson sub-machine gun (tommy gun), light and heavy machine guns and, in particular, their 81-mm mortar, which like the Chindits' 3-inch mortar proved itself the most valuable weapon in jungle fighting. And in the battle at Walawbum the Marauders were able to call on another significant weapon – the fighter bomber. The Chindits had demonstrated the critical importance of air liaison officers both for accurate supply drops and for close support attacks, and now each Marauder battalion had an air liaison officer who was able to call in air strikes against the Japanese units facing them at Walawbum.

The Japanese launched their heaviest attacks on 2 Battalion, which had established a strong road block on the road down from Maingkwan about two miles west of Walawbum. The Marauders were well prepared with carefully constructed slit trenches, and they held their positions with remarkably few casualties in spite of a constant barrage from Japanese artillery. In contrast, the Japanese suffered more than one hundred killed in that one attack. It lasted over thirty-six hours, and when the Marauders ran short of food, water and ammunition Merrill ordered them to withdraw a short distance to take an air drop of supplies and to join 3 Battalion, which was holding the high ground that overlooked the town and dominated the road to the south. While the fighting at the road block continued, the tank unit – which had left the road further north and had been guided along a track by Kachin guides – emerged from the jungle close to the Marauders' position and, more significantly, in a location from which they could attack General Tanaka's headquarters.

The fiercest fighting occurred on 6 March when Tanaka realised the seriousness of his position between the Chinese 22 Division, along with the tank unit advancing from the north, and the strongly held Marauder road block at Walawbum. He therefore attempted to disengage and move as rapidly as possible west and south in order to bypass Walawbum and regain the road to Kamaing. Merrill, who had a brief conference with the commanders of the tank group and the leading Chinese regiment, reckoned that the Marauders had carried out Stilwell's orders to delay the Japanese as long as possible.

The battle in and around Walawbum was valuable as an initial operation for the Marauders and it succeeded in driving the formidable Tanaka off the Kamaing road, but Stilwell had hoped that the whole of Tanaka's division would be trapped and destroyed. In this he was disappointed, partly because Tanaka moved so swiftly in extricating his units from Walawbum but also because the two Chinese divisions, which had arrived during the battle, were too slow to move against Tanaka and close the trap.

Stilwell's had been the clear directing hand in the successful fighting around Walawbum, and although he was disappointed to have Tanaka escape from a well-planned trap, he was pleased with the achievements of the Marauders and the Chinese. Soon, however, he was to be caught up in wider issues and more discussions at top level. The early days of March 1944 were to see the start of momentous developments that did not end until the victorious occupation of Rangoon.

CHAPTER 10

March–April 1944: Crisis

In March 1943, a year before the month of crisis described in this chapter, the Chindits undertook their first operation. In this they should have been backed up by three simultaneous attacks: by the British forces at Imphal, by Stilwell and the Chinese–American divisions in Ledo, and by Yoke Force in Yunnan. The Chindit expedition went ahead and sustained heavy casualties because not one of these supporting attacks took place. In March 1944 things initially appeared remarkably similar. Chiang still refused to advance with Yoke Force, Stilwell was making slow progress in the Hukawng valley, and the British Fourteenth Army at Imphal was still building up its strength and was not ready to advance.

On 4 February 1944 the Japanese had begun an attack, code named Ha Go, in the Arakan. The battle along this coastline between Akyab and Chittagong, although a sideshow compared to what was to come, was significant for a number of lessons which the Japanese failed to learn. Their 55 Division – about 8,000 strong – made a rapid advance against 5 and 7 Indian Divisions and appeared to take them by surprise, eliciting some acid comments from Stilwell. The Japanese advanced for several days, but then the two Indian divisions rallied and, under direct orders from Slim, formed what was known as the 'Admin Box'. This was an all-round defensive position with the defenders supplied by air. The Admin Box held out from 6 to 24 February and inflicted 5,000 casualties on the Japanese. British air superiority was complete and they were able to use the newly arrived Spitfires. The Ha Go attack had forced Slim to move two divisions from the reserves he was building up near Imphal – 26 Indian Division and 36 British Division – to support the defences in the Arakan. Then, on 24 February, the Japanese 55 Division suddenly withdrew because it had run out of ammunition, suffered over 50 per cent casualties and the men were starving.

General Mutaguchi, who commanded the Fifteenth Army and co-ordinated all the subsequent Japanese attacks, made several false assumptions before the Ha Go offensive and he failed to learn the lessons of this small but significant defeat. He assumed that the British would rapidly crumble and surrender as they had done during the retreat in 1942; he failed to realise that the Admin Box, in which the defenders were supplied by air, had introduced a totally new factor into jungle warfare; and he failed to see the crucial corollary of the increased British resistance – that he could not send off a division with a few weeks' rations on the assumption that they would quickly overrun British supply depots. The Japanese retreated from the Admin Box because their men were starving.

Stilwell and Mountbatten, in spite of some brisk exchanges, co-operated well on the strategy in north Burma, but during the early days of SEAC and in his role as Supreme Commander Mountbatten had other battles to fight. His senior army and airforce commanders had informed him that it was not possible to supply forward units by air, that they objected to giving any support to Wingate and the Chindits, and that it was not possible to fight during the monsoon. Mountbatten also had to cope with the preoccupation of the Chiefs of Staff with other plans – such as an attack on Sumatra or the Andaman Islands – and he knew that a major effort in Burma was not their top priority. It is immensely to the credit of Mountbatten and Slim, whose strengths complemented each other, that they overcame the defeatist and negative attitudes of their subordinate commanders and fashioned the Fourteenth Army into one of the most successful British armies of the Second World War.

Soon Stilwell, Slim and Mountbatten were to be forced together into the closest co-operation by the positive actions of General Mutaguchi. As commander of the Japanese Fifteenth Army in Burma, he was operating from his HQ in Maymyo in the very buildings where Stilwell had met Alexander, Wavell and Wingate at the start of the retreat in 1942. Initially, Mutaguchi had under his command 18 Division led by General Tanaka, which faced Stilwell in the north, 56 Division facing Yoke Force in the east, and 33 Division facing the British on the Chindwin. The British may have been inclined to ignore the importance of Wingate's first Chindit expedition in March 1943, but Mutaguchi later conceded that it had changed his entire strategic thinking. Wingate had shown that it was possible for units to attack across the main north–south grain of the rivers and mountains of Burma. This, together with intelligence of the British build-up at Imphal, convinced Mutaguchi that he must attack Imphal and Kohima to pre-empt a British offensive.

Thus was conceived Mutaguchi's grand strategy. He planned a three-division attack: 33 Division under General Yanagida to advance towards Imphal from the south against 17 Indian Division, which had fought in the retreat but was now substantially retrained and re-equipped; 15 Division under General Yamauchi, together with units of the Indian National Army recruited from Indian prisoners of war, to attack Imphal in two prongs from the east; and, most significantly, 31 Division under General Sato, which was to advance rapidly north-westwards to capture Kohima and then advance to Dimapur, the huge supply base – eleven miles long and a mile wide – which provided for the whole of the Fourteenth Army as well as Stilwell's forces. Mutaguchi intended that as soon as Kohima and Dimapur were captured his victorious forces, accompanied by the Indian National Army and its leader, Subhas Chandra Bose, would advance into Bengal where the down-trodden people would rise up, throw out the British and support his triumphant 'March on Delhi'. It is rarely realised how close to success Mutaguchi came in this grand plan, which would also have cut off Stilwell's forces from all contact with the west. An incorrect decision by an otherwise outstanding Japanese commander and the selfless bravery of two Indian and British units at Sangshak and Kohima alone thwarted his plan. His idea of sending off his units with one month's rations and supplies because they would capture plenty at Dimapur became a significant factor in their ultimate defeat.

Mutaguchi's three-division attack on Imphal and Kohima illustrates the significance of the weather and the phases of the moon in modern

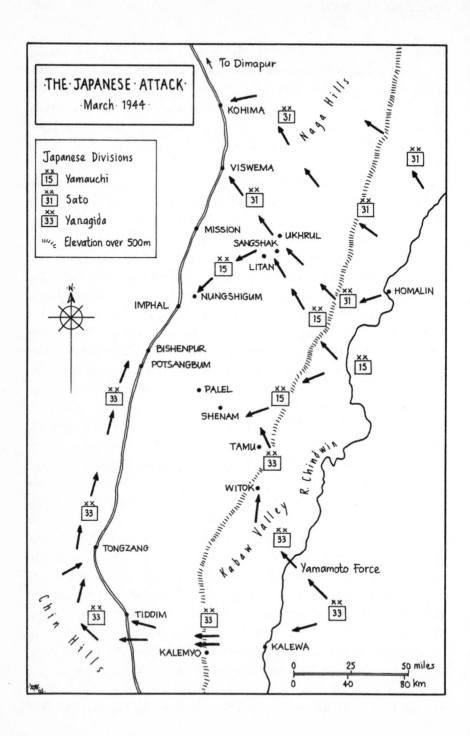

THE·JAPANESE·ATTACK·
·March·1944·

Japanese Divisions
15 Yamauchi
31 Sato
33 Yanagida
Elevation over 500m

To Dimapur

KOHIMA

Naga Hills

VISWEMA

MISSION

SANGSHAK   UKHRUL

LITAN

IMPHAL

NUNGSHIGUM

HOMALIN

BISHENPUR
POTSANGBUM

PALEL

SHENAM

TAMU

WITOK

Kabaw Valley

R. Chindwin

TONGZANG

Yamamoto Force

TIDDIM

Chin Hills

KALEMYO

KALEWA

0   25   50 miles
0   40   80 km

warfare. The first Japanese troops crossed the Chindwin on the night of 5 March. One young Japanese soldier recorded his fear and anguish when, as they reached the west bank of the river, they heard the thunder of the armada of aircraft flying eastwards to launch the Chindits' Operation Thursday. Independently, both sides had chosen the identical date to launch their operations.

Mutaguchi's plan also created a crisis for Stilwell, Slim and Mountbatten. The Ha Go offensive in the Arakan failed disastrously, but it forced Slim to divert two of his reserve divisions from Imphal to the Arakan. This was the main purpose of the attack, and it was soon to have its effect on the situation at Imphal. As the Japanese advanced towards Imphal and Kohima, 33 Division faced serious opposition as it moved up the Tiddim road and 15 Division had to fight hard to advance up the hills towards Shenan, but Sato and 31 Division made dangerously threatening progress towards Kohima.

At this critical moment Mountbatten flew in to see Stilwell and to restore good relations. Stilwell's comments remained critical. He observed that whereas his forces had four fighter planes for their battle, Mountbatten was escorted by sixteen. 'Louis has been up but doesn't like the smell of corpses ... Louis and I get along famously even if he does have curly eyelashes.' American commentators have generally repeated the question that was asked at the time: how could the Fourteenth Army, which for nearly two years had been preparing to advance and attack the Japanese, be plunged into crisis by the approach of three Japanese divisions? Stilwell, still driving forward the advance down the Hukawng valley and demonstrating that the Japanese could be beaten in jungle fighting, was appalled at the prospect of the loss of Kohima and Dimapur, which would put an end to all his plans.

During Mountbatten's visit to the Hukawng valley a trivial incident threatened to impinge on major policy matters. He was driving in a jeep when the branch of a tree swung back and seriously injured his left eye. He was rushed to the nearest American hospital, where he was kept in complete darkness for five days. This happened just when the crisis over the Japanese drive to Kohima was at its height. After five days he discharged himself, against medical advice, and flew to Comilla to see Slim. Here, as Supreme Commander, but after consulting the Chiefs of Staff, he made the decision to transfer thirty aircraft from the Hump operation to fly 5 Indian Division back from the Arakan to bolster the defences of Kohima and Dimapur. The Chiefs of Staff agreed with this proposal, thinking it was better to use the aircraft where they were urgently needed in battle than to support Chiang, who still refused to order Yoke Force to attack. There is little doubt that the airlift of the division by the USAAF and the RAF played a vital role in the defence of Kohima and Dimapur, but even with these reinforcements they were in dire peril.

In the Hukawng valley Stilwell listened apprehensively to news of the unfolding drama around Kohima, knowing that the outcome would affect him decisively and at the same time having to fend off Chiang's fury at the reduction in the tonnage going over the Hump. The first act of the drama to come took place at a little-known Naga village, Sangshak, about forty miles northeast of Imphal. The 50th Indian Parachute Brigade had just moved to Sangshak to complete its jungle training. They were ill prepared for action – they had brought the silver for the officers' mess but no tin hats – and their divisional HQ failed to pass on intelligence about the rapidly approaching Japanese. One of the brigade's Gurkha battalions did not arrive at Sangshak because there was no transport. Then on 19 March the Japanese attacked with nearly one thousand men.

Major General Miyazaki, the capable and aggressive commander of the leading regiment of Sato's 31 Division, had been ordered to drive forward as fast as possible to Kohima, and on the way his unit passed fairly close to Sangshak. Miyazaki was ambitious and conceited. Like Mutaguchi he despised the British and Indian enemy forces and expected to sweep them aside as he had done in 1942. He therefore decided that rather than leave a brigade-strength garrison athwart his lines of communication – and to add to his glory – he would pause to capture Sangshak before proceeding to Kohima. This was to prove a grave and costly mistake that influenced the outcome of the Burma war.*

* Harry Seaman, *The Battle at Sangshak*, Leo Cooper, London, 1989.

The Japanese attacked the leading Indian company at Sangshak on 19 March. The men resisted stubbornly until they ran out of ammunition and were overwhelmed. For seven days the Indian, Gurkha and Maharatta units resisted the Japanese attacks, often in hand-to-hand fighting. On 26 March divisional HQ ordered them to fight their way out, and they found a jungle path which enabled them to slip away. The tough Miyazaki was appalled at the carnage at Sangshak, and he insisted that prisoners and wounded receive good treatment. The effect of the seven-day delay and the more than 50 per cent casualty rate on this leading Japanese regiment will shortly be seen.

An incident at the battle for Sangshak that influenced the situation in Kohima illustrates the importance of intelligence in war. During the fighting a Japanese officer was found with 31 Division's detailed plans, including its proposed attack on Kohima. A brave British officer slipped through enemy lines and got this vital information to corps HQ at Imphal on 25 March. Slim, however, never received the crucial intelligence that the whole of 31 Division was advancing rapidly towards Kohima. Three days later, on 28 March, he held a critical conference in Imphal and made decisions based on the assumption that there would only be a battalion-strength attack on Kohima. This grave blunder at corps HQ could have had catastrophic consequences both for Slim's forces and for the whole of the American supply system supporting Stilwell's divisions lying north of Dimapur.

While the battered survivors of Sangshak sought the safety of their own lines, and while Slim conferred in Imphal, 5 Indian Division from the Arakan was being bundled into the Dakotas that Mountbatten had transferred from duties on the Hump supply route. In a remarkably successful operation, during which the Dakotas flew round the clock, two brigades – complete with weapons and supplies – were landed at Imphal by 27 March and one at Dimapur by 1 April. By 28 March the Japanese advance had cut off Imphal, and from then on the whole of IV Corps could only be supplied by air.

In the final days of March 1944 the leading units of Sato's 31 Division continued their rapid advance towards Kohima and Dimapur, but on the British side there was muddle, if not chaos. The defence of Kohima was to centre on the 4th Battalion of the Royal West Kents, a pre-war Territorial Army unit. They were part of 5 Indian Division and had been heavily engaged in the fighting around the Admin Box in the Arakan. Suddenly, when they thought they might be taken out of the line for a rest, they were rushed to an airstrip, put into Dakotas with their weapons, transport and mules, and landed at Dimapur from where they were marched to Kohima. Then Slim was involved in a decision whether, in view of the rapid Japanese advance, to give priority to the defence of Dimapur or of Kohima. Because of the crucial role of the vast supply base at Dimapur for the supply of Stilwell's forces it was decided to give it priority. This decision involved a hurried transfer of the Royal West Kents from Kohima back to Dimapur. Then, because reinforcements from the British 2 Division arrived earlier than expected, the Royal West Kents were sent back to Kohima. 'The fury, frustration and the language of the soldiers can be imagined.'* As the battalion moved towards Kohima they encountered hordes of terrified refugees fleeing before the advancing Japanese troops. On 5 April, in an atmosphere 'of sullen fury at the way they had been buggered about', they reached Kohima and reoccupied the slit trenches they had started to dig just days before.

This incident has been dealt with in some detail to illustrate the significance of Miyazaki's decision to attack Sangshak and of its week-long defence by 50 Indian Parachute Brigade. During the remaining hours of 5 April the Royal West Kents frantically prepared their defences, and at 0400 hours the following morning the Japanese attacked and captured Naga village, only a mile from Kohima. Thus, if it had not been held up for seven days at Sangshak, 31 Division would have been able to attack Kohima at a time when it had almost no serious defence and when Dimapur was equally defenceless.

Although the Royal West Kents had arrived back in Kohima with just hours to spare before the Japanese attack, the chances of holding up the enemy advance seemed remote and the threat to Dimapur remained dire. There seemed little hope that a single British battalion and a few units of the Assam Regiment could hold up the whole of Sato's tried, experienced and successful 31 Division.

* David Rooney, *Burma Victory*, Arms & Armour Press, London, 1992, p. 75.

The chaos, orders and counter-orders that left the Royal West Kents urgently trying to complete their defences on 6 April 1944 were the inauspicious start to one of the epic sieges of the Second World War. Very rapidly Kohima was completely surrounded and the defences were established on a series of fairly steep hills overlooking the main road. Central to the defence was the deputy commissioner's bungalow and its terraced grounds, including a tennis court which until a short time before had been the scene of relaxed and elegant tennis parties. Suddenly it became the centre of ferocious hand-to-hand fighting, with British and Japanese soldiers hurling grenades across the court. For thirteen desperate days the Royal West Kents and the Assam Regiment units held out against the assaults of Japanese artillery, mortar and machine-gun fire and constant infantry attack. The defenders were gradually driven back into an enclave less than 500 yards long. Close to despair, with food and ammunition running out, they watched horrified as the supplies from an air drop floated gently over to the Japanese lines. On the morning of 15 April, when total collapse was imminent, they noticed a change in the sound and pattern of gunfire and realised that the 25-pounders of the British 2 Division, which had been fighting hard to advance to their rescue, had come within range. Later that day the shattered and emaciated survivors staggered down the hill and were taken away in lorries and ambulances as fresh and well-supplied battalions from 2 Division replaced them.

This was a seminal moment in the Burma war. It halted the Japanese, and they never again made a major advance. Suddenly the threat to Dimapur was removed, and the dire peril faced by all of Stilwell's forces, from Ledo to the Hukawng valley, was removed, and Mutaguchi's ambitious plans for a triumphal march on Delhi were destroyed.

The prolonged crisis at Imphal and Kohima prompted Mountbatten to request Roosevelt and Churchill to renew the pressure on Chiang to order Yoke Force into the attack. Roosevelt sent a strong plea and was infuriated when Chiang sent a dishonest and evasive reply to the effect that he could do nothing because of the threats in the north from both the Japanese and the Communists. When Stilwell heard of this he determined to make a final effort himself to get

Chiang to attack with Yoke Force, and he flew to Chungking on 27 March. This mission failed, but he did succeed in obtaining Chiang's promise of two more Chinese divisions to assist in the advance to Myitkyina, and these were in fact forthcoming. Stilwell was so alarmed at the grave threat to his whole position posed by the Japanese advance to Kohima that as soon as he returned from Chungking he had an urgent meeting with Mountbatten and Slim. This took place on 3 April. In view of the threat to the British position, he offered Slim the use of 38 Division under General Sun, who had worked well with Slim during the retreat in 1942. Although on that day the outcome of the Japanese attack on Kohima was not yet decided, Slim, confident that the advance could be held, refused the offer. Stilwell returned from the meeting and ordered an all-out effort to drive the Japanese back to Kamaing. He then discovered that – as he had suspected for some time – Chiang was secretly communicating with the commanders of the two divisions he had provided telling them not to attack unless he gave permission.

Roosevelt then wrote again, suggesting bluntly that, surely, Yoke Force, which had been armed, equipped and trained by America, and which was facing a severely weakened Japanese division, should now advance. The President added that, if Yoke Force did not attack, the strenuous American efforts in providing arms, equipment and personnel 'have not been justified'. Chiang rarely replied to a serious rebuke, and there was no answer to Roosevelt, but feeling in Washington rose dramatically – veering strongly towards Stilwell's more realistic view. He had written to Marshall – a tower of strength as ever – and received a reply that, unless Yoke Force attacked, the supplies taken over the Hump should stop. Wisely, this threat was not made directly to Chiang but was negotiated at a lower level. This ploy prevented a serious loss of face for Chiang, and it succeeded. On 16 April the order was given for Yoke Force to advance, and it was announced that this was a Chinese initiative made without any outside pressure.

To understand Stilwell's situation, his consistent aim to reach Myitkyina and the factors which influenced this, it is necessary to consider the wider strategic position around Imphal and the dates of the different actions. By the end of 1943, under a rigorous programme of retraining and re-equipment, Slim had built up the Fourteenth Army. In February 1944 he had to decide whether to advance from Imphal and attack the Japanese across the Chindwin or whether to entice them forward towards the Imphal plain where their lines of communication would be stretched to the limit and where his artillery, tanks and air support could be used most effectively. This plan, which was strategically sound but had fierce critics, was pre-empted by Mutaguchi's three-division attack, which started on 5 March. The Japanese, as we have seen, moved more swiftly than expected and created the crisis at Kohima, where they were held up from 6 to 18 April.

While 31 Division advanced to Kohima, Mutaguchi launched a two-pronged attack on Imphal. 33 Division moved to the Tiddim road to attack Imphal from the south. The British there made serious errors. 17 Indian Division, according to Slim's overall strategy, should have carried out an orderly retreat towards Imphal. Scoones, the commander of IV Corps, delayed giving the order, and as a result 17 Division found itself in a bloody fight along seventy miles of road. Slim was always ready to take the blame for the shortcomings of his subordinate commanders and admitted his own mistakes. He took the blame for this blunder although it was clearly Scoones' fault. The effect of Scoones' delay was compounded by the understandable anger of 17 Division, which had established a clear dominance over the Japanese in the relatively static situation around Tiddim and was looking forward to a triumphal advance. By the end of March 1944, 17 Indian Division had retreated to Bishenpur on the edge of the perimeter defences at Imphal. It had sustained heavy casualties but had inflicted far heavier casualties on General Yanagida's 33 Division. Even before the end of March Yanagida had stated that there was no possibility of capturing Imphal in three weeks – as Mutaguchi planned – and that Mutaguchi's entire plan was absurd.

The third prong of the Japanese attack drove from the east towards Tamu and up through a range of hills to the heights of Shenam on the edge of the Imphal plain. 20 Indian Division under General Douglas Gracey defended this approach. Like 17 Indian Division, 20 Division was now well-trained and confident and had played an active part in developing roads and large stores of equipment ready for the proposed attack on the enemy. They expressed their fury and outrage at having to give up millions of pounds worth of stores and territory that had been won in hard fighting. In spite of these objections they accepted their orders and conducted a model withdrawal up to Shenam at little cost to themselves while inflicting heavy casualties on the Japanese 15 Division under General Yamauchi and a specialist force under General Yamamoto. By 1 April, 20 Division was firmly dug in at Shenam, and they realised that their position had to be held at all costs or all the Imphal defences would be at risk.

To Stilwell, as to many later American commentators, these two withdrawals ordered by Slim appeared to be yet another example of the British not being prepared to fight. This was unfortunate because Stilwell was certainly aware of the British plans. He made a typical comment in a letter to his wife in early April 1944. 'Just a line before hopping off to see Louis who, to put it mildly, has his hind leg over his neck. If they don't buck up on their side we will also have our tit in the wringer. What a mess the Limeys can produce in short order.'

Attention was focused on Imphal, where a huge military base had been established around IV Corps' headquarters under Scoones, with a network of roads, supply depots, two general hospitals and basic air-fields. Such a large establishment tended to induce something of a peacetime mentality. Even during the siege there were open-air film shows, and a young doctor wrote home, 'I am having a grand time and I would not miss it for anything.'★ The fighting units – 17 and 20 Divisions and the brave defenders of Sangshak – were fiercely critical of corps HQ for its failure to provide urgently needed supplies, especially barbed wire, but, more significantly, for the failure to pass on intelligence about Japanese movements. As the Japanese approached and Imphal was cut off, 'useless mouths' were flown out but, to the bitter amusement of the fighting units, no staff officers were included.

Stilwell remained highly critical of the refusal of British officers to attack aggressively, but it is understandable that, after the ignominy of the 1942 defeat and the more recent unsuccessful clashes in the Arakan, Slim wanted to be certain that he had sufficient military power to

★ Rooney, *Burma Victory*, p. 143.

ensure the destruction of the Japanese. The build-up may have been slow, but by the middle of April, when Imphal was cut off, Slim had six divisions to face Mutaguchi's three divisions; these were 17 and 20 Indian Divisions, together with 5 and 23 Divisions at Imphal and 2 and 7 Divisions at Kohima. In addition, it should be remembered that on the night of 5 March, when Mutaguchi launched his attack, the equivalent of four brigades of Chindits were sent off to cause havoc behind the Japanese lines.

From the middle of April through May, June and into July, virtually four separate battles raged in and around Imphal and Kohima before the Japanese were destroyed. The situation in Kohima, where the Royal West Kents were relieved on 18 April by the advance of 2 Division under General Grover, suddenly changed. Sato's 31 Division had to turn to urgent defence. The Japanese had accepted horrific casualties when attacking, but they now showed endless tenacity in skilful defensive tactics. Most were determined to hold their positions to the end. Thus the second phase of the battle for Kohima saw 2 Division pushing forwards slowly against the carefully defended positions of the Japanese.

The fierce antagonism felt between some commanders in battle is well illustrated and well known from Stilwell's barbed comments in his diaries. Less well known are the clashes between the other commanders who took part in the long drawn out and vicious fighting that continued right the way through the heaviest of the monsoon storms. Sato, whose division was virtually wiped out by the end of June, clashed bitterly with Mutaguchi and told him that his attack on Kohima was insane and stupid. Sato wrote, 'We have reached the limit of human fortitude ... shedding bitter tears I now leave Kohima.'*
On 5 July 1944 Mutaguchi sacked Sato from the command of 31 Division. Ironically, it was on the same day that General Grover, who had earned the intense loyalty of his men during the gruesome Kohima battles, was sacked by his corps commander for moving too slowly.

The defence of the eastern perimeter of the Imphal defences at Shenam heights, which rose to over 5,000 feet, saw prolonged and

* Rooney, *Burma Victory*, p. 103.

desperate fighting. The Japanese attackers – parts of 15 and 33 Divisions – knew that it offered the quickest and best route through the defences, while 20 Indian Division, consisting of Seaforth Highlanders, Gurkhas, Punjabis and Mahrattas, knew equally well that they had to hold the heights at all costs. The battle raged along a five-mile ridge from 1 April to the end of June. One of the heroes was Neil Gillian, who led an American field ambulance team in the tireless rescue of wounded men. The British recommended him for the Victoria Cross, though as he was not eligible for this award he received the George Medal.

On 28 March, on the northern perimeter of the Imphal defences an advance unit of the Japanese 15 Division cut the road coming in from Kohima and set up powerful defensive positions of its own. Until then more than one hundred lorries per hour had been coming into the Imphal garrison, and afterwards – as it seemed to the Japanese – supplies were flown in by an endless succession of Dakotas. The key battle in this northern sector took place at Nunshigum, one of a range of steep hills whose peaks were lost and recaptured several times. Eventually, with close co-operation between infantry, tanks (Third Carabiniers) and close-support air attacks, the Japanese were slowly destroyed. After one clash at Nunshigum when the Japanese counter-attacked with one hundred men, ninety-eight corpses were found. The Japanese could hardly believe that the British were able to operate tanks in thick jungle and on such steep hills, and one of their commanders remarked, 'Now we are done for.' This illustrates another major blunder by Mutaguchi, who had assured his divisional commanders that they would not face tanks during the Imphal campaign.

While desperate fighting continued at Shenam and Nunshigum, the most prolonged and savage battles took place, if anywhere, on the south and west perimeter of Imphal near the village of Bishenpur. As early as the end of April, 33 Division, originally 4,000 strong, was reduced to 1,000 men. Daily close-quarter clashes continued into May, when the difficult conditions were turned into a hideous nightmare by the arrival of the monsoon on the 15th. For the next months of the campaign relentless rain dominated everything. In constant close fighting the British, who had the advantage of a good supply line, massive artillery and close air support, slowly gained the upper hand.

The Japanese sustained grievous casualties – one 900-strong unit was reduced to 40 men – and many companies were down to two or three men, with all their officers lost. One brief comment, that 'They died apologizing and weeping', sums up the catastrophe that befell them.*

By July 1944 the three Japanese divisions that were intended as the vanguard of the march on Delhi had been savaged and defeated, but the struggle for Burma was far from over. The hard-fought British victories around Kohima and Imphal at least eliminated the threat to Stilwell's position in north Burma. While the battles raged he was back with his Chinese divisions in the Hukawng valley, now even more determined to drive forward, capture Myitkyina and reopen the Burma road.

As he prepared for the drive to Myitkyina, Stilwell had a short period in which he reflected on the psychology of command and measured theory against his experience of jungle warfare. He wrote:

> A good commander is a man of high character (this is the most impor-
> tant attribute), with the power of decision [the] next most important
> attribute. He must have moral backbone, and this stems from high
> character; and he must be physically courageous or successfully conceal
> the fact that he is not. He must know the tools of his trade, tactics and
> logistics. He must be impartial. He must be calm under stress. He must
> reward promptly and punish justly. He must be accessible, human,
> humble, patient, forbearing. He should listen to advice, make his own
> decision, carry it out with energy.
>
> Unless a commander is human, he cannot understand the reactions
> of his men. If he is human, the pressure on him intensifies tremen-
> dously. The callous man has no mental struggle over jeopardising the
> lives of 10,000 men; the human commander cannot avoid this strug-
> gle. It is constant and wearing, and yet necessary, for the men can sense
> the commander's difficulty. There are many ways in which he can show
> his interest in them and they respond, once they believe it is real. Then
> you get mutual confidence, the basis of real discipline.

* Kazuo Tamayama and John Nunneley, *Tales by Japanese Soldiers of the Burma Campaign, 1942–1945*, Cassell, London, 2000, p. 208.

Generals get sharply criticised. They are the birds who shelter themselves in dugouts and send the soldiers out to get killed. They cover
themselves with medals, won at the expense of the lives of their men,
who are thrown in regardless, to compensate for faulty or poorly
thought-out plans.

There are really not many [generals] like that. The average general
envies the buck private; when things go wrong, the private can blame
the general, but the general can blame only himself. The private carries
the woes of one man; the general carries the woes of all. He is con-
scious always of the responsibility on his shoulders, of the relatives of
the men entrusted to him, and of their feelings. He must act so that
he can face those fathers and mothers without shame or remorse.
How can he do this? By constant care, by meticulous thought and
preparation, by worry, by insistence on high standards in everything,
by rewards and punishment, by impartiality, by an example of calm and
confidence. It all adds up to character.

Q: If a man has enough character to be a good commander, does
he ever doubt himself? He should not. In my case, I doubt myself.
Therefore, I am in all probability not a good commander.

This thoughtful piece was accompanied by his normal sharp and often
self-deprecating observations. He mentioned a coloured GI who said,
'It sure is tough to make an old man like you come up and work in
this country.' Sent some war dogs, he commented that he would rather
have had soldiers but joked about training the dogs to smell the difference between Americans, Burmese and Japanese. Then, with his deep
anti-Limey prejudices coming out, he added, 'The British of course
don't smell – they tub regularly. By God the longer I live the more I
appreciate George Washington and the boys of the Revolution.'

During March and April 1944 the main focus was on the battles
around Kohima and Imphal, which set the scene for the next phase
of the campaign. At the same time Stilwell was prodding his divisions
forward and preparing for what he hoped would be a signal victory
that would confound his critics and justify all he had struggled to
achieve – the capture of Myitkyina.

CHAPTER 11

The Drive to Myitkyina

While the crisis at Kohima and Imphal continued, Stilwell concentrated on the hard-fought advance of the Chinese divisions and Merrill's Marauders down the Hukawng valley. At Walawbum they had won a significant victory although Stilwell's hopes of trapping the whole of General Tanaka's 18 Division were not realised. After Walawbum, Stilwell pursued the same tactics of advancing along the line of the road to Kamaing with his two Chinese divisions supported by armour, while the Marauders were divided into two main columns which made flank marches to reach behind the Japanese and block the road further south. The smaller force made a shallow detour and rejoined the road at Shadazup in the Mogaung valley, while a two-battalion group made a wider sweep to reach Inkangahtawng, which lay athwart the Kamaing road and the Mogaung river. These advances brought some very fierce clashes with the Japanese, who now realised the significance of Stilwell's attacks and were determined to prevent him from reaching Kamaing. From there he would have been able to threaten all the divisions attacking Imphal.

The Marauders reached Inkangahtawng and established a road block, but the Japanese, realising that this threatened their whole position, counterattacked with a brigade of troops sent from Kamaing and forced the Marauders to move off to Nphum Ga. At this critical stage of the action Merrill suffered a slight heart attack; Stilwell ordered him to be evacuated, and the ever dependable Colonel Hunter took over. There followed days of confused, vicious close-quarter fighting, and on 3 March the Marauders in Nphum Ga were completely surrounded. This substantial element of the Japanese 18 Division was still

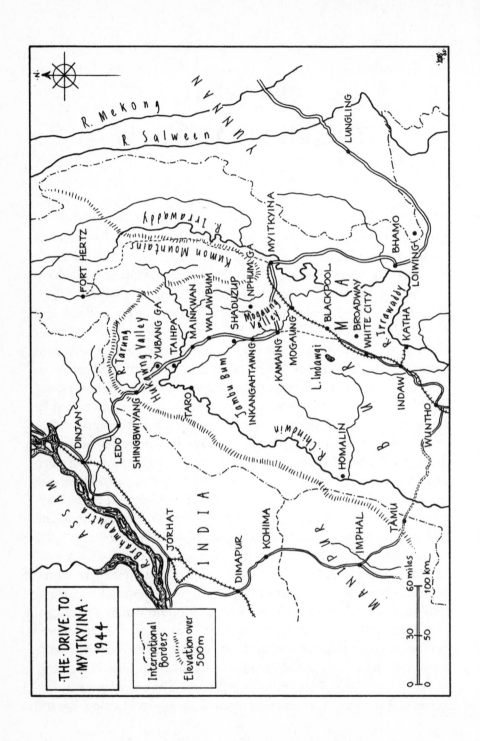

well supplied with artillery, mortars, machine guns and ammunition and subjected the Marauders to a heavy and prolonged bombardment. Inside Nphum Ga the defenders suffered appallingly. They were short of ammunition, food and water, and the whole area was littered with the decaying and putrefying corpses of men and mules, mostly covered by a blanket of flies and an unbearable stench. The gruesome siege dragged on until 9 April – Easter Sunday – which was observed under similar conditions in Kohima. Then the other Marauder units fought their way in to rescue their comrades and break the siege. Surprisingly, in this prolonged fight the Marauders lost just twenty-five killed but killed over four hundred Japanese. Stilwell followed events closely, and when the siege was lifted he ordered a brief halt and special air drops of food and mail. The only comment in his diary is 'Galahad is O.K. Hard fight at Nphum.'

Nphum Ga saw the start of a dangerous new factor in the north Burma fighting. Many survivors of Nphum Ga were exhausted and shell-shocked, and Stilwell was either slow or reluctant to recognise this. His driving passion to reach Myitkyina seemed to sweep aside all other considerations, and this was to have tragic and disastrous consequences for his relations not only with the Marauders but also with the Chindits, who were shortly to come under his command.

On 5 March 1944, the same day that Mutaguchi started his three-division attack on Imphal and Kohima, the Chindits launched their main campaign, Operation Thursday. The chief focus of this was the establishment of 77 Brigade under the intrepid Brigadier Michael Calvert in a 'stronghold' north of Indaw code named Broadway. The stronghold was Wingate's new concept in long-range penetration. It envisaged the setting up of a brigade-sized unit behind enemy lines that would be supplied entirely by air and located in rough country where the enemy could not approach with tanks or heavy artillery. A stronghold would be a powerfully defended base from which the Chindits could spread out over a wide area to cut road and rail links, ambush convoys and destroy supply dumps. A second brigade – 111 under Brigadier William Lentaigne – was flown in to Katha, slightly east of Indaw, code named Chowringhee. A substantial part of this brigade – Morris Force – was detached and sent northeast to operate on the road between Bhamo and Myitkyina. A glance at the map will show that the main purpose of the Chindit operation was to strangle the whole supply system to Tanaka's 18 Division and the forces facing Stilwell by closing the road and rail links at Indaw and the only other road running north from Bhamo. After a few days at Broadway, Calvert felt strong enough to establish a subsidiary base almost astride the road and railway in the narrow valley near Mawlu. This became known as White City because of the number of parachutes that festooned the trees. The Chindit brigades not only destroyed supplies going to the Japanese units facing Stilwell – their first priority – but they also seriously damaged supplies and communications to the three divisions attacking Imphal and Kohima.

When the two Chindit brigades landed near Indaw – 'in the enemy's guts' as Wingate put it – the Japanese reacted swiftly and powerfully. They transferred major units from 18 Division facing Stilwell and from the division facing Yoke Force in Yunnan, along with a special fighting force of nearly divisional strength that was intended for the battle north of Imphal. The main Japanese counterattack fell on Broadway and White City, but Calvert, a Royal Engineers explosives expert renowned for his macabre booby traps, gave outstanding leadership. Over a period of more than ten weeks after 5 March, Broadway and White City repulsed constant and ferocious Japanese attacks. The defences were organised with meticulous care and determination, with mines, barbed wire, fixed-line machine-gun fire and pre-planned 3-inch mortar targets, with the Air Commando Mustangs on ready call. So many thousands of Japanese dead lay around the perimeter that pilots of the light aircraft that flew in to pick up the wounded from Broadway knew when they were close because of the stench from the corpses on the barbed wire.

The role of the long-range penetration units and how long they should operate behind enemy lines was an issue that caused serious friction and intense bitterness between Stilwell on the one hand and the Chindits and Merrill's Marauders on the other. Stilwell pointed out that the Chinese had been in action since November 1943 and asked why the Chindits should be taken out of the line when they had only flown in on 5 March 1944. He failed to see that a unit behind enemy lines and under constant attack was subject to much greater danger and stress than one in normal campaign conditions.

Calvert, the most successful Chindit leader after Wingate, commanded 77 Brigade from early March to the middle of May at Broadway and for a further two months when his brigade moved up to Mogaung. Later he wrote two classic books on jungle fighting,[*] in which he weighs up that difficult issue. He admired Slim as one of the best British commanders of the Second World War but maintained that he had a blind spot about the Chindits and also about the use of parachute troops. One tragic incident brought this issue to the fore.

The Chindits and the concept of long-range penetration were the brainchild of Orde Wingate, who fearlessly espoused their cause. Tragically for them, after visiting Broadway and congratulating the Chindits his plane crashed on 24 March and he was killed. His death was a major factor in the future destiny of the Chindits and Stilwell. The appointment of Wingate's successor involved one of the most bizarre incidents of the Burma war. 111 Brigade under Lentaigne had flown in to Chowringhee but had not been heavily involved with the enemy. Despite this, Lentaigne had apparently lost his nerve and 'his bowels turned to water'. An even earthier comment was that he kept shitting in his pants. John Masters, Lentaigne's Brigade Major and later well known as an author, faced a serious dilemma. He was urgently pondering how he could get a message out to Chindit HQ saying that Lentaigne must be relieved of his command when a signal came in that Lentaigne had been appointed to command the whole Chindit operation. This meant that instead of the fiery and abrasive Wingate arguing the Chindit case with Slim and Stilwell, there was the supine Lentaigne whose nerve had broken. He had been a brave colonel but was now hopelessly out of his depth.

Apart from his weakness, the appointment of Lentaigne had other repercussions that were to cost the Chindits dear. His unit had been transferred to the Chindits against their wishes, and with both Morris and Masters he openly derided Wingate's ideas. When Lentaigne flew

[*] Michael Calvert, *Prisoners of Hope*, Cape, London, 1952, and *Fighting Mad*, Bantam, London, 1964.

out to take over the Chindit HQ, a substantial part of his brigade was detached and sent up to block the Bhamo to Myitkyina road. Then, to the amazement of the brigade's officers, he appointed his crony Masters over the heads of more senior colonels to command the main part of the brigade.

At this stage the role of the Chindits – and particularly their relationship and involvement with Stilwell – was influenced by strategic decisions. On the ground, Calvert's defence of Broadway and White City against all the forces the Japanese could throw at him (including the new 53 Division which had been flown in to support the attack on Imphal but was diverted to Broadway) had completely closed the rail and road supplies to the Japanese army facing Stilwell. Further east Morris Force, which had been detached from Lentaigne's brigade, had hurried north and cut the road to Myitkyina from Bhamo. Thus the Chindit operation had fulfilled the agreement made at Quebec that their main role would be to support Stilwell.

While the battles at Kohima and Imphal were still raging, Slim went to Stilwell's headquarters and discussed the wider issues, including the role of the Chinese divisions. Stilwell continued his disgruntled criticism of the Limeys and their commanders, which was in sharp contrast to Slim's more generous attitude. After the visit Slim wrote:

> In all these actions Stilwell kept a close hand on the Chinese troops, steadying them when they faltered, prodding them when they hesitated, even finding their battalions for them when they lost them ... Stilwell met me at the airfield looking more like a duck hunter than ever, with his wind jacket, campaign hat, and leggings ... I was struck, as I always was when I visited Stilwell's headquarters, how unnecessarily primitive all its arrangements were. There was, compared with my own or other headquarters, no shortage of transport or supplies, yet he delighted in an exhibition of rough living, which like his omission of rank badges and the rest was designed to foster the idea of the tough, hard-bitten, plain, fighting general. Goodness knows he was tough and wiry enough to be recognised as such without the play acting ... Stilwell, thank heaven, had a sense of humour and he could and did, not infrequently, laugh at himself.

One topic that was high on their agenda was the possibility of moving the Chindit brigade westwards from Broadway so as to have a more direct influence on the fighting at Imphal. This would have been a great asset at the time, but Slim rejected the idea and kept loyally to the Quebec agreement. He wrote later that it was a mistaken decision and the Chindits would have been more effective fighting against the Japanese in retreat from Imphal. Next Stilwell, Slim and Lentaigne discussed the proposal that was crucial to the future of the Chindits – that 77 Brigade from Broadway and the main part of 111 Brigade under Masters should move north in order to have a more direct effect on the battles in the Mogaung valley and the approaches to Myitkyina.

The whole issue was bedevilled by the continuing suspicion between the Americans, the British and the Chinese and between the different pressure groups. The Chiefs of Staff in Washington had to decide on priorities between the demands of the build-up for the Normandy invasion in June, of MacArthur's drive across the Pacific, and of Stilwell's fight to capture Myitkyina and reopen the Burma Road. Most Americans were suspicious of British aims and continued to believe that Mountbatten, who previously had commanded Britain's Combined Operations Forces, in fact preferred an amphibious operation that might lead to the recapture of Singapore. This suspicion substantially increased when the headquarters of SEAC moved from Delhi to Kandy in Ceylon (Sri Lanka) in April 1944. Critics reasonably asked why such a huge logistical exercise should be undertaken when the battles for Mogaung, Myitkyina, Imphal and Kohima were still raging.

Stilwell, on the ground in the Mogaung valley, had sound reasons for opposing the idea of moving the Chindit brigades to the north. By blocking the supplies to the Japanese divisions that faced him, the Chindits had made a major contribution to his success – though he never acknowledged this. If they moved north towards Mogaung he feared, correctly, that the large number of Japanese units which were still attacking Broadway and White City would move rapidly north as soon as they were abandoned. He wanted the Chindits to stay at Broadway to keep the supply routes closed and to continue to tie up the substantial Japanese forces in the Indaw area. He argued this case vigorously with Slim and Mountbatten and the Chiefs of Staff. He continued to argue, as he had consistently since the end of the 1942 retreat, that his top priority was to reopen the land route to China. Romanus and Sunderland, in describing this matter, state that 'Stilwell feared that in retreating to the north the Chindits would bring with them the swarms of Japanese they had attacked'.* Slim, in his book *Defeat into Victory*, does not even mention the decision about the role of the Chindits although he was closely and directly involved in it. It is not certain who initially put forward the proposal to move the main Chindit units to the north, though Lentaigne, like Slim a former Gurkha officer, appears to have been the main supporter of the idea. Slim seemed to be happy to go along with it, and in fact had to go to see Stilwell to gain his acceptance. Two factors probably influenced the decision: the difficulty in supplying Broadway and White City by air during the monsoon, expected in mid-May, and Lentaigne's rejection of Wingate's thesis. Shelford Bidwell, who was generally critical of Wingate, wrote that Lentaigne 'would have to change from milling around in scattered columns all over the jungles of Northern Burma in Chindit fashion, and concentrate his forces according to more orthodox tactics'.† Thus, for a variety of complex reasons Slim and Lentaigne implemented the crucial decision: that Broadway and White City should be abandoned, that 77 and 111 Brigades would move north towards Mogaung, and finally – and disastrously for the Chindits – that they would come under Stilwell's command.

From the time that Stilwell took over the Chindits there were four main elements to the north Burma campaign: the move of 111 Brigade to a stronghold, code named Blackpool, near Mogaung; the campaign, under his orders, of 77 Brigade to capture Mogaung; the approach of Morris Force to Myitkyina from the south; and his own main drive down the Mogaung valley and the dramatic approach by Merrill's Marauders to Myitkyina. For the sake of clarity these will be described separately.

* Romanus and Sunderland, *Stilwell's Command Problems*, p. 221.
† Shelford Bidwell, *The Chindit War*, Hodder, London, 1979, p. 206.

111 Brigade and Blackpool

Militarily this was the least important Chindit operation, but it illustrates in dramatic fashion many of the major issues that arose between
Stilwell and the Chindits, as well as the significance of Wingate's ideas
on long-range penetration. The failures of 111 Brigade also gave
ammunition to Wingate's detractors – especially those in the military
establishment, who to this day nurture their unreasoning criticism.
The injustice of such criticism will become obvious because the failures
of 111 Brigade were caused almost entirely by Masters' rejection of
all Wingate's precepts.

The brigade flew into Chowringhee (Indaw) on 6 March 1944
immediately after 77 Brigade flew to Broadway. They made almost no
contact with the Japanese and, largely because of Lentaigne's poor
leadership, spent five days milling around, at the end of which they
had achieved nothing and were totally exhausted. They should have
destroyed the railway south of Indaw but failed to do so. There was much
comment in 111 Brigade that when behind enemy lines Lentaigne
and Masters – and their other crony Morris, who led the group up to
the Bhamo road – were 'excessively timid'.

When Lentaigne, after he took over the whole Chindit operation,
first proposed to send 111 Brigade, now under Masters, to form a block
at Blackpool, Calvert and the other Chindit leaders were aghast because
the plan rejected all of Wingate's ideas. In spite of this opposition, on
23 April Lentaigne ordered the brigade to move north and establish
a block on the railway where it approached Mogaung. At the same time
77 Brigade was ordered to move out of Broadway and, after a brief rest
in the Gangaw hills, to move towards Mogaung. There were now five
Chindit brigades in Burma, and, because Lentaigne and Slim did not
intend to use them in their proper long-range penetration role, there
are fairly solid grounds for the view of the critics that a great many
highly trained troops spent time wandering about in the jungle without achieving very much. Before his death Wingate had foreseen, and
had outlined in detail, an aggressive long-range penetration role for the
Chindits as the Japanese retreated from Imphal and Kohima. These ideas
were ignored, and under Lentaigne and Masters the Chindits were con-
demned to massive casualties because Wingate's precepts were ignored.

Masters described the Blackpool campaign in his book *The Road Past Mandalay*. He wrote that he thought he should have challenged the order to go to Blackpool but felt it would make no difference 'because the hand that pulled us away was not that of Joe (Lentaigne), but of Slim acceding to Stilwell'.[*] This view is inaccurate since, as is now well known, Stilwell strongly opposed the Chindits' move, but it does highlight Slim's responsibility for what happened. Masters describes in detail how he decided on the exact position of the Blackpool base, and his description proves that he totally ignored Wingate's basic rules for a stronghold. The first and absolute rule for a stronghold was to place it in rough country where the enemy could not approach with heavy artillery or armour, with the result that the stronghold could be defended against everything else with weapons that could be flown in – as was brilliantly illustrated at Broadway. Masters ignored this basic precept at dire cost. Before his brigade had time to dig slit trenches at Blackpool or put up barbed wire they were pounded by Japanese artillery. Experienced Chindits felt an atmosphere of trepidation and doom as they approached Blackpool, and 'Underlying all their anger and fury was the conviction that if Wingate had been alive they would not have been at Blackpool at all'.[†] 111 Brigade established Blackpool early on 8 May 1944, and from that moment the Japanese artillery, together with their terrifying 6-inch mortar, continued the daily assault. On 17 May they put down a particularly savage barrage. Louis Allen wrote that the Japanese barrage merely reinforced Wingate's precepts.[‡] Another of his fundamental precepts was the establishment of a serviceable airstrip both to bring in food and ammunition and to fly out the wounded. At Blackpool there was a dangerous hump in the middle of the airstrip that wrecked several aircraft, inhibiting use of the strip. Then the Japanese brought up anti-aircraft guns along with their other artillery and shot down planes coming in to land. Finally the severe monsoon storms made flying very difficult, and during the last disastrous days

[*] John Masters, *The Road past Mandalay*, Michael Joseph, London, 1961, p. 219.
[†] David Rooney, *Wingate and the Chindits: Redressing the Balance*, Arms & Armour Press, London, 1994, p. 139.
[‡] Allen, *Burma: The Longest War*, p. 358.

of the occupation of Blackpool almost no supplies were flown in and no wounded were flown out. Unlike Wingate, who constantly visited his front-line units, Lentaigne, who never visited Blackpool, seemed by his indifference to compound their suffering and became an object of thinly veiled contempt. The troops muttered, 'Had Wingate lived this would never have happened.'

These were the unhappy and disastrous events that led to a major crisis between Stilwell and Lentaigne. Lentaigne's plan had been for two brigades – 14 and 77 – to support the Blackpool base, but because of a particularly severe onslaught by the monsoon neither of the brigades arrived in time to help. 111 Brigade began to set up Blackpool on 8 May. By 20 May, with dwindling supplies of ammunition and food, increasing numbers of badly wounded men and the pounding of the whole area by Japanese artillery and monsoon storms, Masters was sending urgent signals demanding immediate relief or permission to withdraw. Later he wrote harrowing descriptions of the suffering, but he never admitted that most of it was caused by his initial mistakes and his rejection of Wingate's precepts for establishing a stronghold. As often happens in war, he was fiercely critical of everyone else. Of the time when the other brigades failed to reach him he wrote: '40 flaming columns of Chindit bullshit sat on their arses and drank tea and wondered how we were getting on.'*

On 24 May another Japanese attack forced back the perimeter held by a Gurkha unit and the whole position rapidly became untenable. Masters gave the order to withdraw on 25 May and then had to make a heart-rending decision. He agreed that gravely wounded men, some of whom had lost arms or legs and could not possibly be moved, should be shot rather than leave them to the doubtful mercies of the Japanese. The shattered remains of the brigade then moved slowly south towards a village they had passed only seventeen days before. There is ample evidence of the mutinous feelings of many Chindits who thought that Blackpool was doomed from the start. One wrote, 'If Stilwell or Lentaigne or even Slim had appeared they would not have lived to see the dawn.'†

* Masters, *The Road Past Mandalay*, p. 243.
† Rooney, *Wingate and the Chindits*, p. 143.

The disaster of Blackpool and the Chindit 111 Brigade has been described in some detail because Masters' decision to abandon the base became a major issue in the fraught, tense and bitter discussions between Stilwell on the one hand and Mountbatten, Slim, Lentaigne and SEAC on the other. Stilwell demanded further efforts from the Chindits – as he did from Merrill's Marauders – at a time when the men were in such a pitiable condition that further effort was impossible. The doctor with 111 Brigade, an intrepid Ulsterman who was himself recommended for the VC, told Masters that most of the brigade were on the threshold of death from exhaustion, undernourishment, exposure and strain. Men died simply from a cold, a cut finger or the least physical exertion. Stilwell saw the abandonment of Blackpool as another example of cowardly Limeys rejecting his orders and refusing to fight. One wonders if he would have voiced that view if he had had the slightest knowledge of their physical and mental plight.

Romanus and Sunderland described the moment when Stilwell learned that Blackpool had been abandoned. 'While Stilwell and Lentaigne were conferring on 25 May on holding a position (Blackpool) near the railway ... and were agreeing that it should be evacuated only in a case of emergency, the block was already being evacuated. Stilwell's anger at this course of events, together with the steadily declining strength of the Chindits, created a crisis which soon required the attention of the highest S.E.A.C. officers.'* This sorry tale of bitter recrimination between Stilwell and all the Chindit units continued from May through to July. Behind it lay Stilwell's obsession with capturing Myitkyina and his failure to understand the long-range penetration role of the Chindits. He held to his view that if a man could walk he could be used as front-line infantry. And his anger followed 111 Brigade. After leaving Blackpool the brigade reached a location near Lake Indawgyi having lost more than one-third of its strength, carrying nearly 200 badly wounded men and every day losing men who died from total exhaustion. 'They were so spent and drained that at any rate no further operations could be called for. Then came the incredible order: 111 Brigade was to move out and attack Mogaung from the west while 77 Brigade took it from the east.'†

* Romanus and Sunderland, *Stilwell's Command Problems*, p. 221.
† Allen, *Burma: The Longest War*, p. 362.

After a very brief lull during which over 600 casualties were flown out from Lake Indawgyi in Sunderland flying boats, the brigade accepted its orders and moved north through the continuing monsoon towards Mogaung. It was ordered to capture a hill, Point 2171, overlooking the Mogaung river. There, from 20 June to 5 July they endured what many survivors said were worse conditions than at Blackpool. The Japanese held the hill with well-prepared defences, but eventually the Gurkhas – in a wild attack led by a Gurkha officer who won a posthumous VC – finally captured it. Then in July, for no obvious tactical reason and after more than two weeks of suffering and carnage, the brigade was ordered to withdraw – prompting the bitter question, 'What was the point of attacking the hill in the first place?' Increasingly they believed it was the weak Lentaigne passing on the hellish orders of Stilwell. When they withdrew Masters threatened to resign his commission unless his men had a medical inspection. One hundred men were found to be fit for duty out of a brigade of more than 3,000 who had moved to Blackpool on 8 May.

77 Brigade and Mogaung

When Lentaigne first proposed the idea that 77 Brigade should move north from Broadway and, with 111 Brigade, approach Mogaung, Calvert could hardly believe it. He had provided exemplary leadership at Broadway and White City and had repulsed every Japanese attack. 77 Brigade had destroyed the strength of far more Japanese fighting units than Stilwell ever faced. Calvert, like others, was horrified because Lentaigne's orders ignored all of Wingate's precepts, which had been fundamental to the whole Chindit approach. He was warned that his signals came close to insubordination. In the end he had to give way, and with a heavy heart he handed over Broadway to the Nigerian Chindit Brigade and led 77 Brigade northwards to the Gangaw hills. Here they rested for a few days, took additional air drops of food and were able to enjoy relief from the stench of rotting bodies which had been their permanent accompaniment at Broadway and White City.

After a few days recuperation the brigade set out again to march towards Mogaung. They were now under Stilwell's control. Two things should be stressed: Stilwell did not want to have the Chindits under his command, and from the start he used them as normal infantry and appeared to have no conception of their long-range penetration role. No Chindit unit had artillery or tank support, and now they were to be used against a carefully fortified base which the Japanese were determined to defend at all costs.

As 77 Brigade moved towards Mogaung, Lentaigne, who never visited them on the ground, sent Calvert new orders: he should approach Mogaung as swiftly as possible but would detach a part of the brigade to assist 111 Brigade at Blackpool. Calvert sent off a sizable force, including a Gurkha unit, but under the prolonged monsoon downpour they found the Namying river to be a raging torrent which it was impossible to cross. They never reached Blackpool. They had to retrace their steps, and they suffered so much from the bites of leeches picked up in the jungle that many men had to have blood transfusions. Meanwhile, leading patrols from the reunited brigade reported that about 4,000 Japanese were holding Mogaung in a formidable defensive position that covered the rail, river and road approach to Myitkyina.

As he led his brigade north, Calvert heard on 18 May 1944 that Stilwell's forces had captured Myitkyina. This was not in fact true. Rather, Merrill's Marauders had captured the airfield, a couple of miles to the west. From that time on Stilwell was totally obsessed with capturing the town. This warped his judgement and prompted him to make a series of decisions that were to cost the Chindits dear. Calvert still hoped to be able to relieve 111 Brigade at Blackpool, but the raging jungle torrents made this impossible, and on 25 May he too heard that it had been abandoned. On the same day Lentaigne moved the Chindit headquarters to Shadazup in order to be close to Stilwell's HQ, and it was there that he suffered the full onslaught of Stilwell's anger at the news of Blackpool. Then, hoping to appear decisive, on 27 May he issued a peremptory order to Calvert: 'You will take Mogaung.'

Lentaigne, sitting at Shadazup, illustrates one of the classic weaknesses that can beset a commander in the field – a weakness identified by Sun Tsu in China in 400 BC. Although he was now fairly close to the Chindit brigades, he never visited them and he never saw the terrain they had to cover. As a result he continued to issue orders that bore little relation to the situation on the ground and which the brigade commanders increasingly ignored. Two more Chindit brigades – 14 and the Nigerian Brigade – were ordered to the rescue of Blackpool, but they did not arrive in time, and after 25 May they moved slowly on towards Mogaung. It was left to Calvert and 77 Brigade, which had been behind Japanese lines since 5 March, to make the assault on Mogaung.

As the brigade approached Mogaung they had a series of fierce clashes with the Japanese. On one day alone the Chindits lost thirty killed or seriously wounded, but they inflicted heavier casualties on the enemy. Because of the appalling casualties Calvert was determined to seize an area where he could set up an airstrip so that supplies could be brought in and the wounded flown out. He was also determined to build up supplies of ammunition – especially bombs for the 3-inch mortars – so that there would be no shortage in the coming battle. At the same time he received support and valuable intelligence from the local Kachin people, as Merrill's Marauders did further east. The Chindits fought their way slowly forward. In one village about a mile from Mogaung they captured several supply dumps and a well-camouflaged field hospital, complete with drugs. The patients fled or committed suicide. This success improved Chindit morale and they responded magnificently to Calvert's leadership as he was always there in the thick of the fighting. On 10 June the Gurkhas captured the vital railway bridge on the approach to the town despite sustaining more than 100 casualties. Calvert had urged his units forward, hoping to capture the town before more Japanese battalions arrived from their victory at Blackpool. This, however, did not prove possible, and on 12 June two Japanese battalions joined the defenders. The next day Calvert called a meeting of his battalion commanders, who came in with gruesome reports. Most battalions had been reduced to less than half strength and the whole brigade could now muster only about five hundred men who were fighting fit. Most had already been wounded and were suffering from malaria and jungle sores. Supplies of food, medicine and ammunition had become increasingly erratic because requisitions now went through the chaotic headquarters at Shadazup.

The Chindits could not dig slit trenches because the ground was waterlogged and they suffered daily casualties from the Japanese artillery. Determined to eliminate the guns, Calvert organised an attack by Mustang fighter bombers and by all the available mortars, followed by an infantry assault using the newly arrived flame-throwers. The Japanese artillery position was overrun on 18 June, but at the cost of fifty casualties.

For days Calvert had been promised the support of the 114th Chinese Regiment, and that evening the first Chinese troops arrived. Communication problems meant that close liaison was not easy, but Calvert had recruited some Hong Kong Chinese into the Chindits who helped to overcome most of the language difficulties. The most serious difficulty came from an American liaison officer who caused dissension and whom Calvert dubbed Colonel Bluster. Following Chiang's precepts, the Chinese preferred not to make frontal attacks, but just when Calvert was close to despair at his reduced numbers and the loss of so many fine men and close friends he was told that the Chinese had occupied a key sector by the railway station. As this covered a vital flank position, Calvert decided to put in a final attack at 0300 hours on 24 June. Once again the Mustangs started the attack, followed by more than 1,200 mortar bombs. Even with this onslaught the attackers from the Gurkha and South Stafford battalions came under murderous machine-gun fire, but with good covering fire and the use of flame-throwers a final desperate charge drove out the Japanese. As the position was consolidated the Chindits suddenly suffered more casualties from one flank. They discovered, at heavy cost, that the Chinese had not occupied the station area. The source of the false information that cost so many Chindit lives was the odious Colonel Bluster.

In a brief lull after the Japanese were finally despatched and Calvert's troops won the great victory of Mogaung, a BBC newsflash announced that the town had been captured by Chinese–American forces. The Chindits were outraged. The false information had been sent, of course, by Colonel Bluster. Colonel Li, the commanding officer of the Chinese regiment, quickly brought the wretched fellow to Calvert's HQ to apologise. The colonel himself also apologised and stated his clear understanding that it was Calvert's brigade, whose bravery they all admired, which had captured Mogaung. Needless to say this statement did not receive the same publicity as the previous lie. Calvert alleviated a little of the fury by sending a signal to Stilwell's headquarters: 'Mogaung having been taken by the Chinese, 77 Brigade is proceeding to take Umbrage.'* The story goes that an intelligence officer at Stilwell's HQ remarked that Umbrage must be a small place because he could not find it on the map.

Calvert's magnificent leadership, evident since the launch of Operation Thursday on 5 March, has been internationally recognised, but rather than rejoicing at a signal victory he agonised over whether his loyalty to Wingate had made him ask too much of the ever faithful 77 Brigade, whose bones were now scattered along the grim trail from Broadway to Mogaung. British records show serious concern that Stilwell's staff had at this time become sycophantic and that, partly out of fear, they would only tell him what he wanted to hear. The problem is reflected in two highly respected American accounts of the capture of Mogaung. Romanus and Sunderland merely wrote that 'Mogaung fell on 26 June and both units claimed credit for the victory',† while Tuchman records: 'Mogaung was taken, causing a renewed outburst of the public relations war over rival claims for credit.'‡ In modern conflicts such as the Gulf War or the Iraq War the tensions of high command are well publicised – the incandescent exchanges in the First Gulf War between the American commanders H. Norman Schwartzkopf and Colin Powell were there for all to see. If this could happen after a few days of war, who can assess the tension felt by Calvert after leading a brigade behind enemy lines, constantly in contact with the enemy, for 114 days?

Almost immediately after his victory at Mogaung, Calvert received the order from Lentaigne to march his brigade to Hopin. He refused point blank and said that he would stand by his decision before Stilwell or Slim or anyone. The relationship between Stilwell and the

* David Rooney, *Mad Mike*, Leo Cooper, London, 1997, p. 105.
† Romanus and Sunderland, *Stilwell's Command Problems*, p. 121.
‡ Tuchman, *Sand against the Wind*, p. 453.

pathetically weak Lentaigne now broke down completely, and on 30 June, only four days after the capture of Mogaung, Mountbatten was forced to fly in to deal with the problem. Many of 77 Brigade who had kept going to the end simply lay down and died. Horrified by their deplorable physical state, Mountbatten ordered an immediate medical inspection – shrewdly including Merrill in the inspection team. Stilwell had driven the Marauders to such lengths that they refused to fight, so Merrill felt sympathy for the plight of the Chindits. The report was decisive, stating that all the survivors of 77 and 111 Brigades were physically and mentally exhausted. Mountbatten, the only officer senior to Stilwell, ordered that they should be flown out at once.

This decision took some time to reach Calvert who, to prevent any more foolish orders coming through, closed down the brigade's radio. This gave another opportunity to the vile Colonel Bluster, who sent messages to Stilwell saying that 77 Brigade 'were cowards, yellow, deserted, they walked off the field of battle, they should all be arrested'.* Calvert added that Bluster was the logical outcome of Stilwell's anglophobia.

A few days later Calvert was taken to Shadazup, where a nervous Lentaigne accompanied him to an interview with Stilwell. Stilwell, sitting with his son and Boatner, his second in command, began aggressively. Calvert's description continues:

> 'Well, Calvert, I have been wanting to meet you for some time.'
> 'I have been wanting to meet you too, Sir.'
> 'You send some very strong signals, Calvert.'
> 'You should see the ones my Brigade Major wouldn't let me send.'

This was a moment of high tension when Calvert's career and even the future of the Chindits were at stake, but to everyone's relief Stilwell roared with laughter and agreed that he had the same problem sending signals to Washington. Calvert had hit exactly the right note, and Stilwell showed that he respected a man of mettle like himself. Now

* Rooney, *Mad Mike*, p. 108.

he listened while Calvert outlined the achievements of 77 Brigade: the prolonged battles at Broadway and White City, where his brigade fought off far more Japanese forces than those opposing Stilwell. They had completely blocked all the supply routes going north to Stilwell's front, they had hoped that the Chinese–American force would advance down the railway towards them, and they had captured Mogaung at terrible cost, causing tough commanders to weep at the casualties. Calvert explained their fury at the false claim to the capture of Mogaung and concluded: 'I am sorry, Sir, if I disobeyed orders but I think you will realize the strain we were under.'

During this conversation Stilwell sat amazed, interjecting with 'Is this true?' or 'Why was I not told that?' He began to realise how far his staff had concealed the achievements and successes of the Chindits, and he immediately awarded Calvert the American Silver Star. Calvert was strong enough to challenge and enlighten Stilwell, but the American's anglophobia had seriously affected his staff – with dire consequences for the remaining Chindit unit, Morris Force, which was blocking the road from Bhamo to Myitkyina.

Morris Force
After 111 Brigade landed at Chowringhee under Lentaigne, a battalion-strong group, largely of Gurkhas, was detached and marched swiftly northeast towards the Bhamo–Myitkyina road.

This small force illustrates several key issues that affected the role of the Chindits, the leadership of a unit behind enemy lines and the increasingly sour relations between Stilwell and the British. Morris was a lieutenant colonel, transferred with Lentaigne and against their will to the Chindits. The overall failure of Morris Force raised another question – whether the leadership of a unit behind enemy lines demanded a quality of bravery, initiative and determination which few people had. Calvert clearly had this in abundance, as did some of his colonels who were inspired by his example, but certainly Lentaigne and Morris did not. Terence O'Brien, an RAF liaison officer with Morris Force, described Morris as 'excessively timid'.* This consideration of

---

* Terence O'Brien, *Out of the Blue*, Collins, London, 1984, p. 35.

the quality of leadership – which applied equally to the units of Merrill's Marauders – was raised by Charles Carfrae, a column commander in the Nigerian Chindit Brigade. He stated in *Chindit Column* that when placed behind enemy lines some normally sound and brave officers were 'reduced to pathetic ineptitude'.* Sadly, Morris proved to be one of these. In *Out of the Blue* O'Brien made significant comments on the leadership issue. He wrote that Morris's column was always retreating into the wings, while 94 Column under the spirited and energetic Peter Cane was always rushing into action. Cane showed an admirably robust attitude. His column experienced serious problems of wireless communication from the remote hills where they operated. When he demanded a replacement set he was told by HQ to experiment with the aerial in different positions. He replied, 'I have experimented with the aerial in every position except one, and that I leave to you.' The replacement came the next day.

In spite of Morris's inadequacy, Morris Force all but blocked the Bhamo road from the middle of March onwards. Morris's poor leadership was illustrated when Cane's column attacked and destroyed a vital bridge over a gorge. Morris's column should have attacked and sealed off the other side of the village, but instead it moved off without informing Cane. 'Many in the force felt that this was a cowardly action.'†

In his book O'Brien vividly recorded Morris's ineptitude, and also gave evidence of the feelings of the Chindits when they were handed over to Stilwell in the middle of May 1944. They were already aware of the generally hostile view of the British command towards the Chindits, and O'Brien wrote that 'The enticing solution, one that got rid of us, and might also placate the vitriolic Stilwell, was to hand over the Chindits to him completely and let him give them orders direct, rather than keep snapping at high command with his savage criticism'.‡

On 18 May Morris Force received the dramatic but inaccurate news that Merrill's Marauders had captured Myitkyina. This caused

---

* Charles Carfrae, *Chindit Column*, Kimber, London, 1985.
† Rooney, *Wingate and the Chindits*, p. 150.
‡ O'Brien, *Out of the Blue*, p. 217.

rejoicing and they assumed, as did Merrill's Marauders, that they would soon be flown out. They were tragically mistaken. Stilwell's fiery criticism seemed to unnerve Morris, whose leadership became ever more inept, and he created an atmosphere among his officers of simmering resentment close to mutiny. A significant comment came from Peter Cane in *Chinese Chindits*. He wrote that the attack on Myitkyina 'must have been one of the worst managed operations of the whole war, and we had the misfortune to be squandered in its inefficiency. So too were the American troops – Merrill's Marauders – fine, tough, hard troops who knew what was what and were determined to win it. They too were spent uselessly.'★

Morris Force was to be fully involved in the final approach to Myitkyina, but its role in that will be described as part of the main American–Chinese attack.

Merrill's Marauders and Myitkyina

By the beginning of May 1944, and after the bitter and costly fight at Nphum Ga, Stilwell's plan, which had been submitted to the Chiefs of Staff, was clear: to capture the Mogaung–Myitkyina area as soon as possible; to construct all-weather airfields which could be used during the monsoon; and to open the road from Myitkyina to Kunming and link up with the old Burma Road. This link was subsequently called the Stilwell Road. Chiang had at last agreed to send two more Chinese divisions, 14 and 50, so Stilwell now had five divisions and the Marauders to take on the depleted Japanese 18 Division under General Tanaka.

This was the background to Stilwell's passionate determination to capture Myitkyina before the monsoon started in the middle of May. He realised, as his diary entries confirm, that his chances of success

---

★ Peter Cane, *Chinese Chindits*, privately published, 1948, p. 37. Cane's cheerfully robust attitude lasted all his life. After a career with the Gurkhas and the Chindits he served with an oil company in the Middle East. On retiring he took holy orders. When, as a new vicar, he was summoned to see the Bishop of Winchester, he told him, 'If I was God, you would be my sales manager and I would sack you.' (Conversation with the author.)

depended largely on when the monsoon started. On the ground he planned for the Chinese 22 Division and part of 38 Division to drive down the Mogaung valley to give Tanaka the impression that this was the main attack. On 22 April a Chinese regiment took over the position at Nphum Ga to release the Marauder units for a brief rest. The Marauders felt that they had done all that was asked of them and more, and there was considerable resentment when they were told that, rather than being flown out, they were to undertake another demanding operation. On 27 April Stilwell gave Merrill the orders for Operation End Run – a reference to his footballing days.

Because of the heavy losses at Nphum Ga and the depredations of dysentery, malaria and scrub typhus, Stilwell decided to strengthen the main force of the Marauders by the addition of some Chinese units and Kachin Rangers. This brought the total for the dramatic enterprise that was to come to more than 7,000 men, which included some Chinese infantry regiments, artillery batteries and a combat surgical team.

The bitter feelings among the Marauders were not easily assuaged, so Stilwell told Merrill that 'if everything worked out as expected' they would be evacuated after the operation to take Myitkyina. This promise and the emphasis on the significance of the attack on Myit-kyina gave the Marauders the resolution to carry on and to undertake an operation that was far more gruelling than anything they had previously faced. The main group had to cross the formidable Kumon range, which rose to 7,000 feet.

They set out on 28 April along a little-known trail which Kachin guides and labourers had begun to clear for them. Heavy pre-monsoon rain had already started, and the hills were so steep that mules slipped and fell over precipices. One unit lost twenty mules in a day, together with all its supplies. The truly ghastly conditions got worse and, with their lowered resistance, nearly 150 men succumbed to scrub typhus. The Marauders had divided into two main groups, and the eastern prong met some stiff Japanese resistance at Ritpong, which was reached on 9 May, and then on 12 May they encountered a defensive post held by a Japanese battalion. Merrill had to keep to the very tight timetable imposed by Stilwell, so after a vicious clash the eastern group bypassed the Japanese position and rejoined the other Marauders. Both sides were in a desperate situation, and, when the Marauders attacked, a Japanese company commander recorded that although he would engage the enemy at any cost, he had no ammunition for the mortars or heavy machine guns, other ammunition was short and rations were practically exhausted. On 13 May Hunter, leading the front unit, then about twenty miles from Myitkyina, had about 400 Americans and nearly 800 Chinese and Kachins, including an artillery battery. Meanwhile Stilwell, who was fanatically guarding the secrecy of the Marauders' attack even, or especially, from Mountbatten, waited apprehensive and worried.

After the Marauders left Nphum Ga, Stilwell continued to drive forward the main force of 38 and 22 Divisions. He deliberately took the divisional commanders forward to the front-line battle-command posts, but this rarely resulted in the action he hoped for. After one visit he wrote, 'Sun went back. Too much for him.' He frequently went to the front himself to cause the commanders loss of face and shame them into action.

After months of haggling over the advance of Yoke Force, which enjoyed overwhelming numbers against one weakened Japanese division, he merely recorded on 12 May: 'Yoke jumped off yesterday. Maybe.' This comment came at a time when Stilwell had clear evidence that Chiang was interfering yet again and warning Sun and Liao – the commanders of 38 and 22 Divisions – not to advance too quickly.

During May 1944 Stilwell, who confessed that he was a worrier, came under pressure from all sides, but he worried particularly about the Marauders' dash for Myitkyina. He wrote, 'Probably we are getting a bit jumpy.' Then on 8 May: 'Shoved off at 11.30. Picked up Sun at 38th command post and went into 113th [Regiment]. Hot. 1.30 to 3.30 hike up to 114 Regt. Command post. Damned near killed me. All out of shape. No wind. No legs. Swore off smoking there and then. Felt like an old man when I staggered in.' His recurring concern about the Marauders appears in his diary. 'I start them off for Myitkyina. It rains. The resistance grows here. Why didn't I use them on our front? Is the gap too big? Will they meet a reinforced garrison at Myitkyina? Does it mean we'll fail on both sides instead of one? Can I get them out? ... The die is cast and it's sink or swim. But the nervous wear and tear is terrible. Pity the poor commanding officer.' This anguish explains to some extent his incandescent rage when the Chindits appeared not to do all he asked of them.

He had made detailed plans for the Marauders as they approached Myitkyina. They were to keep radio silence until they were close to their target. Then, forty-eight hours before the estimated time of attack, the signal 'Cafeteria Lunch' would alert the air supply system to be ready to fly in reinforcements and supplies. At twenty-four hours 'Strawberry Sundae' would warn the supply depot to be ready with a five-day supply of food and ammunition. When the attack was about to go in the Marauders would signal 'In the Ring', and finally 'Merchant of Venice' would signal that they had secured the airfield and aircraft could land.

On the night of 16 May the advance column, led by Hunter, reached the area of the airstrip west of the town and prepared to bivouac for the night in absolute silence and with no fires. To be absolutely certain about security, all civilians in the immediate local-ity were rounded up for the night. Kachin intelligence suggested that the Japanese had two understrength battalions in the town and about one hundred men at the airstrip. It appeared that although the Marauders had been involved in some fierce clashes on the way, the Japanese had not linked these to an attack on Myitkyina and complete surprise had been achieved.

Back in his HQ Stilwell was recording every signal, and his excite-ment can be imagined. Merrill's Marauders were about to attack Myitkyina, they had carried out his plans to the letter, and soon he would be able to show the Limeys and all his critics in Chungking, in SEAC and elsewhere that he had succeeded in the project which he had pursued doggedly against every setback and disappointment. His exultation is understandable.

CHAPTER 12

The Battle for Myitkyina

On 17 May, from his damp bivouac, Hunter prepared for the attack on the airfield. The Japanese seemed totally unaware of the presence of the Marauders, who gained complete surprise. The Chinese 150 Regiment attacked and captured the airstrip, while an American battalion captured Pamati, a village on the River Irrawaddy just west of the airstrip. Against little opposition another American battalion advanced south to Zigyin, where there was a ferry over the river.

At 1030 hours Hunter signalled 'In the Ring', and then at 1330 the joyful message 'Merchant of Venice', signalling that the airstrip was clear and safe for food, ammunition and reinforcements to be flown in. Until then there had been less Japanese opposition than Hunter expected, and he had only sparse and vague information about the numbers of defenders. The town of Myitkyina was, in fact, held by two weakened Japanese battalions and some labour units amounting to fewer than 700 men. This sounds like a trivial force, but it should be remembered that a few weeks before an understrength battalion of the Royal West Kents at Kohima had held up the whole of Sato's 31 Division.

Back in his HQ, Stilwell waited in a state of almost unbearable excitement. To his relief it was a clear day, and he noted the times when he received the crucial signals. First, he had the message 'In the Ring', but then at noon a reconnaissance plane flew over the airstrip and could see nothing. Finally, at 1330 hours the signal 'Merchant of Venice' arrived (odd of Stilwell in his moment of triumph to choose the title of a play by a Limey dramatist!). His diary continues:

> About 1330 we got 'Merchant of Venice'. Transports can land WHOOPS. Enormous relief to get Merrill's report. At once ordered machinery and

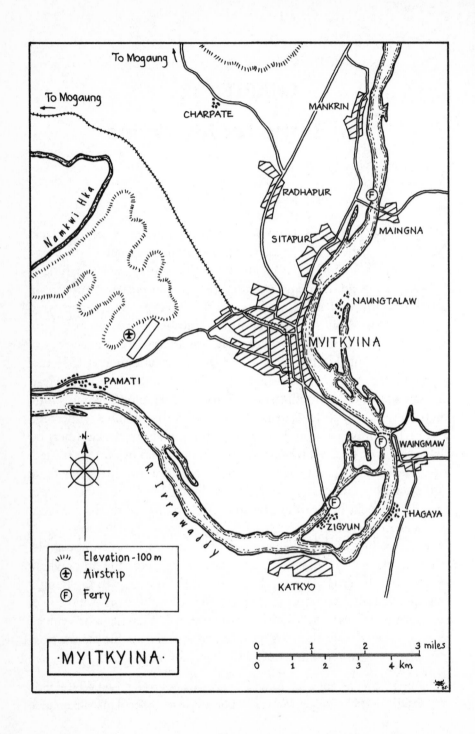

To Mogaung

To Mogaung

CHARPATE

MANKRIN

Namkwi Hka

RADHAPUR

SITAPUR

MAINGNA

F

NAUNGTALAW

MYITKYINA

PAMATI

N

R. Irrawaddy

F WAINGMAW

F

THAGAYA

F ZIGYUN

KATKYO

Elevation - 100 m

⊕ Airstrip

F Ferry

·MYITKYINA·

0   1   2   3 miles
0   1   2   3   4 km

reinforcements started. About 3.30 two transports landed. At 4 saw transports and gliders going over. Thereafter a stream of planes both ways. Told them to keep going all night. We may have 89th (Chinese) Regiment in by morning. WILL THIS BURN UP THE LIMEYS.

Stilwell was determined to have the maximum publicity for his great coup, and on the following day he flew in to the airstrip with twelve war correspondents. It was proclaimed to the world that Myitkyina had fallen, but this was inaccurate. The airstrip had been taken, but from the moment of that brilliant success almost everything went wrong, and Myitkyina town would not be captured until the beginning of August. On 17 May Hunter and the commanders on the ground were disappointed at the pace and allocation of rein-forcements. Engineers, an anti-aircraft battery and a Chinese battalion were flown in that day. Initial confusion was caused because General Stratemeyer, the air commander for the theatre, changed the reinforcement schedules with disastrous results. He sent in more anti-aircraft batteries instead of infantry units, which might have made a quick and successful attack on the town.

Despite the difficulties and bitter frustrations which were to come, Stilwell was justifiably exultant at the success of the strike against Myitkyina. He had been told time and again by the British, the Americans and the Chinese that it could not be done, but he had done it, and supplies were already coming in. The coup caused amaze-ment in London and Washington, where the strategic planners were still dithering over a final decision on Burma. Surprise was total because Stilwell, knowing the very poor Chinese security, had not divulged his plan even to his divisional commanders. He had in fact told Slim but had sworn him to secrecy.

The complete secrecy did cause some problems at the start. Units from three Chinese divisions were the first to fly in, and there was little time to brief them. On the evening of 17 May two Chinese battalions set out to attack the town but lost their way and reached a village, Sitapur, just north of Myitkyina. There, because of muddled and chaotic orders, instead of attacking the Japanese they had a damaging engagement with each other. All the Chinese units soon reverted to Chiang's advice not to advance too quickly.

On 18 May Merrill, who had returned to duty, flew in to Myitkyina and reorganised the units, leaving Hunter in command of the main Marauder force on the ground. Stilwell too flew in to assess the chances of a successful attack on the town. That day provided some ominous signs of the problems which lay ahead. The Chinese units that had fought each other on 17 May were sent off again and, almost unbelievably, ended up fighting each other for a second time, inflicting heavy casualties. In this fraught situation Merrill suffered another heart attack, and then the next day the Chinese units made a third attempt to take the town. They reached the railway yards on the north side but, significantly, the Japanese were able to call up strong defensive units and drove them out.

Stilwell's brief comments during these critical days illuminate his anxiety and tension. On 18 May he wrote: 'Not much sleep. Ants and worry.' After his brief visit with the war correspondents he flew back to his HQ in Shadazup, where he recorded that flocks of visitors were arriving. Here Sun, commander of 38 Division, suggested a plan to take Kamaing. 'I kidded him along and then agreed. Anything to get 38 Div moving. If we get to Kamaing we can tell the Limeys to go to hell.' On 20 May he wrote, 'Japs backed into bazaar section. Resistance now localised, and we are reasonably sure of the place. Japs apparently all in confusion and trying to pull out. Chinese casualties heavy.' This was a serious misreading of the situation because the Japanese were in fact pouring troops into Myitkyina and building up the defences far more quickly than the Americans and Chinese could mount attacks. On 21 May he wrote: 'BAD NEWS. Panic in 150th Regiment; they ran away and had to be taken out. What goes on at Mitch [Myitkyina]? A bad day mentally. Good deal of strain and worry – if the troops are undependable where are we? I'm looking forward to a full stop in this business. Wish it would pour right now.' Next day came 'BLACK MONDAY. Bad news from Mitch.' More than one thousand Japanese were observed hurrying in to man the defences of the town, and the situation was critical. He sensed a general air of discouragement, which worried him more. He anguished over whether to bring in some of the road engineers to replace the Marauders and considered changing the Chinese units. 'If the goddam rain will only let us use the field for a few days. If we can't land planes, can't land troops. This is one of those terrible worry days when you wish you were dead. 10.00 pm still raining heavily.'

During this anxious time an undated note gives an indication of his mental torment. He considered the notion that a coward dies a thousand deaths and the valiant but one, though he added that the valiant who dies but once must be an unimaginative clod:

> Enough will power to dismiss from his mind all the possibilities of trouble and disaster that may occur. That would take balance that I know I could never attain … I think of situations quite needlessly that turn my guts to water. Is it the same thing that makes me worry about covering the flanks, about checking on location of units, delivery of orders, execution of movements, arrival of supplies, etc, etc?
>
> Strangely enough, I do not worry about my own lot. It never occurs to me that my plane will crash or that the next bomb may have my name on it … I know how Win [his wife] would explain it, but if so, why isn't *everyone* taken care of?

The situation in Myitkyina rapidly became static, developing into a battle of slit trenches, mortars and machine-gun fire. By the end of May the Japanese defenders had built up their forces more quickly than the attackers and had over 2,500 troops in the town, including a full-strength battalion and General Mizukami from 56 Division. He came in to co-ordinate all the defences and set up a ferry over the Irrawaddy river east of the town. On the American side Colonel McCammon, in charge on the ground after Merrill's second heart attack, ordered attacks by two Chinese regiments, but they were beaten off.

The decision by Stilwell which almost from the start created the dire situation at Myitkyina should now be assessed. He had focused so much on the Marauders' drive to Myitkyina that he clearly had not planned the follow-up attack on the town. When the airfield fell on 17 May he had to make the vital decision. The tried and experienced British 36 Division was available in northern Burma, was trained for flight operations and could have flown in almost immediately. One American description of Stilwell's decision suggested 'that he wanted to keep an American flavour in the fight'. A modern historian,

Nathan Prefer, stated, generously, that Stilwell considered using 36 Division 'but discarded that idea in the interest of national pride'.* That is too generous. It was Stilwell's paranoia about Myitkyina that coloured the decision. It was not national pride but his own pride and his anglophobia which dictated it. He was not going to see his great prize captured by any Limey unit. This disgraceful decision led to eleven weeks of vicious fighting and countless deaths.

On 30 May Stilwell flew back in and appointed Boatner in place of McCammon. Boatner, whose experience had been largely desk-bound staff work, was not an inspiring leader and he had already made serious blunders, which caused a bitter dispute with General Sun. Boatner faced a crisis. The Japanese had brought up artillery and mortars and were able to bombard the airstrip, causing planes to crash and further curtailing its use. The acute shortage of infantry was made good by bringing in two battalions of road engineers, some of whom had to be instructed in the use of the rifle as they were flown in. Boatner wrote: 'They are in many cases simply terrified of the Japs – they would not follow their officers, refused to attack, and ran under fire.' Stilwell's diary records, 'Terrible letter from Boatner. U.S. troops shaky. Hard to believe.'

The shortage of infantry soldiers was so acute that, on Stilwell's orders, base hospitals in India were combed for convalescent Marauders who were flown straight to Myitkyina. This appalling decision compounded the damage caused by his refusal to use 36 Division. Prefer wrote that 'This incident gave rise to an accusation that tarnished the General's reputation permanently'.† One Marauder officer recorded that by this time Stilwell's name was like a red rag to a bull: 'Stilwell seemed bloodless, utterly cold hearted, without a drop of human kindness.' In another report a Marauder, describing a visit from Stilwell, said: 'I had him in my rifle sights. I coulda squeezed one off and no one woulda known it wasn't a Jap that got the son of a bitch.'‡ By the beginning of June the Marauders had lost ninety killed but 2,000 from sickness and exhaustion. Men suffering from malaria or dysentery had to have a temperature of 102° for three days before they were

* Nathan Prefer, *Vinegar Joe's War*, Presidio, California, 2000, p. 150.
† Prefer, *Vinegar Joe's War*, p. 148.
‡ Tuchman, *Sand against the Wind*, p. 450.

allowed to go sick. In many parts of Myitkyina it was difficult to hold their positions and the initiative clearly lay with the Japanese.

Stilwell's paranoia and Boatner's inadequacy are illustrated from a different angle in their relationship with the Chindit Morris Force, which had virtually closed off the Bhamo to Myitkyina road after flying in to Indaw on 6 March. Boatner seemed to reflect all the worst traits of Stilwell himself. Although he had a preponderance of force, he scattered his units over the area with little plan or method, no concentration of force and no co-ordination. Every few days he would order new attacks, to be carried out at all costs, and the Chindit casualties grew alarmingly. When ordered to attack yet another carefully defended Japanese position Morris went to Boatner, explained the reduced numbers in his force and their pitiful physical condition and asked for artillery or air support. Boatner replied, 'All you lack is courage.' Peter Cane, describing this incident in *Chinese Chindits*, wrote that 'This monstrous remark caused great indignation'. Another comment recorded at the time throws light on Stilwell's original decision. When Morris offered to take part in an attack on Myitkyina he was told that only the Chinese would be allowed to capture the town. Morris himself was weak and tended to pass on Boatner's orders. These frequently demanded an attack with no time for reconnaissance or preparation. In one such attack the Chindits lost twenty-two men killed including Colonel Monteith, a brave and experienced leader who had said only the previous day: 'Boatner will kill us all off before he is finished.'

The desperate effort to bring more fighting troops to Myitkyina went on through June and July. One officer who took part in this operation, named New Galahad, described how men were taken off a troopship and flown directly to Myitkyina, leaving no time for infantry training. The men did not even know their own officers. Within days of taking over Boatner ordered an attack by two Chinese regiments. The attack, for which there was no time to prepare, cost 300 casualties. A week later another joint attack by the Chinese and the Marauders failed to take its objective and the attackers were then barely able to hold the Japanese counterattack.

On 26 June Stilwell flew in, relieved Boatner of his command and put Brigadier General Wessels in charge. Stilwell's brief, grim diary jottings highlight his other problems. The next day he merely recorded, 'Mogaung. We have it.' After a brief visit from Mountbatten, he wrote that the GIs 'were getting a look at the British Empah [sic] with its pants down and the aspect is not so pretty. You can imagine how popular I am with the Limeys.' He referred to the crisis caused by a powerful Japanese attack in southwest China and wrote: 'If this crisis were just sufficient to get rid of the Peanut without entirely wrecking the ship it would be worth it. But that's too much to hope.' On 19 July he noted: 'Japs at Mitch shoving off on rafts.' In a letter to his wife he said that the noose around Myitkyina was good and tight and few would get away – 'then Old Pappy is going to take a day off'. He added, 'I feel guilty about Mitch, but we will get it in due time.'

In Myitkyina, Wessels soon proved himself a tough and professional officer, and he insisted that all units should undertake serious training even as they fought. Despite this there were some disastrous incidents. One New Galahad unit was advancing when it mistook a Japanese scout for a Chinese. The unit was led straight into an ambush and all but wiped out. Gradually Wessel's efficient and determined approach paid off, and towards the end of July there were signs that the Japanese were preparing to pull out. Patrols noticed an increasing number of barges being assembled near the ferry at Waingmaw. Here, as elsewhere in Burma, the Japanese units had their Korean comfort girls, some of whom were captured as their barge floated downstream. On 1 August General Mizukami, who had undertaken to hold Myitkyina, apologised to the Emperor and committed suicide. The town's capture was finally announced on 3 August.

Stilwell's disgraceful decision not to use the British 36 Division at the very start, when Myitkyina had few defences, led to eleven weeks of bitter fighting and 6,000 casualties among the Marauders and the Chinese. Subsequent official inquiries and reports listed grave and costly mistakes, stressing the very poor use of intelligence and the failure to reconnoitre the ground before attacks were launched.

Perhaps General Slim should be allowed the last word. In contrast to Stilwell's constant and petulant sniping at the British, Slim paid a generous tribute to Stilwell and his achievement. 'The capture of Myitkyina, so long delayed, marked the complete success of the first stage of Stilwell's campaign. It was also the largest seizure of enemy-held territory that had yet occurred … When all is said and done, the success of this northern offensive was in the main due to the Ledo Chinese divisions – and that was Stilwell.'

CHAPTER 13

Wider Issues

Even before the final capture of Myitkyina town, Stilwell was called away from his jungle HQ at Shadazup to stand in for Mountbatten at the new headquarters of South East Asia Command in Kandy, Ceylon (now Sri Lanka). The great issues of strategy in the Pacific war were still being fiercely and acrimoniously debated between Kandy, Washington, Chungking and London. Mountbatten had gone to London to argue the case for an amphibious attack on Rangoon after the Fourteenth Army reached Mandalay. Other bitterly contested issues included General MacArthur's advance across the Pacific and Churchill's hankering after an invasion of Sumatra as a step towards Singapore.

Stilwell's reputation had preceded him. Tuchman described the feelings at SEAC HQ as the emotions of Rome awaiting Alaric the Hun. General Pownall, who like Stilwell kept a diary which was later published, was Chief of Staff at Kandy. He wrote: 'Stilwell of course held out against us strongly. He made a pretty fair swine of himself ... he was offensive and proved himself ignorant and obstinate ... he was opposed by everyone else at the meeting, by none more than the Americans.' Stilwell was in good company, for Pownall – not a great commander himself – had nothing good to say about Mountbatten or Slim and referred to Wingate as 'a nasty bit of work'. Mountbatten, while he was away, received reports from all his senior officers that Stilwell 'was pathetically at sea and incapable of taking charge or giving directions'.

Stilwell did nothing to dispel the apprehension. He was met in Kandy by Mountbatten's black Cadillac with motorcycle outriders. He rejected this and ordered a Jeep. Coinciding with his arrival he was

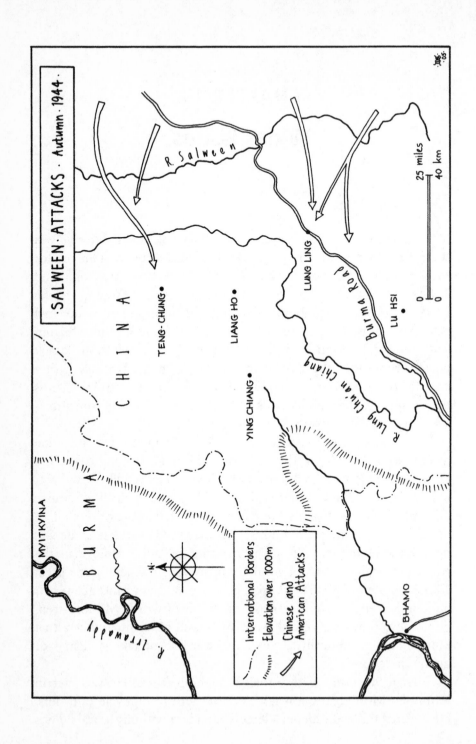

SALWEEN · ATTACKS · Autumn · 1944 ·

R. Salween

CHINA

TENG-CHUNG ·

LIANG HO ·

YING CHIANG ·

LUNG LING

Burma Road

R. Lung Chuan Chiang

LU HSI ·

25 miles
40 km
0
0

BURMA

MYITKYINA ·

R. Irrawaddy

· N ·

International Borders
Elevation over 1000m
Chinese and
American Attacks

BHAMO ·

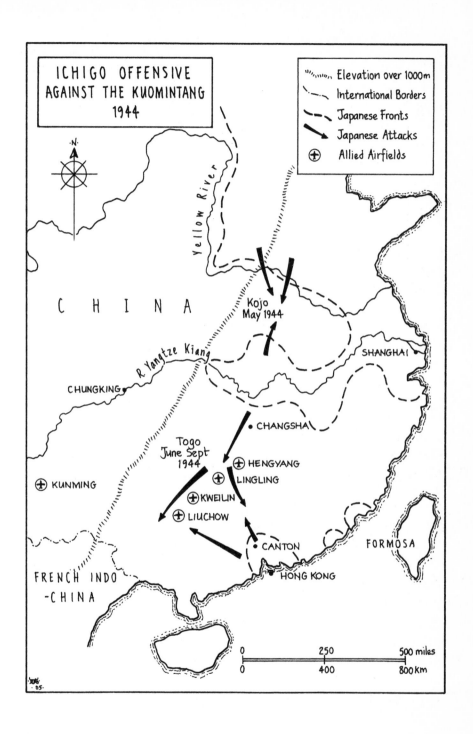

ICHIGO OFFENSIVE
AGAINST THE KUOMINTANG
1944

Elevation over 1000m
International Borders
Japanese Fronts
Japanese Attacks
Allied Airfields

·N·

Yellow River

C H I N A

Kojo
May 1944

R Yangtze Kiang

SHANGHAI

CHUNGKING

CHANGSHA

Togo
June Sept
1944

HENGYANG
LINGLING

KUNMING

KWEILIN

LIUCHOW

CANTON

FORMOSA

HONG KONG

FRENCH INDO
-CHINA

0   250   500 miles
0   400   800 km

·05·

promoted to four-star general, putting him on a level with Marshall, Eisenhower and MacArthur. He clearly saw his time at Kandy as one of rest and recuperation after the jungle campaign, and he never intended to master all the strategic complexities. On 2 August he wrote, 'Saw Pownall and told him to run the show. Went through the crap and beat it. PM. To the Temple of the Tooth – no tooth.' (This was and is the most sacred Buddhist temple in Sri Lanka.) He became lyrical about the beauty of the town and the country around it – comparing it to Yellowstone Park and the climate to Hawaii. He continued this theme in a letter to his wife, which also illustrated his oversensitive attitude. 'Mountbatten has left temporarily, and as heir to the throne, Little Willie the Country Boy, had to come down and take over. This is a laugh. A goddam American in the driver's seat, etc, etc. I am going to read and rest and get a lot of sleep.'

After his brief stay in Kandy, Stilwell was called back to face another crisis in Chungking. Before he left he welcomed Mountbatten back to SEAC HQ. He remarked that Mountbatten appeared ill at ease with him. 'Not surprising because his trip had to do with an operation on his deputy's throat.' Mountbatten's biographer Philip Ziegler considered that they had been in fundamental disharmony. He wrote: 'Mountbatten characteristically assumed that, in spite of their differences, Stilwell still cherished affection and respect for his Supreme Commander. Stilwell was equally sure that Mountbatten viewed him with loathing. Both were wrong.'★ Their relationship had certainly deteriorated since the crisis over the Chindits after Mogaung. At the time Mountbatten considered that Stilwell had treated the Chindits with callous indifference and had overruled him.

During the summer of 1944, when Stilwell was deeply pre-occupied with Myitkyina, dramatic events were taking place in China that led up to his final crisis. As early as March 1944 Stilwell's adviser, John D. Davis Jr, had suggested that America should send a military mission to the Chinese Communists in the hope of gaining their co-operation against the Japanese. An additional purpose was to ascertain how far they were dependent on Soviet Russia for aircraft and weapons. Both the Kuomintang and Mao's forces were building up

★ Ziegler, *Mountbatten*, p. 284.

their strength in northern China, and Japan was doing its best to embroil them in fighting each other. The Japanese then took more positive action and launched two major offensives. In May 1944 they attacked the Kuomintang forces between the Yellow River and the Yangtze. More significantly, from June to September they launched the Togo campaign, which overran the four advanced airfields from which Chennault's Fourteenth Air Force was attacking Japanese troops, shipping, supplies and even the Japanese homeland. The attack included a rapid advance by powerful units that drove northeast from the Hong Kong and Canton area. This is what Stilwell had always predicted and was the kernel of his bitter feud with Chennault. When the advancing Japanese troops captured the first of the airfields, Chennault wrote urgently to Chiang. This contravened the clear regulation on which Stilwell had wisely insisted that all communications from Americans to Chiang should pass through him. Chennault gave a lame explanation for what had happened, and Stilwell demanded his dismissal for insubordination. Stilwell dealt with the matter in considerable detail, pointing out that Chennault had always argued that air power was the full and complete answer and that existing Chinese ground forces could definitely defend the air bases; now that he was proved to be wrong he was trying to excuse himself and put the blame on someone else. 'He has failed to damage the Jap supply line. He has not caused any Jap withdrawals. On the contrary, his activities have done exactly what I prophesied, i.e. drawn a Jap reaction which he now acknowledges the ground forces can't handle, even with the total air support he asked for and got.'

Chennault's reaction to the Japanese advances and their threat to the forward airfields was to demand yet more of the supplies coming over the Hump. Chiang backed up this demand, but when it went to Washington both Stimson and Marshall rejected it. Stimson stated publicly that demands for transport planes to maintain the tonnage going over the Hump had bled America white. When Chiang added demands for more aid now and a promise of Lend–Lease after the war, the American administration stated that there would be no more immediate aid and proposed bluntly that Chiang should make an agreement with the Communists so that both the Kuomintang and Communist troops could join together and fight the Japanese.

In America serious criticism of the Chiang regime was muffled by the powerful pro-China religious groups and missionary-backed relief agencies, but the truth was gradually emerging. During 1944, serious discontent among both junior and senior officers in the Kuomintang flared into rebellion and sixteen generals were executed. Widespread anger and discontent made it obvious that Chiang's regime was rotten from top to bottom. Massive censorship was imposed in an attempt to curb demands for democratic reform, while the warlords spoke openly of independence. American agents reported widespread starvation among both peasants and soldiers as the economy ground to a halt.

America now had to consider new and unpalatable factors. While it urgently sought the co-operation of the Kuomintang and the Communists in fighting the Japanese, the feeling grew that the current situation in China could lead to civil war, and if that happened, because of Chiang's rotten system, Mao Tse-Tung and the Communists might win. This in turn could create a highly dangerous global scenario, with Russia backing Mao and the Communists and the USA backing Chiang, the likely loser. Chiang himself was aware of this danger and tried hard to build up forces with which, after the Japanese were defeated, he hoped to be able to defeat the Communists before either Russia or the Allies could interfere in the internal affairs of China.

The tortuous muddle in China now became further enmeshed in extraneous political factors. Roosevelt, who was facing an election in November 1944, was not keen to have Vice President Henry Wallace as a running mate, so – perhaps to remove him from the limelight – he sent him as a presidential envoy to see Chiang. Wallace's visit in June 1944 sought Chiang's agreement to the visit of an American mission to the Communist forces in northern China. As ever Chiang prevaricated, and since Stilwell was in Burma at Myitkyina, Wallace consulted largely with Chennault and his faction. Not surprisingly Wallace, after a brief and superficial visit, recommended Stilwell's removal. Back in Washington Marshall bluntly and contemptuously rejected the idea, but Wallace's visit did result in a heightened awareness of the disastrous situation in China and the growing opposition at all levels to the corrupt miasma of Chiang's system.

While the build-up to the great crisis continued, the Chinese divisions in Yunnan – because of American cajoling – did at last attack. They made two advances, the first to cross the Salween river and capture a town about 100 miles east of Myitkyina, and a second to cross the Salween lower down and capture Lung-ling on the Burma Road. This should have enabled a force of twelve Chinese divisions to reach Bhamo to link up with Stilwell's forces in the area of Myitkyina and, at last, reopen a major land route into China. These advances had been chronically delayed and only went forward in May 1944 when there were just a few weeks before the start of the monsoon – posing a serious problem to an attacking force that relied largely on supply by air. Stilwell's old friend and colleague Brigadier General Frank Dorn made a most important contribution to this force. He controlled supplies, training, technical advice, and above all training in air liaison techniques. The Chinese had to attack the weakened Japanese 56 Division, which was thinly scattered. Dorn recommended that when the Chinese attacked they should keep going as independent combat teams so as to maintain their momentum and not stop to subdue every Japanese stronghold.

The Chinese attacked on 9 May and crossed the Salween unopposed, helped by bombers and fighters from Chennault's bases near Kunming. Each Chinese division had an American liaison officer to advise, although their advice was frequently disregarded. They were appalled at the casual way in which Chinese soldiers were slaughtered, often because they failed to follow the most basic tactical advice such as providing covering fire or making flank attacks. Reports from the liaison officers gave dramatic evidence of massive waste of ammunition and total lack of maintenance on weapons and vehicles. In spite of these weaknesses the Chinese made good progress against determined Japanese opposition. The divisions approaching Lung-ling captured a map showing details of the Japanese defences for the whole area. They reached the town on 14 June after a prolonged struggle through monsoon rain. Nearly 10,000 Chinese troops were poised for the attack on Lung-ling, but then, in the face of a Japanese counterattack with 1,500 men, they broke and fled and control of the vital Burma Road remained with the Japanese.

During the summer of 1944, when the world's main attention was on the Normandy landings and the Russian drive to Berlin, events took place in Chungking, Kandy, London, Myitkyina and Washington that were to have dramatic repercussions on Stilwell's career. From his early days in the army his career had often been assisted by his old friend George Marshall, and once again Marshall was to play a key role. On a visit to London in June 1944 he was warned by the CIGS, Sir Alan Brooke, that the British wanted Stilwell replaced because he was notorious for his anti-Limey views, because he had seriously mishandled the Chindit issue after Mogaung and because he did not get on with the three British service chiefs at SEAC HQ. In an angry exchange, which reflected American attitudes going back to the Quebec Conference of 1943, Marshall challenged Brooke. He said that Mountbatten had three service chiefs in India, none of whom would fight, yet they wanted to get rid of Stilwell – the one person who had shown that he would fight the Japanese. Marshall's argument was strengthened because at that stage Mountbatten was actually in the process of getting rid of all three of his service chiefs – Admiral Somerville, General Giffard and Air Marshal Pierce.

Marshall had been deeply involved with affairs in China and now, far from just making an angry reply to a British proposal, he was planning on a much more significant scale. He, more than most, was aware of the disastrous situation in China. He pondered over the terrific achievements in the China–Burma–India theatre: Stilwell's drive to Myitkyina, the huge Hump operation, the construction of the road and pipeline from Ledo that followed closely on Stilwell's advance, and the great increase in supplies brought up the Assam railway thanks to the US railway battalions. The impending opening of the Burma Road meant that supplies of all kinds would be substantially increased, and Marshall was determined that they should not be wasted under the control of Chiang and Chennault. He therefore proposed that Chiang should be given a final blunt ultimatum in the following terms: because of the disastrous situation in China that allowed Japanese armies to roam unopposed, Stilwell should be given command of all the Chinese armies with full power to reorganise, discipline, supply and train them. Marshall saw this as the last chance to achieve anything in the country and to justify the vast investment in men, money and machines that America had made in support of Chiang. He believed that Stilwell was the only person who could possibly succeed in this mammoth task.

Before there was any mention of Stilwell's possible promotion, Marshall tentatively broached the subject with him. Stilwell gave a careful and reasoned reply, saying that if the President sent a very stiff message pointing out that desperate cases needed desperate remedies, Chiang might agree to the proposal. He then stressed that without complete authority he would not attempt the job. He felt that the damage done to the Chinese army was so tremendous that there were very few alternatives. He did add that two years previously the Communists had agreed to fight under his command, and a joint offensive with them might possibly succeed. 'These matters must be put before the G-mo in the strongest terms or he will continue to muddle along and scream for help without doing any more than he is doing now, which is nothing.'

After he received Stilwell's unenthusiastic reply Marshall moved rapidly. He submitted the proposal in the name of the Joint Chiefs of Staff, pointing out that the thousands of tons of supplies taken over the Hump for Chennault had been almost completely wasted and that in the major clash of policies Stilwell had been proved absolutely right. The situation in China was alarming and it appeared that the Japanese forces could move around at will almost unmolested.

On 6 July 1944 Roosevelt sent the message to Chiang. He used Marshall's draft unchanged but added: 'The future of all Asia is at stake, along with the tremendous effort which America has expended in that region. Therefore I have reason for a profound interest in the matter.' On that crucial day Stilwell was at his headquarters in Shadazup, where he merely recorded: 'Radio from F.D.R. to Chiang Kai-Shek and from George Marshall to me. They have been pouring it into him about me. F.D.R. told Chiang Kai-Shek to give me full authority to run the show, promotion to full general.' Because previous messages from the President had been altered or watered down by Madame or T. V. Soong, this fateful message was given to Chiang personally by the senior American officer in Chungking.

Faced with the supremely challenging prospect of commanding the whole Chinese army, Stilwell made some interesting comments.

He wrote:

> I never heard Chiang Kai-Shek say a single thing that indicated grati-
> tude to our President or to our country for the help we were extending
> to him. Invariably, when anything was promised, he would want more.
> Invariably, he would complain about the small amount of material that
> was being furnished ... Whether or not he was grateful was a small
> matter. The regrettable part of it was that there was no quid pro quo.

Stilwell repeated his faith in the Chinese soldier and the Chinese people
– 'fundamentally great, democratic, misgoverned. No bars of caste or
religion ... Honest, frugal, industrious, cheerful, independent, toler-
ant, friendly, courteous.' He compared the Kuomintang system of
'corruption, neglect, chaos ... hoarding, black market, trading with
the enemy' with the Communist regime, which aimed to 'reduce
taxes, rents and interest, and to raise production and [the] standard of
living, and to involve the people in government'. He gave an accurate
assessment of the Chinese army, which in theory could muster more
than 300 divisions, although most were at less than half strength. The
troops moreover were unpaid, unfed and shot with sickness and malnutrition, the equipment was old, inadequate and unserviceable, and
there was no artillery, transport or medical services. He concluded by
asking, 'How would you start to make such an army effective?'
     Returning to the theme of Chiang Kai-Shek, Stilwell commented
that he was bewildered by the spread of Communist influence.

> He can't see that the mass of Chinese people welcome the Reds as
> being the only visible hope of relief from crushing taxation, the abuses
> of the army and the terror of Tai Li's Gestapo. Under Chiang Kai-Shek
> they now begin to see what they may expect. Greed, corruption
> favouritism, more taxes, a ruined currency, terrible waste of life, callous
> disregard of all the rights of men.

These strictures are in colourful contrast to Mao Tse-Tung's *Basic Tactics*,
which were issued during his early struggle against both the Japanese
and the Kuomintang in the 1930s. His rules included: do not steal from
people; be neither selfish nor unjust; be courteous; be honest in your
transactions; return what you borrow; replace what you break. The
instructions even included advice on telling jokes – 'not too obscene'.

When Marshall gave Stilwell details of Roosevelt's message to Chiang he added, as an old friend, a fairly stiff rebuke to the effect that there would have been far fewer problems if he had not offended both the Generalissimo and the President on small matters. Stilwell accepted the criticism and promised not to annoy but said that the proposed command was a heavy load for a country boy.

The initial reaction from Chungking gave the impression that Chiang would accept Roosevelt's proposal in principle but wished to discuss further detail because such a command involved far more complex military and political issues than the command in Burma. When Soong, now restored to Chiang's inner circle, heard that America was trying to force Stilwell down Chiang's throat, he commented that 'The Generalissimo will not and cannot yield'. There is now little doubt that Chiang had no intention of accepting Stilwell's overall command but spun out negotiations in order to prolong the supply of American aid and in the hope of vastly increased supplies when the land route up the Burma Road was reopened. He therefore suggested that, as a move towards closer co-operation, there should be a permanent presidential representative in Chungking because political co-operation came before military co-operation. Roosevelt, rather naively, accepted this suggestion, though Marshall objected strongly. After the initial favourable reaction Chiang's real purpose began to emerge.

Towards the end of July 1944, with a pretence of co-operation, he set his first condition: that the Communist forces should not come under Stilwell's command until they accepted the authority of the Chungking government. Nearly everyone realised that this would never happen. The second condition requested clarification over the relationship between Chiang and Stilwell, while the third made plain what had been Chiang's aim from the start: that the Lend–Lease supplies should be entirely under the authority of the Chinese government.

The high-level negotiations took place against the backdrop of continuing advance by Japanese forces towards the airfields in southwest China. They had conquered Changsa but had been held up for several weeks by the spirited defence of Heng-Yang. Chennault's air attacks on their advancing units and supply lines caused serious damage but did not halt their progress. Heng-Yang soon fell to the

Japanese, in early August, despite the fact that there were seventeen Chinese divisions in the area. These were in desperate need of supplies, and this focused attention back on the issue of the allocation of the tonnage coming over the Hump. Stilwell did not duck the issue, and his answer was clear. Chennault had claimed he could drive back the Japanese if he had 10,000 tons of supplies a month. The previous month he had received 12,000 tons, so if his project had failed he had better tell Chiang and leave him to decide what he wanted to do with the available supplies.

When news of the fall of Heng-Yang reached Chungking, a new and serious factor emerged. Marshal Li Chi Shen, a powerful warlord in southern China, contacted the Americans to say that the leaders of all the southern provinces were about to set up a provisional government under his leadership. Its aim was to overthrow the dictatorial regime of Chiang Kai-Shek, to achieve national unity in order to co-operate with the Allies, and to prosecute the war against Japan more effectively. Marshal Li claimed to have about eight divisions to support this move. Such a proposal had to be seriously and swiftly considered. Stilwell received the details while he was still in Ceylon and wrote tersely 'Hooray for Crime', but he warned that while the proposal was being investigated America should remain detached and make absolutely no comment. Urgent enquiries were made to assess the likelihood of the Communist forces supporting the proposal, and fairly soon it was concluded that they would not agree and that in fact there was little solid support among the other warlords in the area.

Despite Chiang's opposition, several American delegations went to visit the Communist-held areas in northern China and were amazed at what they found. The people were working industriously, communities appeared prosperous compared to those in the Kuomintang areas, Communist soldiers cultivated their own patches and did not steal from the local people, and they appeared to be robust, well trained and well equipped. This situation was the result of the brilliant leadership of Mao Tse-Tung, who had linked his views on guerrilla war to an all-embracing political aim.*

* David Rooney, *Guerilla: Insurgents, Patriots and Terrorists from Sun Tzu to Bin Laden*, Brassey's, London, 2004, pp. 141–5.

While these issues were being discussed, Stilwell made some interesting and percipient observations about the situation in China. 'The
cure for the Chinese situation is the elimination of Chiang Kai-Shek
… He hates the Reds and will not take any chances of giving them
a toehold in the government. The result is that each side watches the
other and neither gives a damn about the war against Japan. If this
condition persists, China will have civil war immediately after Japan
is out.'

The Japanese Ichigo offensive (see map on p. 210) provided the
backdrop to the urgent discussions on future policy, but their setbacks
in the Pacific and in Burma prompted an upsurge in other activities
centred on Chungking that illustrate wider aspects of the war. In
Thailand (formerly Siam) the government at the time of Pearl Harbor
had reluctantly given in to Japanese pressure and allowed the passage
of troops to Burma and Malaya although retaining a fairly substantial
degree of sovereignty. During the Japanese occupation a strong resistance movement sprang up. This was in close touch with the OSS
operating out of Chungking, and by July 1944, with strong American
backing, Thai agents were infiltrating into Thailand along a land route
from Chungking. After some initial setbacks they were able to set up
such an effective system that agents could be dropped in safely. Later
there were airstrips in different parts of the country where aircraft
could land safely with supplies. At the same time, with support from
SEAC HQ in Ceylon, and working with SOE and Force 136, agents
were landed on the coast of Thailand by Allied submarines. It helped
that the Thai regent, who was not tightly controlled by the Japanese,
was virtually the head of the resistance movement. The Thai chief of
police was also a supporter, and most communications to resistance
agents were sent out under cover of the police radio system. The Thais
were eager for an uprising against the Japanese occupation forces but
were restrained by Mountbatten and SEAC HQ, which was planning
an amphibious operation and wanted a Thai uprising to coincide with
that. In the end the Hiroshima bomb pre-empted both plans.

In similar vein, the OSS was actively encouraging the Vietnamese
to rise up against their Japanese occupiers. In a well-recorded incident, Ho Chi Minh made contact with Chennault hoping that he
would be able to help the Vietnamese operations. In return for his

support Ho Chi Minh asked for a signed photograph of Chennault and six Colt revolvers – which he gave to his five divisional leaders, keeping one for himself. A refreshing contrast to the greedy and ungrateful attitude of Chiang! American links through the OSS with Ho Chi Minh and the Viet Minh movement were later to lead to serious divisions between Britain and America. Roosevelt and Stilwell were strongly opposed to the Free French and their clandestine activities in Indo-China. When the war finished abruptly in August 1945, the French asked for the return Indo-China, while Britain hurriedly brought in some veterans of the Burma war – 20 Indian Division under General Gracey – to keep law and order. For a brief time in Saigon, in a situation that was quite bizarre, the British using a few French troops and some Japanese were fighting against the Viet Minh supported by the Americans. The final irony was that one of Ho Chi Minh's ablest commanders at the time of his links with Chennault was Vo Nguyen Giap, who was to defeat the French at Dien Bien Phu and ultimately to drive the Americans out of Vietnam.

While the tide was turning against the Japanese and resistance movements in Thailand and Indo-China were gaining in confidence, the final discussions about Stilwell's future and the future of Sino-American relations reverted to Chungking. Roosevelt replied in vague terms to Chiang's conditions about the role of the Communists and the future of Lend–Lease, but he stressed the urgency of making Stilwell's appointment to avert military catastrophe. Chiang for his part prevaricated, with no intention of taking decisive action. He was becoming increasingly isolated even within his own inner circle, and he seemed entirely unaware of the disastrous situation in the army and the country. It appeared that he was hoping – accurately as it turned out – that Japan could be defeated without any major military campaign in China, leaving all his forces and all the American munitions he had stockpiled ready for him to take on the Communists. Thus, little had really changed when Roosevelt's two presidential representatives, Brigadier General Patrick Hurley and Donald Nelson, flew to Delhi on 4 September and were escorted from there to Chungking by Stilwell.

CHAPTER 14

Showdown in Chungking

Brigadier General Patrick Hurley, a tall, imposing man with a white moustache who wore a bow-tie and a homburg hat, appeared to be the ideal Presidential representative. He had been involved with Stilwell at the time of the Cairo Conference and was renowned as a tough negotiator in several major disputes in the oil industry. He made the crack to Stilwell that 'It takes oil and vinegar to make a good French dressing'. He and Donald Nelson had been carefully briefed, and their attitude as they accompanied Stilwell to Chungking was encouraging.

Stilwell remained wary. Noting that Hurley and Nelson were ready to pound the table, he wrote, 'It is one thing to make a brief call on Chiang Kai-Shek when he is on his good behaviour ... It is another to make him take *action* along these lines. (After concessions that give him a blank cheque to tie me up.)' On 7 September Chiang called Stilwell on his own and pointed out that as commander of the Chinese Army the post would be 60 per cent military and 40 per cent political. Then the negotiations started, with Chiang harping on about the issues of Lend–Lease and the Communist forces coming under his control. Hurley and Nelson clearly could not agree to this and went away with Stilwell to prepare an agenda for discussion. T. V. Soong made it plain that Chinese control of Lend–Lease supplies was the central issue. In describing these early stages of the negotiations Stilwell wrote, 'He let the cat out of the bag: "The G-mo must control Lend–Lease."' Pat Hurley told him to write 'DISAGREED' in capital letters. 'We can't even control the stuff we make ourselves. What a nerve. That's what the G-mo is after – just a blank cheque. Now we come to the showdown.' About this time a new nickname for Chiang became popular with American servicemen: 'Cash My Cheque'.

In a memo to Hurley, Stilwell listed the following vital points: that his function should be operational command; that he must have clear support from the National Military Council; that air and ground forces must come under his direct command; that Chiang Kai-Shek must announce his appointment and give him a clear seal of authority; and that Lend–Lease should be handled by an American commission in Chungking, which would have Chinese representatives. At this stage of the negotiations there were also serious discussions with Mao Tse-Tung and Chou En-Lai representing the Communist forces, but the Americans found them as difficult to pin down as Chiang, and little was achieved except a general promise of co-operation against the Japanese.

The threatening background to the talks was the continuing advance of the Japanese against Chennault's air bases, and before the Chinese in Chungking could reply to the blunt memo Stilwell hurried off to make a brief visit to the front. Here the Japanese, driving south after their capture of Heng-Yang and moving northeast from Canton, posed a serious threat to the great air and supply base at Kweilin. He found a situation of chaos; both commanders and troops were unreliable, whole armies made no attempt to fight, and in the few places where there was some determination the effort was hampered by renewed interference from Chiang in Chungking. Stilwell himself had to give orders for the demolition of the Kweilin base, and he realised that there was no hope of holding the other air base at Liuchow.

In the face of this serious military threat, which could have put Chungking itself at risk, Chiang merely demanded that the Chinese divisions at Myitkyina should advance immediately against Bhamo. He even threatened that if Stilwell did not do this he would withdraw the whole of Yoke Force from the crucial area of Lung-ling on the Burma Road. Stilwell made a detailed report of this to Marshall. In spite of his promise to be on his best behaviour towards Chiang, he wrote in his diary for 5 September 1944: 'Wants to withdraw from

Lung-ling, the crazy little bastard. So either we attack Bhamo in a week or he pulls out. Usual cock-eyed reasons and idiotic tactical and strategic conceptions. He is impossible.'

The tense and bitter atmosphere, which illustrated for Hurley and Nelson the kind of problems Stilwell had faced for years, was colourfully recorded in his diary for 16 September:

> The G-mo insists on the control of Lend–Lease. Our stuff that we are giving him. T. V. (Soong) says we must remember the 'dignity' of a great nation which would be 'affronted' if I controlled the distribution. Pat Hurley told him 'Horsefeathers. Remember Dr Soong, that this is our property. We made it and we own it and we can give it to whom we please.' (We must not look while the customer puts his hand in our cash register for fear we will offend his 'dignity'.) Pat said there were 130 million Americans whose dignity also entered the case, as well as the 'dignity' of their children and their children's children who would have to pay the bill. Hooray for Pat. (If the G-mo controls distribution I am sunk. The Reds will get nothing. Only the G-mo's henchmen will be supplied and my troops will suck the hind tit.) ... Gave T.V. the works in plain words. I do not want the God-awful job, but if I take it I must have full authority.

In further discussions the Communists agreed to fight under Stilwell but not under anyone appointed by Chiang. Gradually, American commentators in both Chungking and Washington openly considered making a realistic deal with the Communists. This had no ideological element, as was sometimes alleged in the neurotic atmosphere of later decades in the USA, but was merely an attempt to find any effective forces to fight the Japanese. The Chinese Communists were considered to be somehow different to Russian Communists, and even Roosevelt referred to 'so-called communists'. Stilwell's own view on the issue was clear: 'We must get arms to the communists who will fight.' Serious consideration of using Communist forces was made necessary by the parlous state of Chiang's armies, which was brought home to him when emaciated corpses of soldiers were found lying in the streets in Chungking and Kunming. How many starved to death in the towns and villages across China was never discovered.

The depth and intensity of Stilwell's anger and frustration were evident in a letter to his wife. He referred to the battle with Peanut, which was wearing them out, pointing out that Chiang had thrown away 300,000 men in eastern China without batting an eyelid. He asked:

> Why can't sudden death for once strike in the right place. It would be really be funny if it weren't so tragic. The picture of this little rattle-snake being backed up by a great democracy, and showing his back-side in everything he says and does, would convulse you if you could get rid of your gall bladder. But to have to sit there and be dignified instead of bursting into guffaws, is too much to ask for the pay I get. What will the American people say when they learn the truth?

The issue of Indo-China emerged dramatically at this time after the liberation of Paris in August 1944, and Stilwell strongly opposed the use of Free French undercover units in Indo-China, whose obvious purpose was to recover the country for the former colonial power. This possibility aroused Stilwell's deep and frequently voiced anti-colonial and, especially, anti-Limey feelings. In the same letter to his wife he concluded:

> I see the Limeys are going to rush to our rescue in the Pacific: like hell. They are going to continue this fight with their mouths. Four or five battleships and about ten R.A.F. planes will go to Australia, but in twenty years the schoolbooks will be talking about 'shoulder to shoulder' and 'the Empire struck with all its might against the common enemy', and all that crap. The idea, of course, is to horn in at Hong Kong again, and our Booby [Roosevelt] is sucked in.

Stilwell still had considerable responsibility for the critical situation created by the Japanese advance, their capture of the airfields and Chiang's petulant threat to withdraw Yoke Force, so he signalled Marshall with details of the crisis on the ground in China. The message included the view that Chiang was hoping to bide his time until the Americans defeated Japan. The message reached Marshall during the final Quebec Conference, where Roosevelt and Churchill were involved in serious and often acrimonious discussions about the future of Germany. There is no doubt that Roosevelt was seriously unwell and exhausted and that his attention was focused on major European issues. In view of this preoccupation, the general attitude at Quebec seems to have been that the Allies should merely try to keep China in the war, though there was mention of a plan for the Allies to conduct an amphibious operation to open a port on the Chinese mainland.

Marshall had witnessed how Chiang constantly made promises to Stilwell and then reneged, so he had his staff prepare a three-page telegram from the President to Chiang spelling out the need for immediate action in the clearest possible way. After a brief perusal, Roosevelt signed the document. It referred to the urgent need to reopen the Burma Road and to safeguard air supplies, both of which would be jeopardised by the threat to withdraw Yoke Force. 'I have urged time and again in recent months that you take drastic action to resist the disaster which has been moving closer to China and to you. Now when you have not yet placed General Stilwell in command of all forces in China, we are faced with the loss of a critical area in east China with possible catastrophic consequences.' The message continued, arguing that the only way to stop the Japanese was to place General Stilwell immediately in unrestricted command of all Chinese forces, and it concluded, 'All your and our efforts to save China are to be lost by further delays.'

Because previous messages from the President had not been delivered or had been watered down by Madame or T. V. Soong, Roosevelt had ordered that in future his messages to Chiang should be delivered personally by the senior American officer present. The present fateful message was given to Stilwell, rather than to Hurley, to convey to Chiang. After years of frustration Stilwell felt that at last Roosevelt had spoken bluntly, and he relished the opportunity to deliver the message. His eagerness is understandable, but he did not then consider the consequences that were to follow.

He quickly had a translation prepared and took it to Chiang's HQ, where the latter was in conference with Hurley and Soong discussing, as it happened, details of Stilwell's appointment. Hurley came out of the meeting and Stilwell showed him the text. Hurley, realising what

a bombshell it was, suggested a milder paraphrase. Stilwell rejected
the suggestion. He went in, observed the tea-drinking ceremony and
handed over the document. He expressed his feelings in a diary entry
for 19 September 1944.

> Mark this day in red in the calendar of life. At long, at very long last,
> F.D.R. has finally spoken plain words and plenty of them with a fire-
> cracker in every sentence. 'Get busy or else.' A hot firecracker. I handed
> this bundle of paprika to the Peanut and then sank back with a sigh.
> The harpoon hit the little bugger right in the solar plexus and went
> right through him. It was a clean hit, but beyond turning green and
> losing the power of speech he did not bat an eye. He just said, 'I under-
> stand.' And sat in silence jiggling one foot. We are now a long way from
> the 'tribal chieftain' bawling out. Two long years lost but at least F.D.R.'s
> eyes have been opened and he has thrown a good hefty punch.

Chiang had often reacted violently to bad news, but now he showed
remarkable restraint, at least in front of the Americans, although he
apparently had one of his alarming screaming fits that evening. Soong
considered that Chiang could not appoint Stilwell in such circum-
stances because it would prove his weakness, and if that happened he
might be forced to accept the Communists. There was no official
reaction to the note for some days. Soong, who had received a clear
warning a few days before, believed that Stilwell had arranged the
whole episode in order to humiliate Chiang. The leader's inner circle
at the time were sensitive to some shrewd Japanese propaganda which
suggested that Stilwell was ambitious to take over China himself.
While serious heart-searchings continued Stilwell, in a letter home,
took an almost flippant attitude and included a poem, the first verse
of which read:

> I've waited long for vengeance –
> At last I've had my chance.
> I've looked the Peanut in the eye,
> And kicked him in the pants.

Other verses were even worse.

Stilwell did not realise that Chiang was seriously angry until several days later. Even then, in communicating with Marshall, he maintained that as ever Chiang was stalling in the hope that American advances would spare him from having to recognise the Communists or appoint a foreigner to command his forces. During these days Stilwell was working on detailed plans which he hoped to put into operation as soon as he was given command. The plans, which were produced at his headquarters, aimed at an offensive towards Canton with the present Chinese forces and, it was hoped, a US corps of 10,000 men. Then, with the possible help of units that were still being trained in India and from Yoke Force, a major drive north would capture Hankow and drive on towards Shanghai and the Yangtze valley.

Hurley was actively engaged in these discussions. On 23 September, with Stilwell's agreement, he reported to Roosevelt that he had encouraged Chiang not to produce a deadlock over the document of 19 September, and he hoped that although the situation was still difficult a harmonious solution was possible. On the same day Stilwell conferred with the Chinese chief of staff and produced an interesting memorandum on how to solve the problem. He felt that Chiang was obstinate about control of Lend–Lease because he knew that there were no strings attached to the same supplies going to Britain and Russia. Stilwell therefore suggested that he should go to the Communists and offer equipment for five full infantry divisions in return for the Communists accepting his military command and Chiang's ultimate authority. Second, he suggested that Chiang should handle Lend–Lease material with the following strict priorities: the divisions training in India and Yoke Force would have top priority, following which the next thirty divisions and the five Communist divisions would have priority. No other units would be given supplies until all of these were fully equipped.

This proposal was a genuine and sincere attempt by Stilwell to solve the deadlock and to galvanise both the Kuomintang and the Communists under his command to take effective action against the Japanese. Had it succeeded it could have changed the whole strategic situation in China long before the attack on Hiroshima in August 1945. More significantly, it might have changed the post-war history of China. With Stilwell in charge of over 100 trained and well-equipped divisions there might well have been a very different outcome to the Chinese civil war of 1947–9.

Hurley was impressed with Stilwell's proposals and took them to Chiang, but in the intervening days the Chinese leader had been considering his options. In a fairly early reaction he told Soong that after the note and the way Stilwell had delivered it he was not prepared to offer Stilwell the command. At the same time he realised this had to be done in a way that would not give Roosevelt an excuse for stopping Lend–Lease. He therefore prevaricated for some days – even discussing details of the military action against the Japanese around Kweilin. As a token of his determination he had one army commander executed. With the continuation of Lend–Lease as his top priority, Chiang believed that Hurley and Nelson would remain his supporters as the defeat of Japan and the prospect of a peace conference came closer. He estimated correctly that America would not simply cut its losses in China. Nelson in particular, with lavish promises of post-war aid, had made a big impact on Chiang, who responded by offering him full responsibility for China's recon-struction. Chiang even allowed himself to believe that Nelson had promised him control of Lend–Lease supplies.

Chiang prepared his reply to Roosevelt's memorandum with care. He claimed that the way Stilwell had delivered the memo was insult-ing and was an attempt to make him a subordinate. By refusing the demand for an attack on Bhamo, Stilwell had disobeyed orders. He considered Stilwell unfit to take on a role as complex as commander of the army. Carefully placing all the blame on Stilwell, Chiang was careful to stress his willingness to co-operate in the future and to appoint an American to command the Chinese army.

Hurley, who received Chiang's reply, initially refused to pass it on to the President because it was insulting, but shortly afterwards he accepted an amended version. He added that he regretted his failure to establish harmony between Chiang and Stilwell, but he now felt that they were incompatible. He stressed that the decision to remove Stilwell had not been made until after the delivery of the President's memorandum on 19 September. In the final version that was sent to

Roosevelt, Chiang confirmed his agreement to the appointment of an American as commander in chief but insisted that Stilwell must go. He maintained that Stilwell never had any intention of co-operating but believed 'that in fact he was being appointed to command me ... I can never direct General Stilwell or in all seriousness depend on General Stilwell to conform to my direction.' He continued by asserting that Stilwell was unfitted for the vast, complex and delicate duties of the new command and had always disregarded the mutual confidence and respect that were necessary for Allied co-operation. The previous October he had intended to ask for Stilwell's recall but desisted when Stilwell 'solemnly promised that in future he would unreservedly obey my orders'. Finally, Chiang argued that Stilwell's appointment would cause grave dissensions and do irreparable injury to Chinese–American co-operation. This reply showed clearly that Chiang's view of the appointment was very far removed from the American idea of a commander acting under Chiang but with complete power and authority over the Chinese forces.

For some time Washington did not react officially to Chiang's reply, but then Dr H. H. Kung, Chiang's brother-in-law, who was in Washington, reported a conversation he had with Harry Hopkins – a very senior Presidential aide – during a dinner party. Kung alleged that Hopkins had let slip that Roosevelt was prepared to agree to Stilwell's recall. When Kung's message reached Chiang it had a dramatic effect. He had held back from the public the details of his reply to Roosevelt, but now he announced openly that he had rejected the proposal to appoint Stilwell. He used this opportunity cleverly, stating boldly that in future Lend–Lease must come to him and that any American commander would only command those forces allocated to him. He shrewdly introduced a new element: that Stilwell's claim was an infringement of China's sovereign rights and a new form of imperialism. He even stated that if American aid was withdrawn China could get along without it. Soong in Chungking made sure that the information was sent at once to Hurley and the Americans.

At the same time another interesting aspect was provided by General Merrill, who had just returned from the Quebec Conference. He explained to Stilwell that talk of the Allies making an attack on the Chinese coast was just a cover for major operations elsewhere (MacArthur's attack on the Philippines). America was not interested in the Canton area, it was not going to commit land forces to mainland China, and military operations in China were not now a high priority.

On 24 September Stilwell wrote a fairly relaxed letter to his wife. He referred to Chiang slapping his best and only friend in the face, but added, 'He has at last had one resounding kick in the pants that nearly brought on apoplexy.' Then his diary for the following day records:

> Pat [Hurley] in with bad news. The Peanut reversed the field yesterday. Put in hours talking but you might as well talk to a blank wall. The Peanut lied about me and made astounding statements to the effect that I was bucking him ... he is afraid of my influence on the Army. He had the nerve to say he would have a mutiny on his hands ... 'Throw out General Stilwell. General Stilwell has more power in China than I have, etc, etc.'

The following day his bitterness continued: 'Two years and eight months of struggle and then a slap in the puss as a reward. Jap broadcast said I was plotting to oust Chiang Kai-Shek. Clever.'

As over several days it gradually emerged that Roosevelt was not going to back him up, Stilwell received some indications of the unfolding drama. He heard from Hurley that Soong had asked if Stilwell had got Roosevelt to send the rebuke to Chiang, and added, 'Pat refused to ask me. A-ha! Maybe this is the low-down. It fits in. The G-mo thinks I had it done and then tore his face off with it. So he has to tear me down.' On 30 September, when the news was still not officially public, he wrote to his wife. Unable to give her the whole story, he contented himself with 'We are still floundering around with a gang of morons who can't see beyond their noses ... there may be a loud bang out here before you get this and if you look carefully in the debris ... you may see yours truly with his pants blown entirely off.'

The following day Hurley passed on a report that Roosevelt seemed pleased that another American would be appointed but appeared to accept Chiang's argument that the conditions proposed for Stilwell's appointment were an infringement of sovereignty. Stilwell commented grimly, 'F.D.R. proceeds to cut my throat and throw me out. Pat feels very low about it. I don't. They just can't hurt me. I've done my best and stood up for American interests. To hell with them.'

At the beginning of October 1944 he was able at last to write to his wife and express his real feelings:

> It looks very much as though they have gotten me at last. The Peanut has gone off his rocker and Roosevelt has let me down completely. If old softy gives in on this, as he apparently has, the Peanut will be out of control from now on. A proper fizzle. My conscience is clear. I have carried out my orders. I have no regrets. Except to see the U.S.A. sold down the river. So be ready, in case the news isn't out sooner, to have me thrown on the garbage pile. At least, I'll probably get home and tell you about it. God help the next man.

In more detail, he made notes on the current situation in China as he saw it:

> • Chiang is head of a one party government supported by a Gestapo, secret service, and an S.S. of 100,000.
> • He hates the so-called communists, and intends to crush them by keeping all munitions from them and occupying territory as soon as the Japanese retire.
> • He will not fight seriously. He wants to finish the war with a big supply of munitions so as to perpetuate his regime. He has blocked us for three years and will continue to do so.
> • He has spoken contemptuously of American efforts and has never uttered one word of gratitude.
> • He has been responsible for major disasters in the war.

The depth of his personal feelings was expressed when he explained that he would remain *persona non grata* unless it was made clear to Chiang that he was not responsible for the note of 19 September. 'Ignored, insulted, double-crossed, delayed, obstructed for three years … False charges of disobedience and non-co-operation. Constant attempts to put the screw on us. Use our air force. Borrow our money.'

In Washington, although Roosevelt had more or less given in on the question of Stilwell's appointment, there were still powerful voices in support of his general thesis. Secretary of War Stimson, in particular, maintained that Stilwell was the only success in South East Asia and that the policy of giving Chennault thousands of tons of supplies every month, which were largely wasted, had undercut the supply of aircraft for the main American advance across France and into Germany. Marshall, too, who had always supported Stilwell, continued the fight, partly because he realised that his memorandum of 19 September had prompted Chiang's attack. While the frenzy of tense activity over Stilwell's position continued – and for him the final denouement was close – there were reminders in October 1944 that the war still had nearly a year to run. Stilwell himself flew down to Myitkyina to oversee the on-going campaign against the Japanese, and Marshall left Washington to spend two weeks in France, where hopes of gaining a decisive result against Germany before the winter were rapidly receding.

On 7 October, some encouragement came in a fairly stiff note from Roosevelt to Chiang saying that the situation in China was now so bad that America would not accept the responsibility of overall command. It also proposed that, because of the continuing Japanese threat to the Hump airfields, Stilwell should continue to command the forces in Burma and those in Yunnan – meaning Yoke Force. Chiang and his advisers had been desperately worried that America might curtail or even stop the supplies over the Hump, but to Chiang's great relief this did not happen. Emboldened by this he took a stronger line, saying that as head of state and commander in chief he was entitled to demand the recall of any officer in whom he had lost confidence. He went on to blame everything on Stilwell, even arguing, preposterously, that draining off the best-equipped divisions to Burma had created the problem in east China.

When Stilwell saw Roosevelt's message, he wrote to his wife to say that it was stronger than he had expected, and 'Maybe ole Pap won't get tossed on the pile with the other garbage – We are not yet completely sold down the river.' The tense delay continued through October. On the 13th he wrote: 'Sitting. Waiting. Twiddling our thumbs. Peanut still on a High Horse. Some indications F.D.R. will get tough but I don't trust politicians. Valuable time is lost and nothing done.'

Hurley continued to be the channel for correspondence between Roosevelt and Chiang, and in the next exchange he added two comments of his own: first, he now felt that Chiang and Stilwell were incompatible; and second, ominously, that if Roosevelt continued to back Stilwell he might lose Chiang – and China as well. While these negotiations about his future continued, Stilwell had to carry out his normal responsibilities. He had once again to admonish Chennault for using – without permission – 3,000 tons of petroleum from the strategic stockpile, an action which endangered operations to help MacArthur's advance in the Pacific. At almost the same time Chennault was very stiffly rebuked by MacArthur after his planes flew over Manila docks, compromising security covering actions in the Philippines. Stilwell, with his passion to ensure that every effort was made to fight the Japanese, went off even at this stage to visit the front near Kweilin and to bolster the Chinese leadership.

On 17 October, in an atmosphere of gloom, he wrote to his wife:

> We are in the doldrums for fair, just sitting and waiting for the big Boys to make a decision. If a military commander took two months to make a decision, he would be drawn and quartered, skinned, hung, burned at the stake and otherwise suitably disciplined. But any goddam politician can horn in and keep the war dangling indefinitely. I am in the dark about the attitude our people are taking. But whatever the reason, we are the stepchildren of World War II (Election coming up). I am getting sour enough about this pusillanimous proceeding to warrant being called Vinegar Joe … The Peanut sits on his hands and watches with great glee the fool Americans who actually get out and fight. This is not a letter, I am just scribbling to keep from biting the radiator.

During the next two days Stilwell must have realised that his recall was imminent because Chiang, at Roosevelt's request, was suggesting possible successors – even nominating Eisenhower. On discovering that Hurley was no longer showing him messages from the President, he wrote, 'The thing begins to stink badly.' The next day, which was his thirty-fourth wedding anniversary, he merely noted, 'T.V. says G-mo will be adamant in getting rid of me. A hell of an anniversary. Raining.'

When the final crunch came on 19 October, he wrote:

> THE AXE FALLS, Radio from George Marshall. I am 'recalled'. [General Daniel] Sultan in temporary command. Wedemeyer to command U.S. troops in China. C.B.I. to split. So F.D.R. has quit. Everybody is horrified about Washington ... Hurley feels very badly. Told me he has lost me the command. Sees his mistakes now – too late. Says Peanut accepts Wedemeyer. Everything will now be lovely.

In a letter to his wife he was deliberately low-key, saying that the axe had fallen and he would be on his way to see her in the next few days, though adding that from the start he had thought F.D.R. would sell out. He concluded, 'So now I am hanging up my shovel and bidding farewell to as merry a nest of gangsters as you'll meet in a long day's march.'

After the decision was made things progressed swiftly. He was offered China's highest award but declined because as a senior officer he could not accept a foreign award. Privately in his diary he wrote, 'The Peanut offers me China's highest decoration. Told him to stick it up his ———.' The following day he had a farewell interview with Chiang, who appeared to be full of regret. Stilwell noted, 'I told him whatever he thought of me, to remember my motive was only China's good.' He went to see Madame Sun Yat-Sen, 'who cried and was generally broken up'. He called on the American ambassador, Gauss, who had decided to resign. He left Chungking at 7.15 a.m. on 22 October and flew to Myitkyina, where he met Wedemeyer and Sultan, who were to take over in Chungking and Burma. On 24 October he was in Delhi on his way home.

He wrote a number of papers in the weeks after he left Chungking in which he refuted the report that he left because of friction with Chiang. He justified his whole policy, arguing that while the Japanese held Burma the most urgent task was to reopen the Burma Road to get supplies into China and help them to fight the Japanese. He referred scathingly to the decision of the Joint Chiefs of Staff to give the bulk of the Hump supplies to Chennault and the Fourteenth Air Force. He had opposed this decision from the start, and now in reaction to the air attacks the Japanese had captured all the forward airfields, as he had always said they would. There was now nothing to show for all the effort and expense involved.

Behind all his comments lay Stilwell's fury that, as a patriotic American, he had been unable to prevent the gigantic waste of resources provided by America from being squandered by Chennault's misguided policy; even more, he directed his fury at the deliberate duplicity and deceit of Chiang, who grasped everything he could lay hold of and dishonestly put it on one side to increase his chances of defeating the Communists after the war instead of using it to fight the Japanese.

CHAPTER 15

Finale

Mrs Stilwell heard of her husband's recall in a thoughtful message from George Marshall, and she immediately travelled to Washington to greet him when he arrived back on 1 November 1944. They were quickly given an indication of what was to come. They embraced as Stilwell came off the aircraft, and as they got into the staff car they were surprised to see the crew lined up. A staff officer was haranguing the crew and warning that there must be no discussion of the China situation. They drove to the officers' club and she noticed that he looked thin and weary. When they reached their apartment they were followed in by two generals. Stilwell said to his wife, 'I think they want a word with me.' He was told that the Chinese situation was dynamite; he must not say a word to anyone and must not give any interviews. Next, an impertinent young officer came in and virtually told Stilwell that he must leave Washington at once. Stilwell refused, saying he would not leave until he had spoken to Marshall. He was told that this was not possible because Marshall was away for a few days, but surprisingly Marshall, who lived quite close by, came to the apartment soon afterwards. Marshall brought the same message: 'Not a word. This is dynamite.'

The Stilwells were flown out of Washington. When their plane made a stop-over at a Dallas military airfield they were shocked when they were forbidden to leave the field and quartered in separate rooms. At last, in bright sunshine, they reached Carmel, where they were met by their three daughters.

Sixty years later it might be assumed that tight security and the muzzling of a four-star general were a response to some dramatic

military development, news of which could have jeopardised the lives
of men in battle. The reverse was true. Stilwell arrived in Washington
only a few days before the 1944 Presidential election. During the
election campaign Governor Thomas E. Dewey, Roosevelt's
Republican rival, in an early indication of America's paranoia about
Communism, had alleged that Communists were taking over the
allocation of supplies to China. Roosevelt claimed that it had become
the dirtiest Presidential campaign in history. (Writing in the week of
the Republican convention of George W. Bush in September 2004,
it could be asked whether every Presidential election campaign is the
dirtiest in history.)

On 31 October, the day before Stilwell's arrival, Brooks Atkinson
– a journalist who had been with Stilwell in Chungking – managed
despite efforts to block it to get an article published in the *New York
Times*. It caused a furore. It claimed that Stilwell's recall, demanded by
Chiang, was the victory of a moribund and anti-democratic regime.
It claimed that Chiang's government was totally distrusted and that
China was falling apart; to continue with support for Chiang would
mean that the USA was acquiescing in an autocratic, unrepresenta-
tive regime. The article opened the floodgates of criticism, which for
so long had been suppressed. When forced to comment on Stilwell's
recall, Roosevelt, the consummate politician, cleverly maintained that
Chiang and Stilwell had fallen out some time before and that this
was the result. He denied that it had anything to do with politics, or
strategy, or the Hump supplies; it was just a matter of personalities.
Fortunately for his campaign, this superficial and less than honest
explanation appeared to satisfy American voters.

The frantic political reaction to Stilwell's arrival may in part be
explained by his increasingly outspoken views on the issue of Chiang
and the Communists. He was known to have said that Chiang's
regime meant high taxes, corruption and neglect, and that it was a
petty dictatorship supported by concentration camps, a Gestapo and
a powerful secret service. In contrast the Communists cut taxes,
ruled well and encouraged democratic processes, which was why the
Chinese people were flocking to them. These views were fuelled by
Stilwell's passionate conviction, as a patriotic American, that Chiang's

gigantic deceit and dishonesty towards the American people in the diversion of Lend–Lease supplies for his own ends should be made public. At the same time, with equal passion and patriotic fervour he had devoted all his time and effort to the defeat of the Japanese. To achieve this goal he would have used any forces that were effective and available, and he had realised before anyone else did that the Chinese Communist forces were far more effective than those of the Kuomintang.

Initially, after he reached home, he was appointed to command ground forces in the USA and to oversee their training, but he soon realised that this was just a sop and found it deeply frustrating. He hankered after an active command, but this was not easy to arrange in view of his stature as a four-star general. His feelings are understandable because at the time it was generally assumed that the war against Japan would last another two years. His frustration continued, and his deep hurt at the way he had been treated and by Roosevelt's refusal to see him lingered for the rest of his life. He received a little solace from his new role as a public figure. He was guest of honour at West Point and he had a meeting with Vice President Harry Truman, with whom he established a good rapport.

In January 1945 the road from Ledo finally linked up with the Burma Road – a truly magnificent achievement by the American engineers. General Lewis Pick, who had stoically driven forward the whole project and was a staunch ally of Stilwell, sent out the first convoy, and Roosevelt and Chiang made the most of the publicity. Chiang claimed, 'We have broken the siege of China,' and he announced that the road would be named after Stilwell, who merely mused, 'I wonder who put him up to that?' General Sultan, who had worked with Stilwell in Burma and took over from him on his recall, said that it was Stilwell's indomitable will that had opened the Burma Road. Stilwell himself had the opportunity to pay tribute to the soldiers, aircrew, engineers and labourers, many of whom had given their lives in the great enterprise.

After this he spent many weeks with his staff preparing a very long and detailed report on the history of the China–Burma–India theatre. In this he robustly maintained his theme that America had made a major blunder by providing Lend–Lease without securing a firm commitment to action from Chiang. The report concluded with a severe condemnation of Chiang's government and forecast its downfall. The report was never published because Stilwell refused to cut out his criticism of Chiang and the British. During this depressing period his achievements did gain some recognition. In February 1945 Stimson decorated him with the Legion of Merit and an Oak Leaf cluster to his Distinguished Service Medal. Stimson was a consistent supporter of Stilwell (though for political reasons he did not meet him on his return to Washington), and at the award ceremony he said that no decoration had given him more pleasure.

Events in China were soon to justify Stilwell's views. Assured of American support, Chiang became increasingly unreasonable. By this time Mao Tse-Tung had emerged as a brilliant and successful guerrilla leader, and the powerful position of the Communist forces would soon force America to face the dilemma this posed for its policy in China. In Chungking an increasing number of Americans were suggesting that the decision to co-operate with the Communists should be taken whether or not Chiang agreed. Responsibility for achieving some co-operation fell to Patrick Hurley, who became Ambassador when Stilwell left. He was expected to achieve great things, but he appeared to accept uncritically all the blandishments of Chiang and his circle, and he rapidly alienated most of his staff, who saw all too clearly that Stilwell had been right. Roosevelt clung to the argument, which Chiang had used at the time of Stilwell's dismissal, that American demands could appear to be an infringement of Chinese sovereignty. He therefore insisted that America could not deal with the Communists without Chiang's approval. He held to this position even though other well-informed advisers pointed out that Chiang would never agree to the Communists joining his government because their influence would be too strong. The alternative was that the Communists might overthrow Chiang anyway.

By the time Stilwell received his decoration, the focus of Sino-American relations had moved from the crisis area of southern China and Chungking to the world stage, when Roosevelt and Churchill met with Stalin at Yalta in the Crimea in early February 1945 to plan for the post-war world. Roosevelt travelled on the USS *Quincy* to Malta, where he met Churchill, and they flew on to Yalta. Each leader had different agendas, but clearly the resettlement of Europe after the defeat of Germany had the highest priority. Roosevelt, now very ill and exhausted, wanted to ensure the creation of the United Nations. Churchill, more cynical and realistic, wanted to concentrate on the future of Poland and prevent the spread of communism into central Europe. In sharp contrast Stalin, ruthless and well prepared, was determined to establish – as he argued – an independent Poland under his influence. Because of their differing agendas Roosevelt and Churchill were outsmarted by Stalin. Attempting to be the benign elder statesman, Roosevelt thought he was better than Churchill at handling Stalin, but in fact they were both hoodwinked (it was later discovered that all their rooms and even the garden around the former imperial palace where they stayed had been bugged). By brutal *realpolitik* Stalin achieved his objective over Poland, but the issue of the Far East was more easily settled. Roosevelt wanted Russia to attack Japan as soon as Germany was defeated, hoping that this would save an estimated one million American lives in the final onslaught on Japan. Stalin, for his part, was happy to declare war at that stage, when most of the fighting was over, and, at little cost, to gain a powerful place at the peace settlement where he could advance Russia's interests in Manchuria. The actual agreement for Russia to attack Japan was made privately between Roosevelt and Stalin on 8 February.

Chiang was not present at Yalta and his interests were hardly mentioned, but partly for form's sake it was agreed that when the United Nations was set up China would have a permanent seat on the Security Council. This apparently innocuous decision was to cause bitter international conflict for the next twenty years. Chiang had failed to carry out any of the undertakings he had made at the Cairo Conference, and partly for this reason the promise – made at Cairo – to allow him to take over Indo-China was reversed.

In March 1945, when Stilwell was receiving flattering comments from Chungking saying how greatly he was missed, he did at last meet Roosevelt, who was affable. Stilwell thought the President looked terrible, though not as bad as he appeared in the pictures from Yalta. In Chungking Wedemeyer, now the senior American commander there, failed to grasp the issue of Lend–Lease, and the tonnage that was being flown over the Hump increased to more than 30,000 tons a month, on top of which there were now the supplies that were beginning to move up the Stilwell Road. Still there was no adequate response from Chiang.

By this time it was clear that Germany was close to defeat. Stalin was determined that Soviet forces, not the western Allies, should capture Berlin, and there was intense competition between Zukov and the other Red Army commanders to achieve that prize. More than 150 infantry divisions and over 6,000 tanks raced towards the German capital, determined to exact savage revenge for all the Nazi atrocities. The end came more quickly than expected when, on 30 April, Hitler committed suicide in the Berlin bunker. The defeat of Germany turned attention back to the Pacific and the campaign against Japan.

In the background to the assault on Japan, with its complex military and political issues, lay the development of the atomic bomb – the Manhattan Project – but in the spring of 1945 it was still not known when it would be completed. Already on 1 April American forces had attacked Okinawa, some 400 miles southwest of Japan, and were engaged in a prolonged and bitter fight for this crucial island base. At the same time General MacArthur and Admiral Nimitz, now respectively commanders of land and sea forces in the Pacific, were ordered by the Joint Chiefs of Staff to finalise plans for the assault on Japan. The uncertainty about when the atom bomb would be ready is highlighted by the plan which MacArthur and Nimitz produced. In the first phase, code-named Olympic and to be carried out in November 1945, twelve divisions would take Kyushu, the nearest Japanese mainland island to Okinawa, and in the second phase, Coronet, Tokyo would be taken by fourteen divisions in March 1946.

After a prolonged and bloody fight, the Americans captured Okinawa by the middle of June 1945. They sustained 50,000 killed and wounded, and the Japanese double that number. The very heavy losses of men and ships on the American side were mainly caused

by the kamikaze attacks on the US fleet. This was a new tactic and
difficult to counteract as the suicide pilots would hit their target
unless their plane was literally blown out of the sky. The capture
of Okinawa and the terrific build-up of American pressure had an
almost immediate effect in southern China, an area where Stilwell
was still hankering after active command. Fulfilling all his worst
predictions, the Japanese threatened an attack on Kunming, but
before this happened they started to withdraw from southern China,
destroying all the towns and cities as they left. The Kuomintang forces
slowly occupied the areas the Japanese had left, often with false or
even ludicrous claims of military success. Although Chiang was then
receiving a huge increase of supplies both over the Hump and from
the Stilwell Road, he did nothing, and Wedemeyer came face to face
with the frustrations that Stilwell had suffered for so long

Against this rapidly changing background Stilwell saw Marshall,
who encouraged him to go to the Pacific to familiarise himself with
the situation. After the interview Stilwell, who had known MacArthur
since they were contemporaries at West Point, felt that the Chiefs of
Staff were afraid of MacArthur and uncertain how to control him.
In May 1945 Stilwell flew to the Pacific theatre. MacArthur gave him
a cordial welcome and suggested that he visit the commanders of the
proposed Olympic and Coronet operations. He travelled widely and
visited Okinawa, where he saw the almost total devastation. At the
end of the trip he had a realistic discussion with MacArthur, when
once again his status as a four-star general proved an obstacle. He
declined MacArthur's offer to be his chief of staff because he wanted
an active command. He said he would be happy to command a division so that he could return to active duty with troops in the field.
MacArthur countered this, saying that he would be delighted to
have him as an army commander. With nothing definitively settled,
Stilwell set out to return home. When he reached Guam in the
Marianas he heard that the commander of the US Tenth Army,
General Simon Bolivar Bruckner, had been killed on Okinawa.
On the next leg of his journey to Honolulu he received an urgent
cable from MacArthur to return to Guam and take over the Tenth
Army. He went back to Guam and on 23 June took over command

of the Tenth Army invasion force, planning close naval and air co-ordination. He was delighted to be once again involved in a positive and challenging task.

Meanwhile, proposals for peace had been considered at different levels. As early as May the governing council in Japan considered a plan for peace, hoping to use the Soviet Union as a buffer against the USA. Also in May, Stalin informed Washington that he could be ready to attack Japan in August. In June Japan made the first approach to Russia but received little response. The Japanese Supreme Council resolved to fight to the end, but two weeks later the Emperor Hirohito gave the order that Japan must seek peace. The crisis reached a peak in July 1945. At Potsdam, Truman – President since the death of Roosevelt in April – with Stalin and Churchill issued the Potsdam Declaration demanding the unconditional surrender of Japan. It stressed that the alternative was prompt and utter destruction. At this stage Truman and Churchill knew that the atom bomb was ready but they had not informed Stalin. On 28 July the Japanese prime minister Suzuki declared that the Potsdam Declaration must be rejected because it made no reference to the Emperor. This crucial statement led directly to the dropping of the first atom bomb on Hiroshima on 6 August and the second on Nagasaki on 9 August. This was also the day on which Russia declared war on Japan. Japan surrendered on 14 August.

Stilwell had a few brief weeks to take over command of the Tenth Army, but even then the venom of Chiang pursued him and it was understood that he would not be allowed to set foot on Chinese soil. When Japan surrendered Stilwell, like everyone else, was delighted at the end of the carnage and destruction, which relieved the Allies of the prospect of a ground campaign in Japan with the possibility of horrendous casualties. The casualties on Okinawa had been so appalling and the effect on the morale of the fighting units so severe that some commanders worried whether another hard-fought campaign might lead to a total breakdown of discipline.

Stilwell wrote in his diary, 'SO IT IS OVER.' He was particularly relieved that his youngest son, who was eighteen, would not have to face the prospect of a military campaign against the Japanese – a sentiment shared by the author, then a young infantry officer awaiting the final British offensive in the Far East.

After the announcement of the Japanese surrender, Stilwell quickly found himself buffeted about by the intense rivalry between General MacArthur and Admiral Nimitz. The proposed operations of the Tenth Army were immediately changed, and Stilwell realised that part of the reason was Chiang's last dig. 'So they have cut my throat once more,' he wrote.

In his deep and sincere concern for China and its long-suffering people he soon had to face grim news from all over the country. Japan had occupied Manchuria and Formosa for many years and now there were well over a million troops who had to be returned to Japan from those areas. Within China there was no overall organisation and almost no effective transport for such a mammoth task. At the same time both the Americans and the Kuomintang put a high priority on the need to occupy the territory from which the Japanese were withdrawing before the Communists did so. As America helped Chiang and the Kuomintang with transport to occupy areas in central China, so, in an ominous portent of the Cold War to come, the Soviet Union assisted the Communists. Stilwell, still America's best-informed expert on Chinese affairs, realised better than most the decadence and corruption of Chiang's regime and its contrast to the confident, forward-looking policies of Mao Tse-Tung and the Communists. He foresaw the real danger of America being dragged into a major confrontation on account of the wretched Chiang and his dismal regime, and he advised, 'We ought to get out now.'

The formal surrender of Japan took place under MacArthur on the USS *Missouri* in Tokyo Bay on 2 September 1945, and Stilwell attended as a senior representative of his country. He had a couple of days before the ceremony to inspect the colossal damage in and around Tokyo. He had witnessed the depredations of the Japanese across China from the rape of Nanking onwards, to say nothing of their brutality during the war in Burma. He made no excuse for gloating over the suffering of the people of Tokyo and 'the arrogant little bastards', as he had described them so many years before. Having revelled in the suffering of the Japanese, he viewed the surrender

ceremony with misanthropic bitterness. He noted critically that at the
ceremony MacArthur's hands and leg were shaking with nervousness.
He thought the Allied signatories were a disreputable looking bunch,
and he reserved his fiercest criticism, and anti-Limey prejudice, for
General Percival, the British general who had pathetically surrendered
Singapore to the Japanese and spent the rest of the war in a prison
camp. Stilwell's final damning indictment was that 'The human race
was poorly represented'.

A few days later, as a tribute to the suffering and achievements
of the Okinawa campaign, Stilwell presided over another surrender
ceremony at Ryukyu. With the obvious approval of the troops he
kept the Japanese waiting, standing at attention for ten minutes,
before completing the ceremony with cold efficiency.

When he realised that the Tenth Army was not going to be a
separate unit of the occupation forces, he contacted Marshall for
permission to visit Peking. In replying to his request, Chiang said that
there were both Japanese and Communist forces in the area around
Peking and a visit by Stilwell could be exploited. When things were
back to normal he hoped to issue a formal invitation. That never
happened. Stilwell was amazed that Chiang thought he might start a
revolution, and he noted, 'I would like to do just that.' Soon afterwards he left the Pacific theatre for the last time and returned to
Carmel on 18 October 1945. After a brief and frustrating appointment in Washington he was put in charge of the defence of the San
Francisco area, with a headquarters quite close to Carmel.

Within a few weeks of Stilwell's return home another crisis erupted
in China. Hurley, who had been a major player during the tense discussions over Stilwell's recall, resigned because, he claimed, members
of the State Department were actively supporting Communism
in China. Hurley's resignation highlighted the very strong anti-
Communist feeling among the American people, and certainly
among American military leaders. In an earlier incident another
maverick American commander, 'Blood and Guts' General George
Patton, a contemporary of Stilwell at West Point who now commanded the American troops who met the Russians on the Elbe in
May 1945, publicly refused to drink a victory toast 'with any goddam

Russian son of a bitch'. When reprimanded, he claimed that America would have to fight the bolsheviks some time and they might as well start at once. In this he may have shown remarkable foresight, but at the time it was politically unacceptable and Patton was dismissed – for a second time.* He did, nonetheless, represent very widely and strongly held American views that soon became focused on the situation in China.

Across China the dispute between Chiang and the Communists deepened, and Mao Tse-Tung protested strongly about American planes and ships moving Kuomintang troops to occupy territory in north China evacuated by the Japanese. As Chiang's position steadily weakened, he renewed the demand for the ninety divisions which for long frustrating months Stilwell had sought only to be blocked by Chiang himself. What a different outcome might have been achieved if Chiang had earlier agreed to Stilwell arming, training and commanding the ninety divisions, a proposal that was put forward as early as the Cairo Conference. The American dilemma, which had been highlighted when Stilwell said 'We ought to get out now', became steadily more intractable. Chiang continued to howl for resources, and the Washington administration had to decide whether to pour more money and supplies into Chiang's bottomless pit or to stop Lend–Lease supplies altogether, which would almost certainly mean that the Communists would defeat Chiang and the Kuomintang. Diplomats continued to avoid the harsh reality of this problem, and they fudged an answer, which was to go on sending some supplies to Chiang while attempting to achieve a compromise between the two factions. In America the impact of the China crisis, exacerbated by vicious Republican and Democratic allegations, quickly led to the anti-Communist paranoia that was to divide American society so bitterly. It destroyed the careers of able and honourable people at all levels of public service and led directly to the evil menace of McCarthy, the odious senator from Wisconsin, whom Truman called a pathological character assassin.

* Patton was first dismissed during the campaign in Sicily after he slapped a patient in a military hospital.

As the China crisis intensified, Truman, inexperienced in these dangerous waters, made a clever move. He asked Marshall, who had just retired as Chief of Staff, to undertake a desperate mission to achieve an acceptable compromise. As Marshall saw it his options were limited. If the Communists refused to compromise, America had the power and resources to move Kuomintang troops to northern China, but if Chiang was obdurate he could not be abandoned entirely because that would hand victory to the Communists and would defeat the very object of all the American efforts throughout the war. In a reversal of roles Marshall sent his second-in-command to ask advice from Stilwell. Stilwell was blunt, and forecast that the mission could not possibly succeed. As it increasingly became bogged down in the Chinese quagmire, Stilwell commented, 'George Marshall can't walk on water.'

In July 1946, as a senior American general, Stilwell was invited to witness the testing of the atom bomb at the Bikini atoll. This proved to be his last public engagement. His health began to fail rapidly and he stayed at home, following with interest Marshall's efforts to solve the China problem. American forces transported nearly half a million Kuomintang troops to the key cities of Nanking and Shanghai, and American marines tried, as they had in the 1930s, to secure Chinese ports and transport facilities. Lend–Lease continued with 600 million dollars worth of supplies for Chiang. In July, seeing Chiang's hopeless situation, Marshall stopped military supplies, though this appeared to have little effect on Chiang. He persevered with his hopeless task, and then in October 1946, because of Chiang's intransigence, warned that attempts at mediation would cease. Back in California Stilwell was admitted to hospital in September, where stomach cancer and serious liver damage were discovered. Within days of Marshall's final warning to Chiang, Stilwell died on 12 October 1946.

CHAPTER 16

Retrospect

Stilwell, one of a generation of West Point graduates from the early years of the century who were to achieve high military and political office during and after the Second World War, was driven throughout his career by a strong sense of patriotism. This tended to make him highly critical of other people's efforts. Highly intelligent – witness his fluency in Spanish, then in French and finally in Chinese – he was also prickly, oversensitive and ready to take offence where none was intended. His intense dedication to his country and to the army accounts for some of his criticism of others. This feature of his character, so noticeable when he was a senior general, was certainly present in his early days. When he was awaiting repatriation from Germany in 1918 and President Wilson came to Versailles with his Fourteen Points, Stilwell called him 'an addle-pated boob'.

In weighing up his image as the outspoken, critical, neurotic, tough-guy fighter, it must be remembered that his diary, often jotted down in the midst of battle or under the pressure of wretched defeat by the Japanese, was never intended for publication. Had he lived longer he would doubtless have produced his memoirs in a more balanced and polished form, though it is unlikely that he would have changed his strictures about Chiang Kai-Shek or the British.

His intense feelings about the British, so vividly portrayed in his diary and so highly publicised during the Burma campaign, went back to a time before the First World War. On an early posting to the Far East he visited Hong Kong, and while he admired the tough and competent British soldier, he evinced a deep antagonism to what he saw as the foppish upper-class English officer. This attitude was shared by a number of his contemporaries. Was it perhaps an attitude nurtured at West Point that went back to 1776, or perhaps to the war of 1812 when the British attacked Baltimore, Washington and Pensacola, among others? Initially Stilwell's strong prejudice may have seemed the amusing eccentricity of a colourful character, but in a senior commander and influencing decisions that cost men's lives it was deplorable. There is no doubt that his prejudice against Limeys was a major factor in what was his worst decision – his refusal to employ the British 36 Division to take the town of Myitkyina after Merrill's Marauders had captured the airfield on 17 May 1944. 36 Division was trained in air movement and was ready for action, yet Stilwell refused to use it. Instead he combed American bases and hospitals for sick or wounded men and drafted in building workers who had never used a rifle. This decision cost the lives of hundreds, indeed thousands of men, and Stilwell has been rightly criticised for it by both American and British commentators.

While Stilwell's prejudice against the Limeys is notorious, some explanation of the view from the other side may be seen in the British edition of *The Stilwell Papers*, published in 1949. The well-known British military historian General J. F. C. Fuller wrote a long introduction for this edition. He emphasised the deep cultural gulf between the British and Americans, arguing that whereas Europeans have overcome problems which date back to the Black Prince or even Troy, the Americans have never had to face serious problems, and hence their admiration for the tough-guy, big-shot, billionaire type of character. He then wrote this astonishing sentence: 'We Europeans are grown up and, rightly or wrongly, we look upon all Asiatics, Africans and Americans as barbarians.' Despite this outrageous statement, Fuller went on to say that Stilwell was 'a first rate fighting soldier and one of the few really outstanding characters of the war'. He concluded with the sympathetic statement that few generals have been so disgracefully treated. The most intriguing aspect of Fuller's contribution is why the publishers included it with its outrageous comments. Was it perhaps to give an example of the condescending arrogance of the British military establishment which fuelled Stilwell's views of the Limeys?

From a purely military point of view Stilwell was an outstandingly able leader. As early as 1918 he was frustrated that his linguistic ability landed him in staff jobs when what he really wanted was to earn promotion by commanding a fighting unit. His ability was recognised during the doldrums of the 1920s by George Marshall, who brought him to the infantry school at Fort Benning to revolutionise training. Later, during the Burma campaign, he seems to have been happiest not among the top brass and the splendours of Delhi, Chungking or Ceylon, but with his tough Chinese soldiers on the jungle paths of the Huckawng valley. These were men who appreciated a senior general who shared their privations and their rations and saw that if they were wounded they were not left to die.

Stilwell's intense patriotism, which drove him relentlessly, accounts largely for his reputation as an unpleasant, acerbic and overcritical colleague. He was not popular with many fellow American commanders, and in the final part of the Burma campaign there was serious criticism that his staff were afraid of rousing his ire and would only tell him what he wanted to hear. This criticism was reinforced by the appointment to his staff of his son and son-in-law. It was also highlighted by the colourful and dramatic encounter with Mike Calvert, the intrepid Chindit leader who captured Mogaung, from whom Stilwell learned how seriously he had been misinformed by Boatner and his staff.

Whatever the strengths and weaknesses of this colourful character, any serious assessment must stand or fall on the great issue of China. It seemed from an early time that fate had destined him for a major role in that country. Many other officers were posted to China, but none used the opportunity as effectively or dramatically as Stilwell. On his first visit in 1911 he quickly left what he saw as the stultifying atmosphere of the military headquarters and immersed himself totally in the life and culture of the Chinese, helped by his flair for languages. After 1918, when all officers faced years of frustration and lack of promotion, he eagerly grasped the chance to return to China. Here again he escaped from the HQ atmosphere and undertook work on a road-building programme to support famine relief. There he lived almost like the coolies, and again involved himself totally with his Chinese workers. He also used the opportunity to travel around China and to visit Japan, where he epitomised the Japanese as 'arrogant little bastards', a view he never subsequently changed.

A few years later he undertook a remarkable and highly dangerous journey with a Chinese colleague which opened his eyes to the intense anti-Western and anti-Christian feelings of the Chinese. This may be an indication of one of the fundamental reasons for the ultimate failure of Stilwell's mission and the failure of the great American dream for China – that they were alien impositions, and in the long run were never likely to control China's indigenous development. Barbara Tuchman concluded her book *Sand against the Wind* by observing that 'In the end China went her own way as if the Americans had never come'.

In the years before Pearl Harbor Stilwell again warned America of the dangers of Japanese aggression, which he realised was masked by the better publicised advance of fascist forces in Europe. He witnessed the rape of Nanking and other Japanese atrocities and, reinforcing his outspoken reputation, fulminated against the blinkered attitude in the American embassy and 'the interfering bastards in Washington'. At the same time he began to formulate the view that only America was strong enough to enable China to resist Japanese aggression, and the way that might happen would be for senior commands in the Chinese armies to be held by Americans.

After Pearl Harbor, Stilwell could easily have taken his place along with Eisenhower, Patton and Bradley in the North African and European theatre, but once again fate seemed to direct him to China. After frequent and tedious meetings in Washington, he left for the Far East on 14 February 1942. Some issues, which were to become permanent, appeared almost at once. He found the British apathetic and snooty; he found that Chennault, who was to become his *bête noire*, already had the ear of Madame; and at his first conference in Maymyo General Alexander's attitude made him feel as if he had crawled from under a stone. Another and more significant feature emerged at this time – Stilwell's suggestion that thirty Chinese divisions should be trained and equipped by America.

He was very quickly caught up in the retreat from Burma, but even before that he had submitted to Chiang a plan for 100,000

Chinese troops to be trained and equipped in India. With his previous knowledge of Chiang and China he insisted, as he had with Marshall in Washington, that the one essential was American control of Lend–Lease, with all the bluff and counter-bluff that entailed. Later he discovered another permanent feature – that as early as June 1942 Chiang had tried to get rid of him.

From 1942, through weary years of frustration, Stilwell kept up the struggle to cajole or force Chiang into taking action so that the massive American contribution of money, men and machines could be mobilised into an effective force against the Japanese. From the thirty divisions he had originally suggested the number increased to sixty; and by the time Chiang attended the Cairo Conference in November 1943 it had risen to ninety, and later to more than one hundred.

This crucial issue was soon to be linked to the problem of arming the Chinese Communist forces. Stilwell saw these merely as a group that was more likely to fight the Japanese effectively, and he obtained their agreement to fight under his command. This soon became enmeshed in a graver matter of world significance, which illustrates the catastrophe of the rejection of Stilwell's plan and of his early death. Had Chiang agreed to the plan to equip and place 100 divisions under Stilwell's command, the American administration was already committed to providing the finance and all the supplies. Thus, when the war suddenly ended, he would have commanded a force that would almost certainly have been too strong for the military power of Mao Tse-Tung in the civil war that followed so soon after the Japanese defeat. Ironically, the defeat of the Communists was Chiang's ultimate hope, and Stilwell's plan was the best way of achieving it, but, as Stilwell put it, the dumb bastard couldn't see it.

The double tragedy of Stilwell's dismissal and early death meant that his realistic summing-up of Chiang's corrupt Kuomintang regime, which was only then being recognised as accurate, was silenced just as the China lobby and missionary groups began to play on America's anti-Communist fears. Disastrous results followed.

After Chiang was defeated in the civil war in 1949, he and half a million Kuomintang troops reached Formosa (now Taiwan). There his corrupt and dictatorial regime continued to receive American support, notably from the US navy. From the Korean War onwards, American warships patrolled the Formosa Strait and protected the islands of Quemoy and Matsu close to the Chinese mainland. Another legacy of the rejection of Stilwell's concepts and the consequent failure of the American people to realise the enormity of Chiang's corruption manifested itself in 1955, when the Communist government shelled Quemoy and Matsu. The hawkish US Admiral Radford attempted to pressurise President Eisenhower into launching a nuclear attack on Communist China. Fortunately Radford failed, but, to the amazement of the world, the United States continued to insist that Chiang's regime in Formosa should hold China's permanent seat on the United Nations Security Council. This remained a running sore between America and her allies. The depth of American paranoia about communism during this period is illustrated by some preposterous books published in the 1950s and 1960s. These claimed among other things that Marshall was responsible for sending the 'communist' General Stilwell to China; that Marshall allowed Karl Marx to win the war; that Marshall single-handedly gave China to the Communists; and that in the Marshall Plan, Marshall was the tool of Stalin. An example of the genre is *How the Far East Was Lost*, by Dr A. Kubek.★

Had Stilwell, driven by his intense patriotism, succeeded in his mammoth task he could have changed the course of history in post-war China. Contemplating his failure in this enterprise, he offered his own modest and unsentimental final comment:

> The personal experience of an individual fades into insignificance in the enormous scope and ramifications of war, specially if there is grievance connected with it. And when the general result is success, who cares about the squawks of the disgruntled? If a man can say he did not let his country down, and he can live with himself, there is nothing more he can reasonably ask for.

★ Published by Henry Regnery, Chicago, 1963.

Select Bibliography

This short bibliography suggests books that should be available in libraries and is intended for those who might be interested in reading further about Stilwell's career and the war in Burma.

Allen, Louis, *Burma: The Longest War, 1941–1945*, Dent, London, 1984

Bidwell, Shelford, *The Chindit War*, Hodder, London, 1979

Bond, Brian (ed.), *Chief of Staff: The Diaries of Lieutenant General Sir Henry Pownall*, Leo Cooper, London, 1972

Brookes, Stephen, *Through the Jungle of Death*, John Wiley, New York, 2000

Calvert, Michael, *Fighting Mad*, Bantam, London, 1964

———— *Prisoners of Hope*, Cape, London, 1952

Cane, Peter, *Chinese Chindits*, privately published, 1948

Carfrae, Charles, *Chindit Column*, William Kimber, London, 1985

Connell, John, *Wavell*, Collins, London, 1964

Fergusson, Bernard, *Beyond the Chindwin*, Collins, London, 1945

———— *The Wild Green Earth*, Collins, London, 1946

Fraser, George MacDonald, *Quartered Safe out Here*, Harvill, 1992

Gilbert, Martin, *History of the Twentieth Century*, HarperCollins, London, 2001

Keegan, John, *The Face of Battle*, Cape, London, 1976

Kirby, S. Woodburn, *The War against Japan*, HMSO, 1958

Kubek, A., *How the Far East Was Lost*, Henry Regnery, Chicago, 1963

Lewin, R., *Slim*, Leo Cooper, London, 1972

Lyman, Robert, *Slim: Master of War*, Constable, London, 2004

Mao Tse-Tung, *Basic Tactics*, Pall Mall, London, 1967

Masters, John, *The Road past Mandalay*, Michael Joseph, London, 1961

O'Brien, Terence, *Out of the Blue*, Collins, London, 1984

Ogburn, Charlton, *The Marauders*, Harper, New York, 1959

Prefer, Nathan, *Vinegar Joe's War*, Presidio, California, 2000

Romanus, C., and R. Sunderland, *Stilwell's Command Problems*, Center of Military History, Washington, 1956

———— *Stilwell's Mission to China*, Center of Military History, Washington, 1953

Rooney, David, *Burma Victory*, Arms & Armour Press, London, 1992

———— *Guerilla: Insurgents, Patriots and Terrorists from Sun Tzu to Bin Laden*, Brassey's, London, 2004

———— *Mad Mike*, Leo Cooper, London, 1997

———— *Wingate and the Chindits: Redressing the Balance*, Arms & Armour Press, London, 1994

Seaman, Harry, *The Battle at Sangshak*, Leo Cooper, London, 1989

Slim, Field Marshal Viscount, *Defeat into Victory*, Cassell, London, 1956

Tamayama, Kazuo, and John Nunneley, *Tales by Japanese Soldiers of the Burma Campaign 1942–1945*, Cassell, London, 2000

Tuchman, Barbara, *Sand against the Wind*, Macmillan, New York, 1970

White, Theodore (ed.), *The Stilwell Papers*, MacDonald, London, 1949

Ziegler, Philip, *Mountbatten*, Collins, London, 1985

Index